D0873861

❖TAKES

TAKES ❖ Stories from
The Talk of the Town

by LILLIAN ROSS

Congdon & Weed, Inc.
New York

Library of Congress Cataloging in Publication Data

Ross, Lillian.
  Takes: stories from the Talk of the town.

  "The stories in this book appeared originally in the New Yorker"—Verso of
t.p.
  I. New Yorker.   II. Title.
AC8.R6426   1983   814'.54'08   82–23598
ISBN 0–86553–074–2
ISBN 0–312–92804–1 (St. Martin's Press)

The stories in this book appeared originally in *The New Yorker;* copyright ©
1960, 1965, 1967, 1968, 1969, 1970, 1971, 1972, 1973, 1974, 1976, 1978, 1980,
1981, 1982 by the New Yorker Magazine, Inc.

Published by Congdon & Weed, Inc.
298 Fifth Avenue, New York, N.Y. 10001

Distributed by St. Martin's Press
175 Fifth Avenue, New York, N.Y. 10010

Published simultaneously in Canada by Thomas Nelson & Sons Limited
81 Curlew Drive, Don Mills, Ontario M3A 2R1

Printed in the United States of America by The Haddon Craftsmen
Designed by Irving Perkins
Second Printing

For Erik

❖ Contents

viii

◆ TAKES

❧ Introduction

I LOVE reporting for *The New Yorker*'s Talk of the Town. In many ways, it's the most challenging kind of reporting: the most demanding, the most interesting to do, the most fun, and the most open to humor. Like the longer pieces of reporting for *The New Yorker*—Profiles and A Reporter at Large, for instance—Talk stories can take many forms. From time to time, some people have said of The Talk of the Town that "it all sounds alike." As it happens, the opposite is true. For one thing, Talk stories, like any other kind of writing, vary tremendously in style from writer to writer. A Talk story reveals the very spirit of the writer, and in any given year The Talk of the Town has been written by anywhere from twenty to thirty writers, each of whom has a unique, strongly personal style and feeling. Talk stories usually run to about a thousand words, but sometimes, for one reason or another, they may run twice—even five times—as long. Whatever their length, the writing requires that in a short space one build and reveal a character or a situation or an event or a moment and do so with honesty, with humor, with clarity, with freshness, and with truth.

For me, one of the happiest experiences in writing for The Talk of the Town has been working alongside—and having my writing published alongside the writing of—people whom I happen to regard as among the best writers in the world. Not all of them are well known. Over the years, I have learned much about reporting and writing from my predecessors and colleagues on The Talk of the Town. At the same time, I have always felt inspired by them to push my own efforts forward in ways that I felt were true to me. Because this is an opportunity to put the names of some of them on record, I'd like to list them, in more or less chronological order: E. B. White, James Thurber, Wolcott Gibbs, R. E. M. Whitaker, John Bainbridge, Brendan Gill, Russell Maloney, Geoffrey Hellman, St. Clair McKelway, Emily Hahn, Clifford Orr, A. J. Liebling, Janet Flanner, Gardner Botsford, Eugene Kinkead, Philip Hamburger, Francis Steegmuller, John McCarten, Frederick Packard, E. J. Kahn, Jr., Roger Angell, Andy Logan, Frances Lanahan, Rosanne Smith, Wallace White, Calvin Trillin, Maeve Brennan, Jeremy Bernstein, Whitney Balliett, John Updike, James Stevenson, Anthony Bailey, Burton Bernstein, Jane Boutwell, William Whitworth, Susan Sheehan, John Flagler, Bruce Bliven, Jr., Naomi Bliven, Thomas Whiteside, Tony Hiss, Renata Adler, Constance Feeley, Ved Mehta, Hendrik Hertzberg, Janet Malcolm, Robert MacMillan, John McPhee, Niccolo Tucci, Richard Harris, Jane Kramer, Thomas Meehan, Susan Lardner, Faith McNulty, Alastair Reid, Elizabeth Macklin, Ann Beattie, Michael Arlen, Joan Bennet, Veronica Geng, Paul Brodeur, John Brooks, Henry Cooper, Jervis Anderson, Gerald Jonas, Alec Wilkinson, Mark Singer, Jacob Brackman, Jonathan Schell, Fred Shapiro, Charles McGrath, Stanley Mieses, Garrison Keillor, Israel Schenker, Bobbie Ann Mason, William Wertenbaker, Natacha Stewart, Jamaica Kincaid, George Trow, Ian Frazier, Andrea Lee, Calvin Tomkins, Mary Kierstead, Kennedy Fraser, Patti Hagan, Lola Finkelstein, Daniel Menaker, Wolcott Gibbs, Jr., Lincoln Caplan, William Franzen, William McKibben. I find a special kind of pleasure in reading what the writers for The Talk of the Town, from the oldest (E. B. White, in his eighties) to the youngest

(William McKibben, in his twenties) have done for the department—so much pleasure that it often feels to me as
though I had had something to do with what *they* have
written as well as with what I have written myself. (I have
never talked to any of them about this odd feeling; they may
or may not share it.) In fact, when a reader expresses joy over
a Talk piece and says, "You must have written that one," I
feel flattered, even when I have *not* written that one. I enjoy
having people assume that I did write this or that story,
especially if it is one of the gems contributed these days by
the very young writers. At any rate, writing Talk stories is a
rare writing experience for me precisely because it means
being a part of a group effort, dependent upon many colleagues—an effort that speaks for the magazine, and one that
has, from the start of my experience with it, been led and
molded consistently by *The New Yorker*'s present editor, William Shawn. He has the distinction of having brought forth,
first as managing editor and then as editor, forty-three years
of Talk stories—more than seven thousand—and of having
put together more than two thousand Talk departments, and
also of having, in the middle-nineteen-thirties, written a few
Talk stories of his own, notably those about Buck Rogers and
George Washington's false teeth.

The Talk of the Town deals for the most part with life in
or related to New York, and it is constantly discovering the
excitement and fun in that life. Where there's life, there's
humor. And usually the humor presents itself naturally,
because it's part of the truth; there is no need to alter the
truth to fit one's preconceptions or preoccupations. For me,
the greatest opportunity for humor in writing is presented
by Talk stories. In fact, they offer, on a small scale, an
opportunity for working toward everything I respect and
admire about reporting—what it can be and should be.

Talk stories are not usually "news" stories, as many reporters define the word, and they are not "feature" stories,

as newspapers use the term. Nor are they in the realm of "gossip," which seems to pervade so many books and magazines as well as newspapers these days—to such an extent that the basic meaning of "reporting" has become fuzzy. There seems to be a popular equation now between large sums of money and exploitative book-length pieces of gossip about sensational personalities, and this equation has somehow encouraged more and more excursions—self-deceptive excursions—into fuzziness.

Talk stories are, of course, anonymous. To me, the anonymity one has in writing for the department is very satisfying. I enjoy it not only because I enjoy working quietly, in the knowledge that my work will have to speak for itself in its own way, but also because doing unsigned pieces gives one a special pleasure and a special freedom. One can experiment, one can take chances, one can concentrate on the matter at hand without self-consciousness or the temptation to show off.

A Talk story brings out some aspect of the truth about a person, a situation, or an event. If it is about a person, I try to build the character as one might do in fiction. Quotations help to provide insight. There are three key limitations that make this kind of factual writing difficult:

1. A reporter must have a strong sense of what should and what should not be revealed—a sense of responsibility toward the person he or she is writing about.

2. In quotations, both what is said and how it is said must be conveyed accurately.

3. What is said must be said in the presence of the reporter. It cannot be "reconstructed" from what the reporter *thinks* may have been said or from what someone else thinks he *remembers* having been said. Memory is notoriously undependable. A reconstructed quotation is not a fact; it is a pseudo-fact.

So you are limited in being bound to the *facts* about a real, living person and by your responsibility not to venture too far into the privacy of that person. You must never assume that you have a right to intrude on that person's thoughts and feelings, to violate the inherent secrecy of what is going on in that person's brain. If what you select to report about the person reveals what you *think* is going on in that person's brain, that is another matter. But you must always be aware of the difference between what you know and what you merely *think* you know about a person.

Does a tape recorder used in reporting help reveal any truth? I don't believe so. In fact, I believe that a tape recorder gets in the way of your response to a person, and it is this response that gives an interview its authenticity. Tape recorders almost always take the life out of your response to a person, and the response of the person to the tape recorder may deaden things further. There may be instances when you need to have a record of every word. Most of the time, however, if you depend on your own response you will find in your notes the exact words, the exact rhythms—the exact truth—much of which you might have missed if you had turned over your listening to a machine. Furthermore, the practice of depending on a tape recording makes for a lifelessness in the way you report. It makes *you* lazy and inert.

The roots of good Talk reporting are to be found in the tradition of good reporting in general. Good reporting can be long or short, and I love it whatever its length. A Talk story is a specific yet mysterious literary form, of which brevity is just one element. A Talk story is not a shorter version of something else. It has its own dimensions, and is complete in itself, often compressing into inches the substance of an article of great length. It contains the essence of something. It is a distillation. For me, the definition of good reporting is good writing about real people, real situations, real events. When the reporting, whether short or long, is very good, I find it thrilling to read. Without exception, it directs my attention as a reader to *what* has been written, not to *who* has done the writing. Invariably, the great reporter-writers have wanted it that way. They have given us their reporting, and have been quiet about it. One can read the reporting of some of the great reporter-writers of the past, know that they were telling us the truth about real people, real situations, real events, and find it exciting.

Among the great reporter-writers of the past, certainly, are John Aubrey (1625–1697), Daniel Defoe (1659–1731), Ivan Turgenev (1818–1883), and Henry Mayhew (1812–1887). They were hard-working writers, and they were pretty quiet about their work. Today, the name of Mayhew, one of the world's great reporters, is virtually unknown. He wrote "London Labour and the London Poor," a multivolume work of reporting (for which he did not have and did not need a tape recorder) that should be studied today by anyone interested in factual writing. Here is a quotation from "The Doll's-Eye Maker," one of his many marvellous pieces: "A curious part of the street toy business is the sale of dolls, and especially that odd branch of it, doll's-eye making. There are only two persons following this business in London, and by the most intelligent of these I was furnished with the following curious information. 'I make all kinds of eyes,' the eye-manufacturer said, 'both dolls' and human eyes; birds' eyes are mostly manufactured in Birmingham, and as you say, sir, bull's eyes at the confectioner's. Of dolls' eyes, there are two sorts, the common and the natural, as we call it. The common are simply small hollow glass spheres, made of white enamel, and coloured either black or blue, for only two colours of these are made. The bettermost dolls' eyes, or the natural ones, are made in a superior manner, but after a similar fashion to the commoner sort. The price of the common black and blue dolls' eyes is five shillings for twelve dozen pair. We make very few of the bettermost kind, or natural eyes for dolls, for the

price of those is about fourpence a pair, but they are only
for the very best dolls. . . . Where we make one pair of eyes
for home consumption, we make ten for exportation; a great
many eyes go abroad. . . . They can't make wax dolls in
America, sir, so we ship off a great many there. The reason
why they can't produce dolls in America is owing to the
climate. The wax won't set in very hot weather, and it cracks
in extreme cold. I knew a party who went out to the United
States to start as a doll-maker. He took several gross of my
eyes with him, but he couldn't succeed. The eyes that we
make for Spanish America are all black. A blue-eyed doll
wouldn't sell at all there. Here, however, nothing but blue
eyes goes down; that's because it's the colour of the Queen's
eyes, and she sets the fashion in our eyes as in other
things.' " Henry Mayhew would have written wonderful
Talk stories, I think, if *The New Yorker* had been around in the
nineteenth century.

The reporting in Talk stories is the kind that is deeply
respectful of facts. One of the conspicuous things about
Aubrey, Defoe, Turgenev, and Mayhew is that they were all
enraptured by facts. They tried to set down what could be
seen and heard and touched, what could be tested and
confirmed by others: what was true. They wrote about par-
ticulars; they didn't generalize. They didn't analyze; they
tried to understand but not overinterpret. They did not in-
dulge in flourishes; they did not feel a need to show off. All
of them wrote at times in the first person, but none of them
called attention to himself. Their interest was in *what they were
writing about*. All were people who had a genuine curiosity
about other people and about how things worked. All had
highly developed powers of observation. Not one of them
was mean-spirited. They had no ulterior purposes—no interest in creating a sensation or making a popular success.
Nothing was hidden. They offered a true account, a true
report, a true portrait. Implicit in whatever they wrote was

a firm moral grounding: they were devoted to the truth.

The following is from an exquisite and memorable piece of reporting written in 1870—"The Execution of Tropmann," by Ivan Turgenev, who was, of course, primarily a fiction writer, but who did several notable pieces of factual writing, of reporting: "It was five to seven, but the sky hardly grew lighter and the same dull mist covered everything, concealing the contours of all objects. The roar of the crowd encompassed us by an unbroken, ear-splitting, thunderous wave as soon as we stepped over the threshold. Our small group, which had become thinner, for some of us had lagged behind, and I too, though walking with the others, kept myself a little apart, moved rapidly over the cobbled roadway of the courtyard straight to the gates. Tropmann minced along nimbly—his shackles interfered with his walk —and how small he suddenly appeared to me, almost a child! Suddenly the two halves of the gates, like some immense mouth of an animal, opened up slowly before us— and all at once, as though to the accompaniment of the great roar of the overjoyed crowd which had at last caught sight of what it had been waiting for, the monster of the guillotine stared at us with its two narrow black beams and its suspended axe."

The first writer to do what would today be Talk stories, or even Profiles, of real people was John Aubrey. Here is a sample of his reporting, from his "Brief Lives": "Captain John Graunt (afterwards, major) was born 240 *die Aprilis,* at the 7 Starres in Burchin Lane, London, in the parish of St. Michael's Cornhill, ½ an hour before eight o' clock on a munday morning, the signe being in the 9 degree of Gemini that day at 12 o'clock, Anno Domini 1620. He was bred up (as the fashion then was) in the Puritan way; wrote Shorthand dextrously; and after many yeares constant hearing and writing sermon-notes, he fell to buying and reading of the best Socinian bookes, and for several years continued of that Opinion. At last, he turned a Roman Catholique, of which religion he dyed a great Zealot. To give him his due prayse, he was a very ingeniose and studious person, and generally beloved, and rose early in the morning to his Study before shop-time. He understood Latin and French. He was a pleasant facetious Companion, and very hospitable. He was by Trade, Haberdasher of small-wares, but was free of the Drapers-Company. A man generally beloved; a faythfull friend. Often chosen for his prudence and justness to be an Arbitrator; and he was a great Peace-maker. He had an excellent working head, and was very facetious and fluent in his conversation."

Daniel Defoe, the humane and moral author of works of both fiction ("Moll Flanders," "Robinson Crusoe") and fact ("Tour through the Whole Island of Great Britain"), who "first perfected the art of the reporter" according to the historian George Macaulay Trevelyan, was also the creator, in "A Journal of the Plague Year," of a factual report written in fictional form. Here is a bit from that report: "It is scarce credible what dreadful cases happened in particular families every day; people, in the rage of the distemper, or in the torment of their swellings, which was indeed intolerable, running out of their own government, raving and distracted, and oftentimes laying violent hands upon themselves, throwing themselves out at their windows, shooting themselves, etc. Mothers murdering their own children, in their lunacy some dying of mere grief, as a passion; some of mere fright and surprise, without any infection at all; others frightened into idiotism and foolish distractions; some into despair and lunacy; others into melancholy madness."

Fictional "devices" have been used in reporting for centuries—this is not a recent "invention." Careful observation, significant details, characterization, insight into a character or a situation—all these can be as much a part of good factual writing as they are of fiction. And the basic techniques of both are and always have been the same: exposition, description, and narration. In reporting, there can be not only characterization and character development but also a "story"—even a plot. The two kinds of writing differ in important ways, however. Some fiction contains essayistic passages, in which the writer sounds off about what he feels and thinks. This has no place in reporting. The reporter keeps his opinions, his sentiments, his prejudices to himself. And something else that is, or should be, peculiar to fiction is the author's freedom to say what people think and feel. Contrary to what some writers believe today, what is inside another person's head is "unreportable." The closest a reporter can come is to tell what a person *says* he thinks or feels, or thought or felt.

Two of the great reporters of the present, in my opinion, are Joseph Mitchell and Berton Roueché, and the work of both demonstrates much about every kind of good reporting, long or short. It happens that both men are staff writers for *The New Yorker,* but neither one has written much for The Talk of the Town. Both are outstanding stylists, but neither has a style that calls attention to itself.

For several decades, Joseph Mitchell has been writing his meticulously worked-out, profoundly felt, inimitable factual pieces. Among outstanding stylists, he has the most transparent style of all. In reading Mitchell's reporting, one never stops—or is stopped—to exclaim "What a style!" or "What a vocabulary!" or "What an effect!" Running through all his pieces—about idiosyncratic people in a fish market or in a saloon, for instance—are undercurrents of humor and of a deep awareness of the large enigmas of life and of death. Here is a quotation from Mitchell's "McSorley's Wonderful Saloon": "From the time he was twenty until he was fifty-five, Old John drank steadily, but throughout the last thirty-two years of his life, he did not take a drop, saying, 'I've had my share.' Except for a few experimental months in 1905 or 1906, no spirits ever have been sold in McSorley's; Old John maintained that the man never lived who needed a stronger drink than a mug of stock ale warmed on the hob of a stove. He was a big eater. Customarily, just before locking up for the night, he would grill himself a three-pound T-bone, placing it on a coal shovel and holding it over a bed of oak coals in the backroom fireplace. He liked to fit a whole onion into the hollowed-out heel of a loaf of French bread and eat it as if it were an apple. He had an extraordinary appetite for onions, the stronger the better, and said that 'Good ale, raw onions, and no ladies' was the motto of his saloon.''

For the past forty-odd years, Berton Roueché has been writing, in clean, chaste, utterly clear, beautiful prose, about obscure people who are doing useful and fascinating work (a breeder of Sardinian donkeys, say, or a pair of herb farmers), about extraordinary cases of medical detection, about small towns in the United States. Like Turgenev, Roueché is a writer both of fiction and of fact, but he has demonstrated that he always knows what he has a right to do in the one or the other. Here is a small sample of his exemplary factual writing in his book "The Greener Grass," from a piece entitled "A Cup of Lemon Verbena": "We walked around the greenhouse, across a dusty barnyard, and up a short, steep lane to the drying house. It is a small wooden building, overlooking a scrubby pasture. The truck, a little jeep pickup, was at the door, with its engine idling, and a quaking heap of dull-gray-green sage in back. An elderly man in overalls was standing beside the truck, lifting the sage out and dropping it into a vat of water. He gave us a placid glance, nodded to Miss Thomas, and then fished a dripping clump of sage from the vat and carried it over to a shoulder-high tier of wire-mesh trays that stood just outside the door—they looked like short-legged iron cots, stacked one on top of another—and spread it out in one of them. 'I have an idea a lot of herb growers don't bother to wash their cuttings,' Miss Thomas said. 'As a matter of fact, I don't know of any others that do. Fresh herbs aren't really dirty, but we always give them a good dunking just the same. That's one big difference between our herbs and most others. There just isn't anything that's too much trouble when you're going in for quality, you know.' "

I am proud to be a part of a tradition of writing which goes back several centuries. I am proud, too, to be a part of *The New Yorker's* special tradition of highly disciplined, literary, thorough, honest reporting, which includes Joseph Mitchell, Berton Roueché, and many other writers who have written Profiles and Reporter at Large pieces intended, in one way or another, to cast some light on what this world is about. And certainly I am no less proud to have contributed something of myself to the modest and great tradition of The Talk of the Town.

❖ *Takes*

IT'S always an adventure to watch John Huston directing one of his movies—or, for that matter, to watch John Huston —and we didn't pass up the chance last week when he spent a few days here shooting some scenes for his latest movie, "The Kremlin Letter," which is his twenty-ninth, and is about spies and spying and various forms of low-life skul- duggery. At sixty-two, Huston seems to have as much of a tendency as ever to attract dramatic characters and movie- like scenes to himself, so that he seems constantly to move as the leading character in one of his own movies. We started out with him on the morning after his arrival, riding with him in a limousine up through Central Park toward his first location, the Museum and Library of the Hispanic Society of America, at Broadway and 155th Street. He sat in a corner of the rear seat, his face browned, weather-beaten, fur- rowed, his hair gray and cut short, and his eyes narrowed against the smoke of a little cigar in his mouth. He wore a pale-yellow turtleneck under one of his self-designed bush- jacket suits (this one khaki-colored). Through the window, he regarded Central Park as though it were Kenya bush country. Next to him sat his eighteen-year-old daughter, Anjelica, a very beautiful, very tall, brown-eyed girl with elegant, Roman features and wearing an up-to-the-minute mini-costume; she is in New York understudying the part of

Ophelia in a British production of "Hamlet." In what appeared to be considerable rapport with her father, she, too, looked at the Park through half-closed eyes. On one jump seat sat the producer of "The Kremlin Letter," an anxious but amiable young man, wiry, slightly built, and growing a villainous-looking beard—Carter De Haven III, grandson of a famous vaudeville performer of that name. Up front with the driver was Ernest Anderson, a longtime friend and aide of Huston's, who joined him in 1950, after combining Madison Avenue advertising and the production of concerts by jazz musicians in the nineteen-forties. This was the first day since Huston made "The Asphalt Jungle," in 1949, that he had arranged to shoot scenes for a movie in New York.

"Well, how does New York look to you?" we asked him.

Huston's face registered profound consideration of the question. He maneuvered the cigar to one corner of his mouth. He crossed his legs. He nodded to De Haven. Anderson half-turned in the front seat and waited for the answer. "Well, I'll tell you," Huston began. "My heart, my heart always *leaps* when I set down at Kennedy Airport!" He gave his full body as well as his full face to a laugh, uniquely Hustonian, and leaned toward us, putting his face right up to ours and taking a long time to let his laugh subside. *Cut.*

Heading north on upper Broadway, past the supermarkets and the tenements and the warm-weather sidewalk life of housewives, children, truck drivers, and loafers, we asked, "Do things look different from the way you remember them when you lived here?"

This time, Huston just talked. "When I was a kid, in the late twenties, there was such a wonderful variety of lives you could live in New York. I had the boxing at St. Nick's, the literary world of O'Neill and Anderson, the poetry of E. E. Cummings and Edna St. Vincent Millay, and the East Side social life, and it was wonderful to go from one to another. Harlem was one of the most creative places in the world. I used to love to go to the little clubs in Harlem. When I was twenty-two or twenty-three, I had a friend there named Billy Pierce, who ran a dancing school with a dancer named Buddy Bradley. Billy was getting old And he walked with a cane. And Billy and I became very good friends. I used to go there in the middle of the night to watch Billy and Buddy make up dance routines." Huston paused dramatically. He puffed on his cigar. "One day . . ." He paused again. "One day, Billy said to me, 'Colored people fall out when things is going bad. White people fall out when things is going *good.'* " Pause. Hustonian, close-to-our-face laughter. *Cut.*

We stopped for a traffic light at Broadway and 144th Street. Two small boys crossing the street in front of our car looked at its occupants with a certain unfriendliness. One of them banged on the fender with a small stone and skipped away.

"New York has always been changing," Huston said. "In one's youth, one thinks it stands still, and one believes in absolutes. I came on a lovely metaphor this morning."

"What is it?" De Haven asked.

"I'm going to tell it to you," Huston said, lowering his voice mysteriously, then letting his laugh rise up in a nice crescendo, to subside in a fit of coughing. "I wouldn't dream of *not* telling it to you," Huston said. "I became very *fond* of this metaphor. It was 'These manifestations are just coming to the surface. Time is a slow-moving centrifuge.' " Pause. Laugh. Cough. *Cut.*

Into the Museum of the Hispanic Society of America. A bronze sign on the iron gates to the museum steps had been changed, for the scene in the movie, to read "The Tillinger Foundation." According to the complicated story of "The Kremlin Letter," the Tillinger Foundation was the front for a band of old-time spies who were enlisting a young American to take part in some anti-Communist dirty work. The young American was being played by Patrick O'Neal. Two of the old-time spies were being played by George Sanders and Nigel Green. The set was the front room of the museum —dark-red marble, with an open balcony running around the entire room, and, on the walls of both the ground floor and the balcony floor, large oil paintings by Goya, Velázquez, and others. Camera, dollies, lights, cameramen, crew, assistant directors, and the actors were waiting for Huston in the front room, along with the curator and overseers of the museum. Huston greeted everybody, then walked slowly toward a painting of the Duchess of Alba by Goya. He stood there quietly for several minutes, shaking his head in awe and disbelief. The Duchess of Alba looked coolly at him, a black lace mantilla covering her head and shoulders, one golden-sleeved hand on her hip, the other with a heavy-ringed forefinger pointing down to her delicate silver-and-gold shoes. "My God!" said Huston. "My God, isn't she *some*thing!" *Cut.*

The next morning, we met Huston at the location of his next set—the Central Park Zoo, in front of cages occupied by two baby gorillas, a black panther, and a lioness. In the movie, Patrick O'Neal and Nigel Green were going to be spying there on the daughter of a United Nations delegate from the Soviet Union. The early morning had been cloudy, threatening rain, and some of the crew were struggling with lights in case it stayed dark. As soon as Huston arrived—cigar in mouth, and wearing a light-blue version of his bush suit—the sun broke through the clouds.

"How do you do it?" one of the crew asked Huston.

"I make medicine in the morning, that's all," Huston said.

"It doesn't pay to monkey around with God," said the man.

"He smiled on this picture more than He did on 'The Bible,' I'll tell you that," said Huston, and he walked over to the cage of the baby gorillas and greeted them graciously. "Well. My goodness. Hel-*lo,* babies. How are *you* this morning?"

The baby gorillas leaped at the bars, as though Huston were a mother gorilla. De Haven came over and stood next to Huston, watching the gorillas, who were now working their mouths at Huston.

"Those are the babies," Huston said. "Aren't they the dearest, gentlest, most wonderful creatures?"

"Well, yes," said De Haven.

"A friend of mine has eight gorillas as pets," Huston said. "John Aspinall. He runs the Clermont, on Berkeley Square —the biggest gambling house in England. Just a beautiful house. And John Aspinall is a gentleman, an Oxford man. He lives out in Kent, near Canterbury. He invited me out to meet his gorillas. And I went into the cages with them. And, I tell you, they're the nicest people I've met in a long time." Hustonian laugh. "There was one young lady in the cage," Huston said, lowering his tone. "And she made it clear to me, if I sent her flowers—why, she'd go to the theatre with me."

"I see," said De Haven.

"You go for walks with Aspinall's gorillas," Huston said. "He takes the gorillas out for walks, two at a time, holding each by the hand. I tell you, I'd love to spend the night in the cages with those gorillas, spend the whole *night* with them. To penetrate the *mys-*tery of it."

"Couldn't they break your neck?" we asked.

"Yes, but they wouldn't," said Huston.

"How come?" we asked.

"Because they aren't that kind of people," Huston said, very softly. *Cut.*

Patrick O'Neal and Nigel Green were sitting on a park bench, the camera trained on them as they glanced around furtively, watching the Russian delegate's daughter while she sketched on a pad in front of the lioness's cage. Huston stood near the camera, waiting for the lighting to be ready. He was joined by Gladys Hill, the co-author, with Huston, of the screenplay for "The Kremlin Letter."

"I've just been to the Hispanic Museum," Miss Hill said. "It's just great. Tremendous."

Huston stepped away from the camera. "Did you see the Goyas?" he asked her.

"I did," she said.

"Three of the greatest Goyas I've ever seen," he said. "Unbe*lie*vable Goyas. And those two Velázquez. Don't they make you *weep?*"

"They do," Miss Hill said.

"And they've got half a dozen El Grecos in there!" Huston said. "My God, those El Grecos! And the Roman glass! The doorknobs! The furniture! Everything! And done in absolute, beautiful taste. And all those people taking care of the place! All those wonderful, gentle, charming people."

"Anything in there you'd want to own?" we asked.

"Yes," Huston said, as though we were giving him an argument. "Everything!" *Cut.*

Another day of shooting "The Kremlin Letter" in New York. The Village. Location: Interior of a small coffeehouse on Macdougal Street. On the steps of a building across the street stood a large group of watchers—neighborhood people, mostly young, bearded, and costumed more outlandishly than a group of extras playing their counterparts, who were seated for the camera inside the coffeehouse. Huston came out of the coffeehouse for a breather. He was now wearing a short-sleeved version of his bush suit, in khaki. Someone had pinned an "Irish Power" button on his lapel. He peered at the crowd across the street. A boy wearing a boater and a sleeveless red undershirt waved to Huston, and he waved back. De Haven came over to him, and Huston said that Anderson was going to take him to one of the few places left in the city where jazz was being played.

"Ernie knows them all, and all the musicians love Ernie," Huston said. "You know, I want to tell you a story." He leaned toward De Haven, his manner highly conspiratorial.

"One day, in Paris, Ernie introduced me to Dizzy Gillespie, and we spent a wonderful evening in one of those jazz places listening to Dizzy play. Some months later, I was in New York, and, through Ernie, I met Louis Armstrong, who invited me to be his guest at ringside at the Patterson-Johannson fight in Yankee Stadium. We arrived and sat down, and then Louis spotted Dizzy a few seats away. Louis called Dizzy over and introduced me, saying, 'This is Walter Huston.' " Huston paused, grinned, drew on his cigar. "Well, Dizzy shook my hand, and he said, 'Glad to meet you. I met your son in Paris.' " Laughter from everybody around, with Huston's loudest of all. *Cut.*

On the way back to his hotel, Huston stopped at an apartment-house development on La Guardia Place, south of Washington Square, to look at a huge, three-story-high stone sculpture, a reproduction of a head of a young girl by Picasso. Without saying anything, Huston walked around the sculpture a few times. It was late afternoon, and sunny, with a soft wind blowing. A small boy went past dancing, having a good time by himself. An old woman walked by with a Great Dane on a leash. A couple of teen-agers were playing handball against a wall of the nearest apartment house. Still not talking, Huston started to leave. He rounded the corner of the apartment house, and when the Picasso sculpture was out of sight, he took us by the shoulder. We stopped. He looked secretive. He jerked his head in the direction of the sculpture. Very slowly, he drew us back toward the corner. "She's peeking at us," he said, in a whisper. Under his direction, we peered around the corner of the building, and, sure enough, there was the face of the sculpture, peeking at us. *Cut.*

❖ Revels

JOHN HUSTON was in town last week for the opening of his thirtieth movie, "Fat City." Huston is, of course, an original. He moves, as we've noted more than once in the past twenty-odd years, like a bigger-than-life character in one of his own movies, and it's always a pleasure to watch him go. So we were delighted to accept his invitation to accompany him, his twenty-two-year-old son, Tony, and a few other well-defined characters, to round out the scene, to the opening of—and later a party for—"Fat City." Both were held at the Museum of Modern Art.

There was the usual limousine transportation provided by the producer—in this case, Ray Stark. We rode with the two Hustons, both of whom were wearing crisp seersucker jackets, the father with a white shirt and a rakish black bow tie, the son with a brick-red shirt and a multicolored Art Nouveau tie. The son, six feet four, has a couple of inches on his father. Both men have beards, Tony Huston's being new, spare, and black, and John Huston's gray, scraggly, and somewhat shorter than the one he wore as Noah in his movie "The Bible." Also in the car were three handsome, elegantly attired, horse-loving non-movie friends from California—Celeste Shane, Darlene Pearson, and Bill Gardner. They talked about how *Harper's Bazaar* had said there was a beautiful woman to be found on every street corner in New

York but they couldn't see *any*. It was apparent that they liked California better. John Huston listened, laughed with them, smoked a Montecristo, and saved his conversation for later. We complimented Tony Huston on his appearance. (We might add that Tony, whose full name is Walter Anthony Huston, and his sister, Anjelica, both have faces that remind us of their mother, the late Enrica Soma Huston, who was a strikingly beautiful woman.)

"I just got this jacket at Abercrombie & Fitch," Tony said, in a kind of light and subtly mixed English-Irish-perfectly-enunciated way of speaking that sounded all his own. "I came over here from London to keep Dad company, and I brought London summer clothes—thick tweeds, suitable for the Highlands."

"Tony's been going to all the museums," Huston said, regarding his son with unconcealed admiration, very much the way the late Walter Huston and John used to look at each other. "While I stay behind and do what Ray Stark and Columbia, the distributor, want me to do for 'Fat City.' " The two Hustons laughed in their individual ways.

"Today, I talked to Frederick Dockstader, at the Heye Foundation, about some American Indian art I've started collecting in my little flat in London," Tony said. "I've always been interested in antiques, but I'm only learning now. I thought prices in London might be better than they are here, but I learned today that the reverse is true."

Huston *père* again laughed appreciatively.

In the few remaining blocks to the Museum, we asked Tony to bring us up to date on his activities in general and his falconry in particular.

"I've trained about thirty birds of prey since I was about ten," he said. "Falconry is the blood sport that intrudes least upon nature. I've read just about everything ever written about the art. It hasn't died in me at all. And I'm still writing poetry, which I started doing when I was seven or eight. My interest has never died out. But I'm writing more prose now. When I graduated from Westminster School, I went to London University to study English Literature. I ended up after a year feeling that one way *not* to end up as a writer was to study English Literature."

Two more Huston laughs.

"I wasn't a dropout," Tony continued. "I can always go back. But I felt I might have got into a hole. An opportunity came up for me to travel around America with Buckminster Fuller, going with him from campus to campus. I was transcribing his tapes. I ended up with three hundred hours of tapes. I stayed with him for six months. I feel that Bucky Fuller is one of the very few great men I've ever met. He's got so many things. This great energy. And what you might call his optimism. It was quite wonderful to be with him."

"How did you find the response to him at the colleges?" we asked.

"Very good among the young people," Tony said. "The faculty people were different. I was disappointed by quite a number of them. They would be a little bit mean in the way they tried to find fault with him."

Out of the car at the Museum. Tony stepped aside quickly and the friends from California faded into the Museum as a small crush of young admirers—bearded, bluejeaned, long-haired, and sweaty—advanced on John Huston and told him they had been watching the free day-long showings of many of his old movies at the Columbia I and II, and thought the movies were great. Into the Museum's lobby, where the movie business took over. Columbia beaters. Assistant beaters. Ray Stark. Leo Jaffe, president of Columbia Pictures Industries, and his wife. Stanley Schneider, president of Columbia Pictures, and *his* wife. Distributors. Theatre owners. Agents. Television reporters with TV lights, portable cameras, and portable mikes. Still photographers with flashbulb cameras. Rich supporters of the Museum of Modern Art. Publisher Sam Newhouse and *his* wife. His son Donald Newhouse and *his* wife. Everybody milling around John Huston and shaking his hand and making remarks.

" 'Fat City' isn't my subject, but I'm here anyway."

"Let's hope to God it gets them coming to the theatre."

"The film was a smash at the Cannes Film Festival."

Then the head of the Museum's film department, Willard Van Dyke, came over. "I'm Willard Van Dyke," said Willard Van Dyke to Huston. "I'm going to introduce you tonight. This is my wife, Barbara."

Huston smiled, laughed, posed for the cameras, shook everybody's hand, and looked at his watch.

"It's about eight o'clock," Huston called over to Ray Stark, who was separated from him by a four-foot-high ribbon. Stark, a very friendly stocky man wearing a royal-blue jacket and horn-rimmed tinted glasses, paused in front of the ribbon.

"Ray, jump over that thing!" Huston called to him. "Jump!"

Ray Stark hesitated.

"Jump!" Huston called, giving one of his throaty laughs.

Ray Stark jumped. Huston received him with a hug.

"Say, I have a cast of that sculpture," Stark said, of a piece of sculpture in the Museum garden.

"Let's go look at it!" Huston said, making a whole production of his brief line, and guiding Stark into position in front of the Gaston Lachaise figure of a flying woman. The photographers had a field day getting pictures of the sculpture behind the two men.

"This is *John's* night," Stark said happily, moving back toward the lobby. "The director is the important one."

"They're the artist. Right, Ray?" a heavily suntanned man said to Stark.

"Right," Stark said.

"I hope to Christ it goes, this picture," said the suntanned man. "I hope this is the year for pictures about fighters."

Ray Stark looked a little worried.

Late arrivals. The stars of "Fat City." Stacy Keach, with the singer Judy Collins. John Huston hugged Stacy Keach, and vice versa. Then came Keach's co-star, Susan Tyrrell, escorted by her agent, Bill Barnes. Huston hugged Susan Tyrrell. Everybody hugged everybody else. Tony Huston appeared again and shook hands with Judy Collins.

"Stacy is wonderful, just wonderful," Tony said to Judy Collins. "Not only as an actor, I mean, but as a person."

Everybody in the vicinity expressed agreement.

"I'm from Columbia Pictures," a calm, bespectacled woman said to us. "I met John Huston when he was making 'We Were Strangers.' There's Beverly Adams. She was a Columbia starlet. She's with her husband, there—Vidal Sassoon, the famous hairdresser. She married him and stopped working. Boom! Just like that."

TV lights were on Huston. Kevin Sanders, the WABC-TV critic, was asking him, "Mr. Huston, just what does the expression 'fat city' mean?"

"It's a jazz musician's term," Huston said. "It's a dreamer's term, meaning no boundaries to the possibilities. It's the pot of gold at the end of the rainbow."

"Everybody into the theatre!" a Columbia man was yelling.

Standing in front of the screen, Willard Van Dyke made his introduction: "I want to welcome one of the most favorite of all film directors, Mr. John Huston."

Big applause from the audience, which looked like Museum of Modern Art members and goers. We saw more celebrities, including Mr. and Mrs. Otto Preminger.

"I have a peculiar nostalgia tonight," Huston was saying in front of the screen. "I was coming to the Museum of Modern Art when it was in the old Heckscher Building. . . ."

The lights dimmed, and the movie started. Lovely pictures. Terrific characterizations. Wonderful faces. Good acting. Real Huston stuff.

The end. Applause. Everybody into the garden for the party, described in the invitation as "a champagne supper and reception for Mr. Huston."

There was plenty of curried chicken and rice and shrimp salad and drinks, all catered by Robert Day-Dean's, and there was plenty of talk about "Fat City."

"Very authentic."

"A beautiful picture."

"It's too down. I don't like down movies. I like up movies."

"How come Henny Youngman is at *this* party?"

"I'd book it. How about you, Al? You book it?"

"It's like one of those goddam foreign pictures. No pace. No momentum."

"I loved the picture, John," Otto Preminger said to Huston.

"We loved it," said Mrs. Preminger. "It's beautifully done."

There were a lot of critics there, official and unofficial, and all gobbling chicken and rice and shrimp salad. Everybody eyed everybody else. Woody Allen stood off to one side with his own private group of friends, but they all eyed everybody, too. Almost everybody came and talked to Huston about one thing or another. A young man named Mike Sragow, of the *Crimson*, told Huston he was writing an honors thesis at Harvard about him and his movies. Leo Lerman, a bearded editor of *Mademoiselle*, came over and told Huston he loved the picture. "And I love your beard," he added.

Anjelica Huston, who works as a model in New York, and who was wearing a white chiffon shimmery gown and pearls, hugged her father from behind, and Huston looked happy. Mike Sragow asked Huston if it was true that he might make a picture with Leslie Fiedler. Huston laughed deeply. At least seven heavily suntanned men came over and introduced their wives to Huston. One of the men said, "Good luck on the picture. I hope for your sake it makes money."

"Thank you very much," Huston said, graciously making his usual big production of the line.

Huston ducked out of the party fairly early. Tony Huston walked out of the Museum with him. The sidewalk was now empty of fans. Tony's face was glowing with enthusiasm.

"Good night, Dad," Tony said, and the two men hugged each other. "It was the best, Dad," Tony said.

Huston drew away slightly from his son, looked at him, and then drew him close again and gave his deep laugh over the younger man's shoulder.

Tony then drew away and looked straight into his father's eyes. "It was really the best, Dad," he said. "And you know I don't lie."

❖ Bartók in the Morning

ONE rainy midmorning last week, Benny Goodman ar
ranged a couple of antique music stands alongside the
Mason & Hamlin baby-grand piano in the large living room
of his apartment high up in Manhattan House. Mr. Goodman, at seventy-one, was suntanned and looked almost exactly as he has looked for decades the same lip, the same
quick grin, the same just about everything, except for a bit
of grayness and wispiness of hair. He was wearing a light-
blue worsted suit over a khaki safari shirt open at the collar.
He cleared the top of the piano, scooping up a half-dozen
framed pictures of his family—his late wife, Alice; his
daughters, Rachel and Benjie, both now in their early thirties and married, and living in Florence, Italy, and East Deer-
field, Massachusetts, respectively; Rachel's daughter,
Naomi, one and a half—and put them all on a coffee table,
next to a battered and peeling brown leather-covered clarinet case. He lifted the lid of the piano and fixed it open. One
of the music stands, which he had placed close to the piano
bench, was a double one of oak, early-nineteenth-century
French, with candelabra, and with an inlaid edging of birch.
The other stand, near the tail of the piano, was of indetermi-
nate age, was painted mostly black, and was inlaid with
mother-of-pearl. Mr. Goodman set chairs, taken from
around his dining-room table, in front of the stands. Then

he tossed worn-looking sets of sheet music onto each of the music stands and onto the piano rack. The sheet music bore the following heading:

BÉLA BARTÓK
Contrasts for Violin, Clarinet and
Pianoforte
Written for and Dedicated to Benny
Goodman and Joseph Szigeti
September 24, 1938

The piece, which takes about twenty minutes to play, was the final one on an all-Bartók program to be presented later that week in Orchestra Hall, Detroit, where the Detroit Symphony Orchestra, conducted by Antal Dorati, was celebrating the hundredth anniversary of Bartók's birth. Mr. Goodman ambled around the living room picking up, examining, testing, and discarding clarinet reeds. Reeds and more reeds seemed to be scattered all over the place: on the mantel of a fireplace, under a large Vlaminck still-life showing sheets of music, books, a pitcher, a cup, and a boxwood clarinet; on the floor, near a clarinet stand holding a boxwood clarinet just like the one in the painting; on a table holding pre-Columbian sculptures of two drummers and a man playing a clarinetlike instrument; on the shelves of a cabinet displaying some Meissen frogs playing various musical instruments, including the clarinet.

There was a buzz at the front door, and Mr. Goodman opened it to admit his two fellow-performers—the violinist Yehudi Menuhin, in a dark-blue raincoat, and the pianist Paul Coker, in a mustard-colored raincoat who had come for a rehearsal of "Contrasts" in preparation for the concert.

Mr. Menuhin, holding a brown canvas-covered violin case under one arm and supporting the case with the other hand, greeted Mr. Goodman, introduced Mr. Coker, and made a beeline for the piano. "Oh, a Mason & Hamlin!" he said happily, in a light British accent. "Such a good firm, isn't it, Benny?"

"Yeah," Mr. Goodman said. He spoke in his familiar hoarse, drawling voice and added his characteristic hoarse laugh.

"They gave three pianos to my sister and me," Mr. Menuhin said, with a beatific smile.

Looking very serious, Mr. Coker, who is twenty-one and has been a student at Mr. Menuhin's music school near London since he was nine, sat down at the piano and tried it out.

"Lovely," Mr. Menuhin said. He is sixty-four, and his face—now also framed in wispy gray—looked the same as it does in the familiar photographs of the eleven-year-old Yehudi Menuhin, in short pants, making his historic New York début, at Carnegie Hall. Still carrying his violin case, he walked over to the pre-Columbian sculptures. "Oh, I like your figurines here, Benny," he said. "Where do they come from? Are they new or old?"

"Mexico," Mr. Goodman said. "Old."

"Extraordinary," said Mr. Menuhin. "They're in such good condition, Benny. And look at these figurines!" He headed for the display case. "Frogs!" he said, with joy.

"Usually, you see monkeys, in the Meissen," Mr. Goodman said, grinning.

"Frogs make good sense," Mr. Menuhin said.

Mr. Menuhin set his violin case down on a chair and took off his raincoat. He had on a multicolored sports shirt open at the collar and flopping over blue pants, and a heavy royal-blue cardigan with pockets at the bottom. He opened his case and took out his violin, which had been tucked in among assorted handkerchiefs, potions, lotions, and papers, including a passport and many snapshots of children. Mr. Coker, who had on a brown suit with white pinstripes, a tattersall shirt, a necktie, and a brown sweater, took off his jacket and reseated himself at the piano.

"I even got you Szigeti's music stand," Mr. Goodman said, indicating to Mr. Menuhin that he was to take the stand with the candelabra. "I bought it from his wife about thirty years ago, when they had to move away."

"It's a beautiful stand, Benny," Mr. Menuhin said. "Very pretty."

"I use it as an end table," Mr. Goodman said, with his laugh. He took off his jacket and put it around the back of a chair.

"Are we going to sit or stand?" Mr. Menuhin asked.

"I like to stand," Mr. Goodman said.

"So do I, Benny," Mr. Menuhin said. "Do you find you have more breath when you stand?"

"Yeah," Mr. Goodman said.

Mr. Coker, at the piano, sounded the A. Mr. Menuhin put on a pair of heavy horn-rimmed glasses, picked up his violin, and drew his bow over the A string. Mr. Goodman sounded a quick and mellow A and then played a fast run from the top to the bottom register.

"I've got to change violins near the end," Mr. Menuhin said, smiling.

"Yeah," Mr. Goodman said. "At the beginning of the 'Sebes,' the 'Fast Dance,' at the end, Bartók wanted the violin to be deliberately mistuned."

"Fortunately, I just bought a copy of my Guarnerius—of this one, 1742. It's not bad. Not bad."

"I've got to change clarinets, too," Mr. Goodman said, picking up the A clarinet and setting the B-flat clarinet, now without a mouthpiece, at the ready on the floor near his feet.

Mr. Coker warmed up with some scales. Mr. Menuhin echoed him on the violin, and Mr. Goodman played a few more runs. They all opened their sheet music to the first movement, titled "Verbunkos," or "Recruiting Dance."

"Shall I set the tempo?" Mr. Menuhin asked. "Hadn't I better begin?"

He started off with a little pizzicato, and then Mr. Goodman sounded the melodic theme, which was picked up by Mr. Coker. They went right at it, stopping now and then to replay some parts. Occasionally, Mr. Menuhin would make a remark, such as "Let's play very quietly, Benny," or "Shall we do the three-two bar together?," or "Once again. I didn't do it right," or "You're only a little late on the third beat," or "That's it! That's it! Perfect!"

Mr. Goodman made most of his remarks by singing them to the others. "Dee-da-da-dee," he would sing to Mr. Menuhin. Mr. Menuhin would respond by playing the passage that way and then saying, "Oh, that's very nice. That's so nice. I like the fingering." He would play it again and then say, "Do you like it, Benny? Or would it be cleaner—" And he would play it another way.

"Daddle, deedle, daddle, da, da," Mr. Goodman would sing to him.

"Wonderful!" Mr. Menuhin would say, and he would play it that way.

After Mr. Goodman played a long, melodious cadenza, Mr. Menuhin responded with a short pizzicato passage that was practically jumping.

"You must have had wonderful experiences working with Szigeti," Mr. Menuhin said when they took a rest. He sat down. "I'm sure if you had recorded your rehearsals with Szigeti you would have had twenty hours of wonderful conversation. Is it a nice hall in Detroit, Benny?"

"Pretty nice," Mr. Goodman said. "We're not playing in the big hall."

"That's good," Mr. Menuhin said. "It must have been exciting, Benny, to play it with Bartók and Szigeti—the experience of playing it for the first time."

"Bartók was a wonderful piano player," Mr. Goodman said. "We made a recording of 'Contrasts' with Szigeti, and with Bartók at the piano. It's interesting to play the piece after all these years. I think I remember what he wanted. I studied the piece so much that I know the whole thing. Jóska

—Szigeti—would tell me, 'Play the slow movement the way you would "Body and Soul." ' In those days, I was a little bit inhibited. Bartók was very reassuring. He wasn't as fussy as a lot of composers. On one difficult passage, I cracked that I might need three hands, so he said, 'Don't worry. Just approximate.' "

"How wonderful," Mr. Menuhin said.

Mr. Goodman gave his hoarse laugh. "He meant 'Don't take it too seriously.' He was content. He didn't put many instructions in the music. Neither did Mozart. Not like Beethoven," he added. Mr. Menuhin and Mr. Goodman laughed, and Mr. Coker, who seemed to be leaving the talk to the others, joined in. Mr. Goodman glanced out at the rain, which had started to come down heavily. "The first public performance of the piece was at Carnegie Hall. In 1939. I was playing with the band at the Paramount, and I was practicing the piece backstage between shows. Five shows a day. Six on Saturday and Sunday. Then, for the première of the piece—the concert, at Carnegie Hall—we couldn't get anybody to go. In those days, the music publishers were beholden to performers, so we got them to take a block of tickets. Bartók was in Hungary, and Szigeti and I played it with Endre Petri at the piano. The next year, I played the piece again, this time with Szigeti and Bartók himself, at Jordan Hall in Boston. I was so busy with the clarinet that it didn't occur to me that it was history. I last played the piece sixteen years ago, at a music festival at Stratford."

"But you made the record with Bartók," Mr. Menuhin said, standing up. "In 1940?"

"Yeah," Mr. Goodman said. "And I can still hear him. He was a real swinger." He gave his laugh and transferred his mouthpiece to the other clarinet.

They continued playing for a while. Suddenly, Mr. Menuhin broke off. "Should I play louder?" he asked. "Do you want me to play louder, Benny, in this part of the

'Sebes'? You play Bartók with expression, Benny. Beautiful expression. Shall we run through it again, Benny?"

"That'll do it," Mr. Goodman said. "I don't like to rehearse much anyway. Don't leave the fight in the gymnasium, as they say."

"That's a good one," Mr. Menuhin said, with his smile.

"Did you have the disc operation, Yehudi?" Mr. Goodman asked.

"Yes. Twenty-five years ago. In Cape Town, South Africa. I had gone there to give a concert for the blacks. The hospital there was wonderful. When was yours, Benny?"

"Mine was forty-one years ago," Mr. Goodman said.

"You have to keep limber. Do you do exercises, Benny?"

"I swim," Mr. Goodman said. "I know the pools all over the world. It keeps you in better condition. Do you still stand on your head?"

"Oh, yes," Mr. Menuhin said. "And if I find, on airplanes, that I can lie down across the empty seat next to me, that's good."

"I do that, too," Mr. Goodman said, once more changing the mouthpiece on his clarinet.

"Shall we run through it once more?" Mr. Menuhin asked.

"It's a pleasure to play with you guys," Mr. Goodman said.

They started from the beginning and played the piece all the way through.

"Lovely," Mr. Menuhin said at the end.

"Yeah, better, wasn't it?" Mr. Goodman said.

"You play Bartók with such feeling," Mr. Menuhin said.

"The cadenza you played," Mr. Goodman said. "Beautiful."

No one said anything for a moment.

Mr. Menuhin slowly put down his violin, and then he said, "The piece is so full of life and humor."

❧ *Halloween Party*

A LETTER has arrived from a woman we know:

My thirteen-year-old son gave a Halloween costume party for a bunch of boys and girls. I became his financier as he talked endlessly about his Count Dracula costume. Count Dracula seems to have been the most popular Halloween costume for the past ten years—a black satin Count Dracula cape ($18.95), Count Dracula fangs ($1.25), clown whiteface makeup ($2), and Zauders stage blood ($2). The menu for the party included fried chicken, spaghetti, Cokes, salad, and cupcakes with orange or chocolate icing (cost per guest: $7). The candy, for visiting trick-or-treaters as well as for the guests, was orange and black jelly beans, sugar pumpkins, Candy Corn, Tootsie Rolls, Raisinets, Almond Joys, Nestlé Crunch, Baby Ruths, Milky Ways, Heide Jujyfruits, Peanut Chews, and Cracker Jacks (total: $38.65). My son also had eight cookies, six inches in diameter and decorated with black cats ($1.25 each); eight little plastic pumpkins full of hard candies, each with a trembly plastic spider on top ($2.50 each); eight orange-colored balloons that blew up to resemble cats (eighty-five cents each); eight orange-colored lollipops with jack-o'-lantern faces (seventy cents each); a large paper tablecloth showing a black witch standing over a black caldron with spiders popping out of the caldron ($2.25); matching napkins ($1.10); matching paper

cups ($2); matching paper plates ($1.75); a "HAPPY HALLOW-
EEN" sign ($1.25); a dancing skeleton ($3.99); something
called a Happy Spider ($4); a classic jack-o'-lantern, made of
a real pumpkin ($4, plus labor). Total investment in props:
$181.59. Total investment of labor in jack-o'-lantern,
kitchen cleanup, and laundry: $35. Total investment in emo-
tion and puzzlement: indeterminable.

I watch the guests arrive. The first one, A, comes as Darth
Vader, of "Star Wars." B comes as Luke Skywalker, of "Star
Wars." C comes as The Incredible Hulk. D comes as a tramp.
E comes as a ghost. F comes as a ballerina. G comes, in one
of her mother's old evening gowns, as Bette Midler. All are
in an advanced stage of hysteria. A pulls at C's costume. G
immediately starts throwing sugar pumpkins at E. They've
given themselves an hour before they move the party out to
ring doorbells and see what they get. They tear into the fried
chicken, most of them eating three bites and wasting the
rest. They sprinkle jelly beans on the chicken and on the
spaghetti. They pick at the spaghetti, which is on the menu
because my son said everybody likes spaghetti. They eat it
one strand at a time, dropping a strand on the floor for each
strand they consume. They gulp down the Cokes, another
"must"—their appetite for the caffeine insatiable. And what
are they talking about, these eighth graders who are eying
each other fishily? They are talking about their *careers.* They
are talking about getting into Exeter. They are talking about
Yale and Yale Law School. They are talking about how to
get in here and how to get in there. They are talking about
who makes more money, the president of Chase Manhattan
or the president of General Motors. Nobody is talking kid
talk. Nobody is talking about the present time and what to
do with it. Nobody is talking about learning. Nobody
sounds *young.* A, a pudgy boy who tries to find out the marks
of every other child in his class, wants to be "a successful
corporation lawyer." He doesn't say just "corporation law-

yer." It's success that he's bent on. He informs my son that
he intends to have more money than his uncle, who is a
corporation lawyer in Philadelphia. Next, A tells my son
that he wants to go to Exeter. Why? "Because Exeter is a
stepping-stone to Harvard," he says. Not Exeter for the
wonders of Exeter but Exeter because it will be useful *after*
he leaves it.

B, with his mouth full of Almond Joy, is asking the others
a question: "Do you want to be a little fish in a big pond or
a big fish in a little pond?"

What has that got to do with getting an education? How
about the excitement of learning algebra? How about that
wonderful grammar teacher who showed you how to recognize the participle absolute? Why aren't you talking about
your French teacher's getting you to speak French with an
accent that would wow them in Paris? I want to butt in with
my questions, but I keep my mouth shut.

Now A is talking. His mother, he is saying, has taken him
rock climbing, because rock climbing is an impressive activity to put down as his "interest" on the application to Exeter.

"But you *hate* rock climbing!" says D, who is a mischief-
maker with the face of an angel under his tramp makeup.
"You hate to move your *ass,*" D adds.

All right, who else is here? C, who is wearing a mask of
The Incredible Hulk. C is the jock of the group. He has been
in training since the age of two in the craft of giving nothing
away. He's wary and tight and already immunized to the
teeth against charity for its own sake. He, too, wants to be
a corporation lawyer; so do B and D. The girls, though—the
ballerina and Bette Midler—both want to be big-corpora-
tion presidents. They are both relaxed, being well aware of
what women's lib has done for them. E, the ghost, is the only
one with a simple costume, made of a sheet. A, talking to B,
points out that E doesn't have to bother about a costume,
because he's rich, very rich. His grandfather lives in Texas

and owns real oil wells—not new ones but very old and very productive oil wells. E wants to be a movie director and has promised to give my son, who at the moment wants to be an actor, a starring part in his first movie. They are pals. Both of them are regarded with suspicion by the ones who want to be corporation lawyers.

What else are they saying? They're still talking about Exeter. Apparently, A is obsessed by Exeter—it is he who keeps bringing the conversation back to it.

"They ask you to write a 'personal letter' to them," this little busybody says. "They say, 'This letter should represent you as accurately as possible.' But then they tell you in the catalogue what they want, so all you have to do is tell it back to them."

C finally talks. "The way *you* always figure out what the teacher wants and give it right back to *him,*" he says.

D squirts a little Coke at A, and the future lawyers get up and make for the door. They cram their loot bags with the orange and black jelly beans, the Candy Corn, the cookies, the trembly spiders, the balloons, the jack-o'-lantern lollipops, and the rest. They make a big point of thanking me loudly. The girls amble out, smiling knowledgeably at each other. E and my son run to catch up to them. They, too, thank me extravagantly. And they all go off, in their disguises, to do their tricks and get their treats. I am left wondering what it's all about.

❖ Nixon's Walk

WE want to make one thing perfectly clear. President-elect Richard Nixon walks to his pre–White House office, in the Hotel Pierre, from his home, at 810 Fifth Avenue, every time he goes to his office from his home. The walk, by our measurement, comes to two hundred and forty-eight steps— more or less, that is, allowing for a few side steps every once in a while to make way for some nursemaid pushing a baby carriage or some boy or girl or other person walking a dog. Now, to be specific, the two hundred and forty-eight steps include twenty-one steps going west from Mr. Nixon's residence—No. 810—which happens to be on the north side of Sixty-second Street, and the twenty-one steps bring Mr. Nixon to the northeast corner of Sixty-second and Fifth. To be specific again—and we'll get to his destination in just a minute—Mr. Nixon takes exactly one hundred and sixty-nine steps going south to the Fifth Avenue entrance of the Hotel Pierre, at the southeast corner of Sixty-first Street and Fifth Avenue. Now, this is what we mean: Mr. Nixon's walk is composed of two hundred and forty-eight separate and distinct steps, and the steps are not too long—roughly about fifteen, maybe sixteen, inches. What happens is that these steps take him to the Hotel Pierre, where he goes into the lobby and into an elevator and up to his office, and that's that. He's arrived. He's in his office.

Now, here's a description of what Mr. Nixon sees in the course of managing to take these two hundred and forty-eight steps to his pre–White House headquarters. First of all, we have to say that Mr. Nixon may give the appearance of walking briskly, but steps measuring fifteen or sixteen inches each step means—and we want to be perfectly clear about this—steps measuring fifteen or sixteen inches means that he is not stepping too quickly. He is certainly stepping cautiously, and all the time he is stepping he is moving his legs. He also happens to be moving his arms, but we'll get to that in just a couple of minutes. All the time he is stepping, he is looking, observing, staring, gazing, and, we might add, he is seeing what there is to be seen on the whole block —block and a fifth, that is—from his home to his office. Now, bear with us while we take just a minute to explain something that's really quite important if we're going to give you the best possible description of Mr. Nixon's walk to his pre–White House office. If Mr. Nixon looks *north* when he reaches the northeast corner of Fifth Avenue and Sixty-second Street—but *only* if he looks north—he sees No. 815 Fifth Avenue, and on the ground floor of that building there is an office shared by three dentists. If Mr. Nixon looks, he sees the names of the dentists posted in the window of the ground-floor office shared by these three dentists. Their names are G. W. Hindels, D.D.S.; L. Marder, D.D.S.; and M. R. Schoenberg, D.D.S. The reason Mr. Nixon can see these names is that the names are printed in large black letters on the sign in the ground-floor window of the dentists' office. But the fact is that Mr. Nixon usually doesn't bother to take the time to look north, because usually he's thinking about getting to his office, and since the office is south, he's doing his best to go south, because that is what he wants to do.

Let us point one thing out, however: Mr. Nixon *does* look a little bit to the west, even though his gaze is generally directed south. And if Mr. Nixon looks a little bit to the west, he's going to see a number of things in Central Park, not including, we want to make clear, the Children's Zoo, which is three blocks to the northwest. Mr. Nixon happens to see the stone wall bordering the Park, with benches stationed alongside the wall and some dirty newspapers that Mayor Lindsay's Parks Department attendants neglected to pick up, and he also happens to see the tops of some elm and maple trees. If he takes a deep breath—and if the wind is blowing from the northwest—Mr. Nixon will get the odor of some of those baby goats and mama goats and baby pigs and mama pigs that live in the Children's Zoo, on that pretty valuable real estate northwest of 810 Fifth Avenue. If the wind happens to be of gale force, of course, it's pretty clear that Mr. Nixon is going to get a pretty darn strong odor of a lot of baby ducks and mama ducks along with the odor of the baby goats and mama goats and baby pigs and mama pigs.

Keeping his eyes straight ahead as he takes those steps south, Mr. Nixon sees the big sign on the R.C.A. Building that consists of electric lights, very much like the electric-light sign that said "NIXON" during the Presidential-election campaign. The R.C.A. Building sign says "R C A," but we want to explain that this "R C A" sign is clearly visible in the daytime, too. Because Mr. Nixon can, so to speak, see out of the corners of his eyes, he can spot the entrance to the B.-M.T. subway on the west side of Fifth Avenue between Sixty-first and Sixtieth. To make it quite clear, that is the entrance to the Broadway B.-M.T. over to Queens and downtown to Whitehall Street and Brooklyn. It's a pretty fine ride on the B.-M.T. if you don't get shoved into a train during the rush hour, but obviously Mr. Nixon isn't going to be able to take a subway ride to Brooklyn or to Queens during the next forty-four days, and he's certainly not going to be able (ha-ha!) to take one of those rides, much as he'd like to, after January 20th.

Between the Broadway B.-M.T. subway entrance and the side of Fifth Avenue that Mr. Nixon is walking on, there are, of course, a good number of buses, with people riding in them. The buses pretty well obscure the subway entrance from time to time, but Mr. Nixon sees it anyway—at the same time, we might add, not missing many of those advertisements plastered on the sides of the buses. On some of the buses, the "Hello, Dolly!" advertisement is plastered right alongside the "Shouldn't your brand be True?" advertisement. We'd like to point out that the latter advertisement is for True cigarettes and is quite an interesting and clever advertising slogan. But that's getting just a little bit ahead of our story. The first big and quite important sight that Mr. Nixon sees when he emerges from his residence is the Knickerbocker Club, at 2 East Sixty-second Street. Now, the Knickerbocker Club is a large, rectangular building only three stories high, with a nice private garden all walled in by a high brick wall. The Knickerbocker Club happens to be a gentlemen's social club that was founded on October 31, 1871, which means that Mr. Nixon will be nearing the end of the third year of his Presidential term when the Knickerbocker Club will be celebrating the hundredth anniversary of its founding.

Mr. Nixon doesn't take more than twenty-one of his two hundred and forty-eight steps before he sees five potted small fir trees set into large concrete pots. There are nice ivy plants flowing down the sides of the concrete pots, which happen to be set along the front of 812 Fifth Avenue. There are good light poles in front and along the side of his residence as well. On the light poles are signs that Mr. Nixon can read on the way to his office. They read, "Tow Away Zone," and "No Commercial Traffic," and "No Parking Anytime Except Authorized Vehicles," and "No Parking 8 A.M.–6 P.M.—Dept. of Traffic—Official State Vehicles Only." Mr. Nixon can study these signs, or he can notice, and really see, the cars of all the Secret Service people who keep their cars parked on Fifth Avenue—both sides of Fifth Avenue, that is—between Sixty-second and Sixty-first Streets. They just don't pay any attention to those signs. It's high time for all of us to be aware of the fact that the Secret Service cars have signs in their front windows reading, "Official U.S. Secret Service," and they often have little stickers of American flags pasted in the corners of their car windows, both front and rear. Some of their license plates—New York license plates, that is—are Y 2 7567, XD 7455, and Y 2 7612. Other cars bearing government license plates have license plates like G 114 3635 and G 114 3628. There are dozens of cops, members of the New York City Police, stationed along the way from Mr. Nixon's home to his office, and that means that they're stationed there whether Mr. Nixon is here, there, or in Florida, and they have a lot of wooden barriers handy, on which Mr. Nixon can read the inscription "Police Lines Do Not Cross—Police Dept."

Along about—well, we'd guess the hundred-and-forty-fifth step of Mr. Nixon's steps, give or take a step or two, Mr. Nixon passes a light pole on the southeast corner of Sixty-first Street and Fifth Avenue, and it's a light pole that is obviously broken and in need of repair. But we'll get to that in just a minute. First, it's essential to note that there's not another building on Fifth Avenue between the Knickerbocker Club and the M. Hartley Dodge mansion on the northeast corner of Fifth and Sixty-first Street. And that happens to be a good thing, not a bad thing, because there's a high-value piece of property on which *nothing* stands. It happens to belong to the Dodge estate, which refuses to sell it, but we say it's a good thing and not a bad thing because for once, for one time, on this one block, there's a nice piece of private property that's just clearly and simply private. But as soon as you've crossed Sixty-first Street to the southeast corner, there's this light pole, with the bottom part broken, and inside Mr. Nixon can see a mess of wires and junk like that. There's the usual wire trashcan, which happens to be just about midway between the light pole and a mailbox. The trashcan has a copy of the *Times* in it. The mailbox is painted, but not freshly painted, in red, white, and blue, and Mr. Nixon can see that somebody has got to start thinking about the problem of getting some fresh paint, not only for that mailbox but for thousands and hundreds of thousands of mailboxes all over the country. They need painting. Mr. Nixon makes his study of the mailbox on his—well, about his, we'd say, hundred-and-fiftieth step. He probably notes the message, too: "U.S. Mail. Use Zip Code Numbers. Mail Early in the Day." It's quite clear that Mr. Nixon goes along with Mr. Johnson in probably not wanting to make any changes in the message on those boxes—at least, not for the time being—and certainly he doesn't want to make any move that would get in the way of or disrupt the Christmas-rush mail.

Now, bear with us while we get Mr. Nixon past the entrance to the Pierre Café, which happens to come just before he reaches the entrance to the Hotel Pierre. As he steps by the Pierre Café, if he just looks a tiny bit to his left, just a *tiny* bit, out of the corners of his eyes, on that left side, he sees a sign posted near the checkroom at the entrance to the Café, and that sign reads as follows: "Occupancy by More Than 125 Persons Is Dangerous & Unlawful." If he sees that sign, he probably thinks about it. Next, Mr. Nixon takes about twenty steps past five potted trees on the Pierre's side of the sidewalk and two potted trees on the curb side that are substantially the same as the potted trees near Mr. Nixon's residence.

The steps are running out now, and Mr. Nixon goes inside the Pierre, where, we should point out, it takes him another fifty-eight steps to get along that Hotel Commodore–like arcade on the way to the elevator that will take him up to his pre–White House office. He happens to step along on carpets that are cream-colored and decorated with pink roses, and there's a friendly glow from the Pierre's indirect lighting coming down on Mr. Nixon and everybody. If Mr. Nixon reads very fast, he can take in the fact that the Pierre Café, according to a sign on the left side of the arcade, is "New York's intimate rendezvous for luncheon, cocktails, dinner, supper, and dancing, featuring Stanley Worth and his orchestra, with songstylist Susan Brady and pianist-singer Ellen Harwicke Wednesdays–Sundays—Phil Wayne and his orchestra Mondays & Tuesdays—Continuous Entertainment nightly from 5 P.M." It's sort of interesting to realize that Mr. Nixon passes arcade window displays for the Carole Stupell Salon Table Settings—showing gold-rimmed water glasses and a plate with a reproduction of a Grandma Moses painting of a winter farm scene on it—as well as displays of Fabergé and Max Factor perfumes and Dior lipstick.

When Mr. Nixon goes home from his office, of course—and we'd like to especially emphasize this last point—he sees pretty much the same things he saw on his way from his home to his office.

◆ Secretary Shultz

THE other day, we arranged to meet George Pratt Shultz, the eleventh Secretary of Labor, when he came to town. He is forty-eight years old, a graduate of Princeton (class of 1942), a veteran of the Second World War (Marine Corps), a former professor of economics and industrial relations (Massachusetts Institute of Technology, 1948–57, and the University of Chicago's Graduate School of Business, 1957–62), a former college dean (the University of Chicago's Graduate School of Business, 1962–69), a Republican (lifetime), an arbitrator of labor-management disputes (in textiles, in chemicals, in food products, in farm implements, in electrical equipment, in metal fabricating), co-author of two books ("Causes of Industrial Peace Under Collective Bargaining" and "Strategies for the Displaced Worker"), and a husband (of the former Helena M. O'Brien) and father (of Margaret Ann, Kathleen Pratt, Peter Milton, Barbara Lennox, and Alexander George).

Secretary Shultz was going down to City Hall to call on Mayor Lindsay, and he invited us to go along.

"What's been the high point of your life up to now?" we asked him during a ride down the East River Drive in a limousine driven by a chauffeur.

"Being sworn in as Secretary of Labor," Mr. Shultz replied quickly. "Sworn in by the Chief Justice, in the presence of the President, with my wife holding the Bible. It was a dramatic and gripping moment."

"How have things been for you since then?" we asked next.

"Busy. Interesting. And with a level of activity that is wild," he said. "When I go home and my wife asks 'What did you do today, George?' I have to say, 'I can't remember anything about this morning. It was too long ago. I can only tell you what I was doing at five o'clock.' "

A very nice man. Soft-spoken. Trying to overcome his built-in stiffness. Seemingly bland, with a quiet, unobtrusive face. A little flabby here and there, but with a freshly sunburned forehead. Alert eyes, and an expression somewhat defensive and discouraged. A not well-fitting navy-blue suit. A light-blue shirt with a button-down collar. A dark Paisley necktie.

"How does your job compare with being a dean?" we asked.

"As a dean, I worked in ways that were similar," he replied. "As you well know, a dean doesn't dictate. Being an administrator, a dean works with the alumni, with the faculty, with the students. But there are certainly differences. People are not interested in meeting deans or in talking with deans. I'm still not used to it."

"Had you known any of your fellow Cabinet members before January?" we asked.

"I knew David Kennedy, Secretary of the Treasury. He's a trustee of the University of Chicago. And, incidentally, I knew Bob Mayo, Director of the Budget, who is an official of the Continental Illinois National Bank—Kennedy's bank. I had met Governor Romney, Secretary of Housing and Urban Development, on one or two occasions, briefly. I had met Secretary of State Bill Rogers once, briefly. Maurice Stans, Secretary of Commerce, I had met in the White House when he was Director of the Budget under Eisenhower. In those days, I was working as a consultant to Jim Mitchell, Secretary of Labor, helping out in a study of collective bargaining in the basic-steel industry, and I would see Stans and others at the White House staff mess. Mel Laird, Secretary of Defense, I had met on a number of occasions. I saw quite a bit of him at a two-day meeting that Senator Percy held in Chicago before the Convention, when we spent all of a Saturday and all of a Sunday tossing ideas around for the Republican platform."

"Where do you sit at Cabinet meetings?" we asked.

"Between the Postmaster General and the Ambassador to the United Nations," Secretary Shultz said. "Between Winton Blount and Charles Yost, that is. I had never met either of them before we all became members of the Cabinet."

"Anything go on at the meetings in the way of fun?" we asked.

"The meetings are all very serious. Very dignified. Very formal. As they should be," Secretary Shultz said. "Our wives attended the first Cabinet meeting, as you know. They all really enjoyed it, as you might expect."

City Hall. Into the Mayor's office. Mayor Lindsay gave his caller a breezy, bouncy, energetic, informal greeting. The Mayor stood straight and looked dapper, in a pin-striped navy-blue suit and a shirt of wide blue and white stripes which, although this was late afternoon, didn't have a suggestion of wilt in it. Secretary Shultz's suit was pretty limp, and he himself was sagging slightly. He sat down heavily in an armchair. The Mayor sat on the edge of a sofa facing him. A couple of his aides, Gordon Davis and Peter Tufo, came in and were introduced. Both Davis and Tufo were young, thin, alert, enthusiastic, and casual. They took chairs facing the Mayor and Secretary Shultz. We sat at one end of the sofa. Coffee was served. Everybody sipped it black.

"Glad to see you looking so well, George," the Mayor said.

"Yes, well . . ." Secretary Shultz said. He took a sip of coffee and sighed. "I had one of those lunches," he said. "With newspaper people."

"I did, too," the Mayor said, slapping both his kneecaps and then waving a hand in the direction of the window. "I had the C.B.S. news guys."

"I've got a dinner tonight," Secretary Shultz said. "The American Arbitration Association."

"I'll be stopping by," the Mayor said. "I'll be happy to denounce you," he added, slapping his knees again. "It might do you some good these days to be denounced by *me*." The Mayor, Davis, and Tufo laughed loudly. Secretary Shultz smiled.

"I've been pounded on all weekend long," Secretary Shultz said. "By my kids, Margaret and Kathleen. All they talk is civil rights. They're very impatient with us. They're very impatient with everybody."

"With good reason," said the Mayor.

Secretary Shultz sighed again. He looked over his shoulder at the Mayor's desk, behind him.

"That's a handsome desk," he said. "Is it traditional? Or what?"

"It's a replica of George Washington's desk," Mayor Lindsay said. "The federal people are trying to steal it, but I'm not letting them get it. Well, I've got a couple of topics, George."

"I've got a couple of good-news topics, too," Secretary Shultz said. "But you go first."

"O.K.," Mayor Lindsay said. "Number One, the Neighborhood Youth Corps. We asked for funds for fifty thousand bodies. Double what we had last year."

"The funds appropriated by Congress will be no different from last year," Secretary Shultz said.

"You've got Congress in the palm of your hand, hey?" the Mayor said. He and his aides laughed loudly.

"Well . . ." Secretary Shultz said.

Mayor Lindsay laughed again, and then said, "Seriously, George. Remember last summer, when the kids jumped all over the cars outside City Hall here?"

Secretary Shultz nodded.

"We couldn't get the checks out in time to those kids," the Mayor continued. "And, being brand-new, we weren't staffed up. These kids are poor, and they're hungry. And to them getting those checks means the difference between eating and not eating."

"We had this idea of using the unemployment-compensation offices for distributing the checks," Secretary Shultz said.

"Let me see if I understand it," Mayor Lindsay said. "Where would the kids go to get their checks?"

"It would be sort of a coal-and-ice deal," Secretary Shultz said. "The seasonal low point of these offices is the summer."

Mayor Lindsay turned to Gordon Davis. "How do you see that, Gordon?" he asked.

"We're going to be ahead this year," Davis said. "Our management system is pretty solid. We'll be ready this year."

"We're in a position to handle fifty thousand kids," Mayor Lindsay said.

"Start from the idea that the money will be the same this year that it was last year," Secretary Shultz said.

"Plus supplements," Mayor Lindsay said.

Peter Tufo looked up from making some notes. "Plus supplements," he said.

"We've tried to call people's attention to other kinds of manpower programs in addition to the Neighborhood Youth Corps," Secretary Shultz said. "Thinking of kids in the age-eighteen-to-nineteen category."

"We had very few kids above the age of eighteen," Gordon Davis said quickly. "These jobs are for kids who are going back to school in the fall."

"We're going to have nearly three hundred thousand teen-age kids pouring out of the schools and into the streets next month," Mayor Lindsay said.

"You should get the information soon," Secretary Shultz said.

"It's a rough year," Mayor Lindsay said. "The statewide cuts have done damage. Let me ask you, George. Do you smell any supplemental budgets in the wind? Any summer funding? It's very important that we know where we stand."

"It's one of the things we need to work on," Secretary Shultz said.

"Highly commendable," the Mayor said. "Great. This planning in advance. And advancing the timetable. We're pleased, George, with the MA-4 program for training the unemployed and underemployed. How many bodies will Con Edison be training in that program, Peter?"

Tufo looked up from his notes. "Four hundred," he said.

"Good," the Mayor said. "Very good." He turned to Davis. "Gordon, what were the federal limits last year for the Youth Corps?"

Davis laughed. "That's part of the great debate," he said. "They gave us almost eleven million dollars initially, but it was two million less than what we got in 1967, which meant the program could go for only eight weeks instead of ten. Then there was the big battle to get a supplemental appropriation of eight hundred thousand."

"We then made the decision to pump in three to four million bucks that we didn't have," the Mayor said. He gave a low sigh.

Secretary Shultz gave a louder sigh.

"I've been yelling and will keep on yelling about the need for funds for the cities," the Mayor said. "It's no secret that I've been opposed to the war in Vietnam for years and that

I think that funds going into those channels are needed desperately in the cities. Nixon was elected President because the people of this country are fed up with the war in Vietnam. George, I wish you'd go back and tell your gang there that they need the guys like me who are doing the yelling about funds for the cities."

Secretary Shultz nodded. "Be glad to," he said. "I'll tell them."

❖ Two People in a Room

HAROLD PINTER, the English playwright, is living on Fifth Avenue, in the Seventies, during the Broadway run of his twelfth, and latest, play, "The Homecoming." With his wife, Vivien Merchant, who is acting in the play, and their nine-year-old son Daniel, he occupies a twentieth-floor apartment—a sublet, furnished with hundreds of somebody else's books along a wall of built-in bookshelves, and things like mahogany sculpture, ivory miniatures under glass, and antique gilt-trimmed ebony tables. A picture window in the living room offers a blinding panoramic view of most of Central Park and miles of skyline. We called on Mr. Pinter in his apartment one afternoon last week, while his wife and son were attending the Dog Show. A handsome, amiable-looking man of thirty-six with black hair, black sideburns, and eyeglasses that are rimmed with horn on top and color-less plastic on the bottom, Mr. Pinter was wearing house slippers, black trousers, and a pale-blue shirt, open at the collar, with French cuffs and onyx cufflinks. He pointed out a small shelf of books in the foyer and said he had brought most of *those* books with him from England, along with his Olympia portable typewriter. The Olympia, uncovered, stood on an ebony table facing the view. There were four-teen of his own books: "Letters of James Joyce," Volumes II and III; "La Maison de Rendez-vous," by Alain Robbe-Grillet; "Plain Pleasures," by Jane Bowles; "Casualties of Peace," by Edna O'Brien; "A Delicate Balance," by Edward Albee; "Story of O"; "The Man in the Glass Booth," by Robert Shaw; "The New Poetry," edited by A. Alvarez; "The Poems of John Donne"; "Love Poems," by Thomas Hardy; "The Less Deceived," by Philip Larkin; "The Whitsun Weddings," by Philip Larkin; and "The Selected Letters of Dylan Thomas."

Mr. Pinter told us that he and his family liked the apartment and thought the view quite beautiful, especially at night. "I find myself in a little bit of a trance in New York," he said. "Occasionally, I roll down the Avenue in a taxi, and I realize: 'I am in New York.' I've been here for six weeks, but I haven't been able to work. I haven't done a thing here. When we were in Boston with 'The Homecoming,' I started working on a new play. I had started something. It was there. On a few pieces of paper. It was just born. I enjoy writing when I can manage it. But it becomes more and more difficult. In the last five years, apart from all the considerable distractions and extra demands of life—the telephone, the correspondence, new productions, correcting proofs, turning down invitations to go to Timbuctoo and give a lecture, all that—I find that writing has become more demanding. I've been at it ten years, but in the last five years, quite apart from the question of time, the writing itself has been more difficult. Writing my first play, 'The Room,' was comparatively easy. Now that I'm ten years older, I've become more aware of my limitations. When I was thirteen and started writing poetry, I had quite a considerable freedom of language. I was very much under the influence of Dylan Thomas then, and I didn't care a damn what the hell was going on. As I've got older, I've developed a concern for economy and discipline."

We asked him where he lives in England.

"London—Regent's Park," he replied. "Right *in* the park.

In a very beautiful Nash house. Built in 1820. It's a very tall house—five floors—and it looks over the lake. My wife has a remarkable talent for decoration. We put in bathrooms and kitchens. All that. And plumbing and electricity. The drawing room, on the first floor, is forty feet long. Very classical. It's a very calm house. Calm. Calm colors. White and blue. It's pleasurable to be in. I have a study at the very top of the house, and there's no lift. In the morning, when I take my son to school, we sometimes walk through the park to the tube station, and we pass extraordinary hostile geese. Driving is faster, but it's nice to walk through the park. Life at home has another kind of rhythm."

We asked Mr. Pinter whether he had grown up near Regent's Park, and he said no—that he was born (on October 10, 1930), and had grown up, in Hackney, in the East End of London. His father, Jack Pinter, who is now retired, was a ladies' tailor, with a small shop, also in Hackney. "I lived in a brick house on Thistlewaite Road, near Clapton Pond, which had a few ducks in it," he said. "It was a working-class area—some big, run-down Victorian houses, and soap factories with a terrible smell, and a lot of railway yards. And shops. It had a lot of shops. But down the road a bit from our house there was a river, the Lea River, which is a tributary of the Thames, and if you go up the river two miles you find yourself in a marsh. And near a filthy canal as well. There is a terrible factory of some kind, with an enormous dirty chimney, that shoves things down to this canal."

We asked Mr. Pinter to tell us about his childhood.

"My mother was a marvellous cook, as she still is," he said. "My father worked terribly hard. He worked a twelve-hour day, making clothes in his shop, but eventually he lost the business and went to work for someone else. In the war, he was an air-raid warden. When I was nine, I was evacuated to the country. I went to a castle in Cornwall—owned by a Mrs. Williams—with twenty-four other boys. It had marvellous grounds. And it was on the sea. It looked out on the English Channel, and it had kitchen gardens. All that. But it wasn't quite so idyllic as it sounds, because I was quite a morose little boy. My parents came down occasionally from London. It was over four hundred miles there and back, and I don't know how they made it. It was terribly expensive, and they had no money. I came home after a year or so, and then I went away again—this time with my mother—to a place closer to London. On the day I got back to London, in 1944, I saw the first flying bomb. I was in the street, and I saw it come over. It looked like a tiny airplane. It was an innocent-looking thing. It just chugged along. And then I saw it come down. There were times when I would open our back door and find our garden in flames. Our house never burned, but we had to evacuate several times. Every time we evacuated, I took my cricket bat with me."

"What was the name of your school?" we asked.

"The Hackney Downs Grammar School," he said. "It was a ten-minute walk from home. All boys—about six hundred of them. It was a good building. It was pretty awful, but it had great character, and some of the masters had, too. Especially my English master, Joseph Brearley. He's a very brilliant man. He's a great fellow. He's still there. He was obsessed with the theatre. I played Macbeth when I was sixteen, and he directed me, and then he directed me when I played Romeo. I went in for football and cricket at school, and I was always chosen to run. My main ability was sprinting. I set a new school record—a hundred yards in ten point two—but it's been broken since. The only universities I was thinking about were Oxford and Cambridge. But you had to know Latin, and I didn't know Latin. I went to the Royal Academy of Dramatic Art, but I left after three months. I didn't care for it. I was out of my element there. I was a very unsophisticated young man, and they all seemed to be very sophisticated there. And then I was full of contempt for so many things in those days. I'm not as full of contempt now. It's very difficult to feel contempt for others when you see yourself in the mirror. I have a certain sympathy for myself, but it's modified. I bore myself a great deal. The fact of myself overwhelms me by its tediousness. Dragging yourself around day after day is a hell of a burden. I can be full of high spirits, nevertheless. I enjoy things greatly."

"How long did you live on Thistlewaite Road?" we asked.

"Until the age of eighteen," he said. "At the age of eighteen, back then, you were supposed to join the Army for two years, under conscription. I decided not to join. I was a conscientious objector. I went before two conscientious-objector tribunals, and then I had two trials. At both trials, I took my toothbrush along. My father respected my point of view, but when prison loomed, he thought I should cut my losses and go into the Army. For me—well, you know, the idea of rearming was preposterous. I was aware of the suffering and of the horror of war, and by no means was I going to subscribe to keeping it going. I said no. And I will still say no. It's even more stupid now. At both my trials, the decision about what to do with me was left to the magistrates' discretion. I was fined on both occasions. Ten pounds the first time, and twenty pounds the second. At my second tribunal, I took one of my close friends, Morris Wernick, to speak for me. The others took reverends. But I had no religious beliefs by then, although my parents still go to the synagogue informally, and I used to go, too. There were a lot of colonels with mustaches at the tribunal. It was very, very stuffy. I took Wernick, and he made an immortal speech on my behalf. He said, 'Now, I *am* going into the Army, so I am not a conscientious objector, but I can assure you that you will never change *him*. It's a waste of time to try to persuade him to change his mind.' Wernick became a schoolteacher. Schoolteachers in England are very poorly paid, so he went to Canada. He lives and teaches in Sault Sainte Marie, in

Ontario. Wernick is married and has three children. I haven't seen him in several years, but the day after tomorrow I'm going to meet Wernick in Toronto."

"What happened after you left the Royal Academy of Dramatic Art?" we asked.

"I wandered about a bit, and then I answered an advertisement and got a job with a Shakespearean repertory company in Ireland, run by Anew McMaster," Mr. Pinter said. "He was a remarkable man. Among other things, he was the best Othello I've ever seen. It was my first job on the stage. I was young and tough in those days, and we did an extraordinary repertory. I played in 'Hamlet,' 'King Lear,' all that. Anew McMaster meant a good deal to me. He died a few years ago. I went over to the funeral. After two years in Ireland, I got a job with Donald Wolfit's Shakespearean company, where I met my wife. We didn't get to know each other very well then, but we met again, in 1956, in the Bournemouth Repertory Company, on the Channel coast. I was the leading man, and we played opposite each other. She played Jane Eyre and I played Rochester, and that year we got married. That same year, I was at a party in a house in London, and I was taken up to a room in the house and introduced to two people in the room. The two people remained in my mind. It was my first dramatic image. I told a friend, Henry Woolf, who was studying in the Drama Department of Bristol University, that I would write a play about them. I was working in a repertory company in Torquay, Devon, rehearsing one play in the morning and playing in another one at night. Woolf telephoned me and said he had to have the play, so I wrote it. It was 'The Room.' It took me four days, working in the afternoons. Woolf directed it. On a Sunday night, when I wasn't acting, I went down to see the play. It seemed to go well. It excited me. 'The Birthday Party' was the first play I had produced in London—at the Lyric Theatre, Hammersmith. It went off in a week. Most of the critics massacred it. No one came. At the Thursday matinée, there were six people in the audience. The box office took in two pounds nine shillings. But after it was off, Harold Hobson, the critic on the *Sunday Times,* wrote a long and encouraging piece about the play. He just liked it, and stuck by it for years."

"How do you like writing for the theatre?" we asked.

"I'm not interested in the general context of the theatre," he said. "The fact that other playwrights do things differently doesn't strike me as terribly illuminating. My main interest, actually, is poetry. Reading poetry. The poetry of John Donne and Philip Larkin. And W. B. Yeats I always read. Reading aloud is one of my indulgences. That and a little drinking. I try to keep to the opening hours of the pubs in drinking. This morning, I was up at nine-thirty, and had grapefruit and a cup of tea. Then, before lunch, I had two beers and a Scotch. But it was a calm morning. It was quite a modest morning. My doctor advises me against drinking, but I'm ignoring his advice. It's a short life. And I have no wish to be eighty-eight. I feel pretty exhausted now that I'm thirty-six."

"How do you regard your writing?" we asked.

"I can't regard what I've done as singular," he said. "I'm continually surprised at the response of a number of people to my plays. All I know is that blank sheet of paper in front of me, and then, when it's filled, I can't believe it. I don't throw away many sheets of paper that are filled. I do, of course, go over the sheets of paper many times. I regard myself as an old-fashioned writer. I like to create character and follow a situation to its end. I write quite visually—I can say that. I watch the invisible faces quite closely. The characters take on a physical shape. I watch the faces as closely as I can. And the bodies. I can't see a consistency in my work. I have no idea whether the plays have a consistency or have not. Each play is quite a different world. The problem is to create a unique world in each case, with a totally different set of characters. With a totally different environment. It's a great joy to do that."

"Do you think you may eventually get some work done in New York?" we asked.

"I've been here quite a number of times," he replied. "I've found it, as everyone says, 'stimulating.' On my first visit, in 1961, when rehearsals started for 'The Caretaker,' it was August, and it was a terrible time to be introduced to New York. But it was 'stimulating.' This time, New York is simply a place. I'm bored by what New York thinks of itself. I wish it would shut up. There's a little village in Gloucestershire, in the Cotswold Hills, that I like better. The village is called Bibury. It's very English. It just exists."

❧ *An Educated Person*

HARVARD'S Faculty of Arts and Sciences voted earlier this year to approve a proposal introduced by the faculty's dean, Henry Rosovsky—and developed and refined by a series of committees—to reform the undergraduate curriculum. The Dean had repeatedly pointed out, before the vote, that Harvard and other leading colleges and universities were graduating young people who were unable to think or write clearly, let alone appreciate the ways in which one gains knowledge and understanding of oneself, of society, and of the universe. The faculty's reforms, which immediately struck a responsive chord in liberal-arts colleges throughout the country—with reverberations in primary and secondary schools as well—set some clearly defined standards for what the Dean calls "an educated person." The new program, which will gradually be put into effect for Harvard freshmen next fall, struck a responsive chord in us, too, so when Dean Rosovsky came to New York the other day to address the annual meeting, at the Waldorf-Astoria, of the College Entrance Examination Board, we sought him out. Shortly before he was scheduled to speak—at a luncheon of twelve hundred educators—on the subject of "The Core Curriculum," which is what the new program is called, we had a talk with him in a quiet corner of the Waldorf lobby. The Dean is a sturdy-looking, friendly, cheerful man of fifty-one, somewhat cherubic of face, with a classic, old-fashioned short haircut. He wore dark-rimmed glasses, and he had a lighted pipe in his mouth and a worn-looking briefcase under one arm. He was dressed in a dark-blue suit, a white shirt with a button-down collar, and a dark-blue necktie with yellow stripes, and he was the happiest-looking dean we've ever seen. We asked him if he would mind telling us more about his standards for an educated person.

"I don't mind," he said, setting his briefcase on the floor beside him. "I'm beginning to get used to saying some of these things more than once." He took a quick breath, and his eyes, behind the glasses, literally sparkled. "An educated person should be able to communicate with precision, cogency, and force," he said. "He or she should have an informed acquaintance with the mathematical and experimental methods of the physical and biological sciences; with the historical and quantitative techniques needed for investigating the workings and the development of modern society; with some of the important scholarly, literary, and artistic achievements of the past; and with the major religious and philosophical conceptions of what man is. These ideas were included in a report to the faculty a couple of years ago. I said at the time that I thought an educated American could not be provincial; he should know about other cultures and other times. He should have some understanding of, and experience in thinking about, moral and ethical problems. He should have high aesthetic and moral standards. He should be able to reject shoddiness in all its many forms, and to defend his views effectively and rationally." The Dean gave us a serene smile and puffed at his pipe. "I was quite critical of the state of undergraduate education, and everybody seemed for the most part to agree with me. When you say things are bad, you don't get much disagreement, I learned. It's when you start offering solutions that things become more serious." The Dean gave us another calm smile.

"When did all this get started?" we asked.

"Roughly four years ago, when I wrote a letter to the faculty pointing out that we needed a fresh and realistic statement of the purposes of undergraduate education," the Dean said. "Earlier in the nineteen-seventies, before I became dean, Derek Bok, now Harvard's president, was president-elect, and we had long conversations about our dissatisfaction with the state of liberal education. We both felt that the nineteen-fifties and nineteen-sixties, while they had some very desirable features, were adverse to liberal education. We had experienced a tremendous expansion of the college and university. We had an explosion of professionalism. A chemistry professor, for example, might think of himself as a chemist, not as a professor. In the turmoil of the nineteen-sixties and early seventies, universities had become highly politicized. I felt that the time had come to focus again on educational issues. I never intended to have my original letter go beyond Harvard. But I asked the faculty to respond, and we also made the letter available to students, so that we might hear from them. Well, we received hundreds of letters—all thoughtful letters—from the professors and from the students, and pretty soon all this was in the newspapers. There were also political reactions. Political reactions from the left. Political reactions from the right. What we had started talking about, it seemed, was on other people's minds, too. The student press opposed the new curriculum. They viewed it as recapturing authority. And some scientists were not sympathetic. They're not high on teaching science to non-scientists. We've had a lot of talking about the subject at Harvard since the spring of 1977. Very serious discussions—among the best I've ever heard. It made one feel pleased to be a member of that body. It was an elevating experience, talking about the business of education. As a result of all the discussion, some people who were opposed to our program have now offered to teach in it. I've had some praise from quarters I don't particularly want it from—from people who oversimplify or from reactionaries who want to bring things back to what they call the good old days. The whole back-to-basics approach needs to be defined. I'm in danger of becoming a hero to some Neanderthals." The Dean, looking a little pained, leaned forward and went on, "We've heard from so many people by now, from all over the world, that I've had to appoint a special man—Charles Whitlock, Associate Dean for Special Projects of the Faculty of Arts and Sciences—as a kind of Minister of Foreign Affairs on this issue." The Dean drew on his pipe and smiled again. "We've got a tremendous amount of work ahead of us to carry out the program," he said. "And now we're getting into graduate education, which is at least as important as the undergraduate program."

"What is actually going to be changed in the curriculum?" we asked.

The Dean leaned forward again, looked at his wristwatch, and puffed at his pipe. "The new curriculum will reflect the priorities revealed in the simple proposition of what we mean by an educated person," he said patiently. "The core curriculum will be designed to give all students a better sense of intellectual sympathy for one another. No college can remedy the damage of poor secondary education, but we are determined to give those eighteen-year-olds who need it *a second chance.* The liberal-arts college plays a very special and important role in American society. In England, the student begins to specialize at the age of fifteen. His life is set at that point. In Japan, getting into the right *kindergarten* can be the determining factor. It would be easy for Harvard to imitate the universities of Europe—to set the entrance standards so high that students from many regions of the country and from many backgrounds would be excluded. We are not interested in that kind of élitist education."

Dean Rosovsky looked at his watch again and put his briefcase on his lap. "A liberal education should provide a common core of intellectual experience for all students," he said. "I'd rather have a doctor who understands pain and love and suffering than a doctor who knows only about the latest drug to come on the market. The core program will be remedial only in the sense that it provides for courses in math, expository writing, and foreign languages. Math is our addition; the others have been with us for a long time. Since the Second World War, all students have been required to take, in addition to a major—which we call a field of concentration—a general-education requirement specially designed to provide a broad liberal education. But this program had become outdated, and it lacked definition and vigor. Too many science courses were *about* science instead of being basic science, and many courses were no longer general in the good meaning of that word. The program we're now setting up is divided into five fields: Letters and Arts; History; Science; Social and Philosophical Analysis; and Foreign Languages and Culture. Walter Jackson Bate, the author of the great biography of Samuel Johnson, is head of the committee working on Letters and Arts; Bernard Bailyn, Winthrop Professor of History, is on History; James Q. Wilson, Shattuck Professor of Government, is on Social and Philosophical Analysis; Otto Solbrig, Professor of Biology, is on Science; and Ezra Vogel, Professor of Sociology and Chairman of the Council on East Asian Studies, is on Foreign Languages and Culture.

We had read in the papers that within the past year Dean Rosovsky had turned down the jobs of president of the University of Chicago and president of Yale, in order to remain at Harvard as dean. We asked him why.

"I'm still in the middle of the reform of undergraduate education at Harvard," he said. "I love Harvard. It would be a privilege to be connected with Yale or with Chicago, but they are not mine. Harvard is *mine.*"

We asked the Dean if he would give us a rundown on his own educational background.

"All right," he said. "I was born on September 1, 1927, in
the Free City of Danzig. In the same year and in the same
place, by the way, as Günter Grass. I found that out when
we gave him an honorary degree in 1977. My dad was a
graduate of the University of Kiev. So is my mother. I'm a
Rosovsky on both the maternal and the paternal sides of my
family, all of whom came from a small village called Rosovo,
near Minsk, in White Russia. The Rosovskys—some of
whom, including my brother, Alexander, changed their
name to Ross—are a close, often inbred clan. The inbreed-
ing, however, seems to have done things for our lifeline. My
mother's great-grandmother, for instance, died at the age of
a hundred and seven."

"Did she eat yogurt?" we asked.

"No, she drank vodka," the Dean said. "She used to drink
vodka and tell my mother stories about the retreat of Napo-
leon—about the collapse of his army, in 1812, at the
Berezina River. When the Russian Revolution started, my
dad had just graduated from law school, and, under Ke-
rensky, he became a judge in Bobruisk. Six months later, he
had to flee. He settled in Danzig with my mother in 1920 and
went into the timber business, setting up a branch of the
business that *his* father had set up in Latvia. My brother was
born in 1922, and in 1934 he was sent to boarding school in
Belgium, because under the Nazis life for Jewish children
was becoming impossible in the secondary schools. The
Jewish community in Danzig set up its own elementary
school, which I attended for four years. In 1937, my parents,
running from Hitler, moved to Brussels, where my dad reës-
tablished his timber business. In May, 1940, when the Germans invaded Belgium, we made the classic refugee trek to
France, to Spain, to Portugal, and then to the United States.
That period was one of great excitement for me. No school.
Travel. Uniforms all around us. My poor father was a refugee three times in his life. But for me it was really fun, except
that whenever we stayed more than a few days in one place

my mother insisted on putting me in a school. There were eleven of us in a 1936 Ford with Belgian license plates— including an uncle, his wife, their daughter, and people from another family. In Saint-Amand-Mont-Rond, in the center of France, my mother sent me to school right away. When Belgium surrendered to the Nazis, the French yelled *'Sales Belges!'* at us in the old Ford. But within three weeks France had surrendered. We made it into Spain.

"My mother had wanted to go to America since the rise of Hitler. In Portugal, we found a ship, the S.S. Nyassa, which they told us the Germans had given to the Portuguese as reparations for the First World War. We all got on for five hundred dollars each. We landed in Hoboken on December 4, 1940. Right away, there was school. Before that Christmas vacation, I was at Joan of Arc Junior High School, at Amsterdam Avenue and Ninety-third, in my short pants and long woollen stockings. Then somebody told us to go to Klein's and get some American clothes, so my mother bought me a lumberjacket and long pants. From that point on, I felt very much at home, even though I knew no English. Six months later, I took the exam for admission to Stuyvesant High School and got in. My dad, in the meantime, had set up and was running some sawmills, for a Belgian baron of Jewish origin, in Kinston, North Carolina, and elsewhere in the South, and was spending more and more time there. We didn't speak English at home, and so, even though middle-class Jews for the most part didn't send their sons to boarding school, I was sent, in 1942, to the Cherry Lawn School, in Darien, Connecticut. It was run by a Swedish noble-woman who was married to a Russian emigrant. It was not a St. Paul's or an Andover, but I had a marvellous education there, played touch football, and graduated in 1944. My brother, meanwhile, had graduated from William and Mary. I went there for a year, and then I was drafted into the Army. I served in Europe—in Paris and in Wiesbaden, mostly—

with the Counter Intelligence Corps, because I spoke German, French, and Russian. I met Henry Kissinger for the first time at Oberammergau, when I was in the European Command Intelligence School and took a course he gave in the German paramilitary organizations. When I got out of the Army, I took a reserve commission and went back to William and Mary, where I majored in economics and history. I graduated in 1949. Under the G.I. Bill of Rights, I enrolled in graduate school at Harvard, studying economics, but in 1950, on the outbreak of the Korean War, I was called back into the Army and was shipped to Korea. At that point, I started developing my interest in Asia. In 1952, I went back to Harvard, where I became a Junior Fellow, elected to the Society of Fellows."

"What's that?" we asked.

"That is a lucky break," Dean Rosovsky said, and he gave us the genuine eye sparkle again. "It means you have three years in which you do what you want to do. You get a silver candlestick, you attend a fancy dinner every Monday night, and you study what you want to study. I started out studying Russian economic development in the last half of the nineteenth century. Then I became interested in Japan. At that time, very few people were following the tremendous economic achievement of Japan in the last hundred years. I decided to study Japanese. In 1956, I got married—my wife, Nitza, is a seventh-generation Jerusalemite—and the day of the wedding we left for Tokyo, where I did work for my Ph.D. thesis, on 'Japanese Capital Formation, 1868–1940.' " The Dean paused for a moment and looked at his watch again.

"What happened after Japan?" we asked.

"Berkeley," the Dean said, and he shook his head and gave a hint of a sigh. "In 1958, I became an acting assistant professor of economics and history there, and by the time I left, in 1965, I was a full professor. It was the beginning of the student troubles, and I was unhappy about what was going on. I strongly believed in high-quality public education. I had gone to Berkeley in the first place for ideological reasons. But I began to feel that many students and faculty did not believe, as I did, in that great institution. They were pecking away at the administration. They were abandoning important academic principles. I felt we were there to study and do research. So I resigned. Without having another job." The Dean laughed. "I had a number of attractive offers, including one from Harvard. I loved Harvard. I owed the greater part of my education to Harvard. So I went there. But what I thought I had left behind me at Berkeley I found existed at Harvard as much as anywhere else. I became chairman of the Economics Department there in 1969, at the time of the greatest trouble. The year before that, I had given a report, as chairman of a committee on black studies, saying that Afro-American culture should be incorporated into serious studies but should not be kept separate and apart, and that caused a lot of discussion, a lot of controversy. I seem to have difficulty staying out of controversial things. In 1973, while I was in Indonesia—I've done a lot of work there from time to time, and a number of my former students are now in high government or industrial positions there—I heard that John Dunlop, then the dean, was going to Washington to be director of the Cost of Living Council. When I got back, President Bok asked me to take my present job. I said yes within twenty-four hours. I don't believe in introspection."

"What do you do as dean?" we asked.

"I'm custodian of a national treasure," Dean Rosovsky said. "I have the Faculty of Arts and Sciences under my jurisdiction—everything except the professional schools. I have sixty-five hundred undergraduates at Harvard and Radcliffe; twenty-three hundred graduate students; eight hundred and fifty faculty members, including five hundred full professors. I sit on top of a large bureaucracy, including the dean of the college, the dean of the graduate school, the dean of applied sciences, and so on. Arts and Sciences has an annual budget of a hundred and twenty million. We have to balance our own budget, and we have our own endowments. If we have a deficit, we have to borrow money, at interest. We had a big deficit when I took over, of two or two and a half million."

"What did you do?" we asked.

"Got rid of it," the Dean said, with a grin. He looked at his watch once more, and got up to head for the twelve hundred educators waiting to hear him speak. "I'm in my sixth year in the job now," he told us. "It's been a fantastic education."

❧ Hits

AT the age of thirty-eight, Burt Bacharach, the composer of maverick song hits—propulsive, wry, engaging, rhythmically unpredictable songs that somehow combine elements of bossa nova, calypso, rock, and traditional pop, and end up sounding unimpeachably contemporary—disembarked at nine-forty the other night at Kennedy Airport from T.W.A. Flight 840, which had left Los Angeles about five hours earlier. He was met by a special T.W.A. chauffeur named Jerry Blackman and by us. Mr. Bacharach, whose hits include "Alfie," "What's New Pussycat?," "What the World Needs Now Is Love," and "Reach Out," was carrying with him, in a small pale-green fabric-covered, zippered overnight case, the score he had composed for the new Broadway musical "Promises, Promises," which will open in late November—the first show he has composed music for—and we were going to watch him deliver it to people connected with the show. Waiting for Mr. Bacharach's music were David Merrick, the producer of "Promises, Promises"; Neil Simon, who had adapted the book from the 1960 movie "The Apartment"; the cast of actors, singers, and dancers; and numerous other people who had some direct interest in the fact that Mr. Bacharach was arriving with the score. Mr. Blackman, a friendly, deferential man about the same age as Mr. Bacharach, took the green overnight case from the composer and led the way to his company's Lincoln. We got into the back seat with Mr. Bacharach, who had a Beverly Hills tan, and who was wearing Italian black-rimmed sunglasses pushed up on top of his hair. His hair was a curly dark brown with a lot of gray in it. He had a rugged, handsome face with an aquiline nose, and what seemed to be a chronic expression of remote thoughtfulness, or puzzlement, which was no doubt aggravated by five hours of dazed flying through the clouds with a T.W.A. showing of the movie "Thoroughly Modern Millie." Mr. Bacharach was wearing bright California clothes: a green jacket, rust-colored slacks, a brown-and-yellow striped tie, a dark-blue shirt. In the car, driving to the city, Mr. Blackman asked Mr. Bacharach about his race horse—his first, a two-year-old named Battle Royal.

"It was the kickiest thing I've ever done," Mr. Bacharach said. "It was something I had always wanted to own—a winner. He won the first time I raced him. Then he was entered in a fifteen-thousand-dollar claiming race at Del Mar. I was fearful of his being claimed, but my trainer didn't think he would be. I got absolutely obsessed with that horse. He ran his heart out. And he lost by a nose. I saw the jockey get off, and they slapped that red tag on my horse's nose: CLAIMED. It was heartbreaking. Jerry, I just can't tell you how heartbreaking it was. Everybody said to me, 'You made *money*. He even *won* once.'"

"How much did you pay for the horse?" we asked.

"I paid fourteen thousand five hundred. But I'm not in it for money. It's like love. First love. I want to get that horse back so badly, Jerry."

"I know," Mr. Blackman said.

"I became fully committed," Mr. Bacharach said. "There's nothing kickier than owning your own horse. I bought another horse that very same weekend. I was thinking about naming him Alfie. But I may name him Reach Out. Isn't that a great name for a horse?"

"Great," Mr. Blackman said.

We accompanied Mr. Bacharach to his apartment, on East Sixty-first Street, where he placed the green overnight case on a baby-grand Steinway in a music nook, which looked out on a terrace that ran around a good part of the apartment. Mr. Bacharach looked into the kitchen. "My folks stocked the place for me," he said to us. "Isn't that nice? Scott's paper towels. Pepperidge Farm bread. Eggs. Six lemons. I wish I could say I'm happy to be home. But I'm really sad. I had to leave my wife and little girl in Beverly Hills, and I'm not ashamed to say I miss them very much. Our little girl is two, and, you know, it's better for a two-year-old girl to be home, running around on the grass, having the pool and yard and everything. And, besides, my wife, Angie Dickinson, is an actress, and she's just finishing a movie. I believe in dual careers. And my wife is a real actress. I can tell. I saw her in that Lee Marvin movie where she plays this girl he sends to sleep with somebody he wants to kill, and I forgot she was my wife. She had me feeling so moved. She was very sympathetic. She captured me very much. Imagine seeing your own wife up there on the screen and having her touch you that much. And with her sitting right there next to me while I'm watching her on the screen. Working on this show means that the next three months are wiped out, and I wasn't keen on the concept of living in New York, either, let me tell you. But it's a very exciting thing, working on this show, and Angie will fly in and join me a few times anyway. I'm not one of these guys who resent a wife's career. Not that I like the very strong, very ambitious kind of woman. Angie isn't like that. But I love the idea of a lady working. I really love it. Excuse me just for a minute. I've got to call my folks."

Mr. Bacharach dialled a number. "Hi, Mom. Hi, Dad. How are you? . . . Not bad. . . . No, we didn't circle too long, and, besides, it didn't matter. It's such a beautiful night. . . . The apartment's fine. You did a beautiful job. The apartment looks beautiful. . . ."

We looked at framed things on the walls of the apartment: A three-foot-square blowup of a photograph of the singer Dionne Warwick. Three different photographs, signed with varying expressions of affection and esteem, of Marlene Dietrich. A framed certificate that read, "Presented to Burt Bacharach to Commemorate the Sale of More Than One Million Copies of the Scepter Records Pop Single Record 'I Say a Little Prayer.'"

"The first album I made as a recording artist, three years ago, sold thirty-five hundred copies," Mr. Bacharach said to us. "My second one has been out for nine months, and it's already sold over a hundred and thirty-five thousand copies. The wild thing about my songs is that they cross the two age gaps. They're hits with people my parents' age and they're hits with the kids, too."

"How do you explain that?" we asked.

"They're *songs,*" Mr. Bacharach said. "The songs are basically sophisticated. I write the music the way I feel. Hal David, my lyricist, writes the words the way *he* feels. No matter how groovy the electronic devices are these days, there's got to be a song. Electronic devices are marvellous. But nobody's going to whistle electronic devices. You've got to have a song."

Mr. Bacharach went over to the baby grand and touched the green overnight case. "All my original sketches. The rhythm patterns. And about fifteen or sixteen songs for the show," he said, and the chronic look of thoughtfulness, or puzzlement, seemed to deepen. "I think the songs are consistent with the way I've been writing. If you asked me have we changed gears for the show, I'd say I hope not. I would like to feel there's been no compromise."

"When did it all start?" we asked.

"Well, in London one day two years ago, David Merrick came over to me at a party," he said. "I was in the middle of scoring 'Casino Royale.' I wasn't thinking about doing a show. I was just getting my feet wet scoring movies, which is fantastic. All the things you can do to the action in a movie with the music! Working with the movieola! All that. Later on, Merrick asked me if I'd be interested in working on a musical version of 'The Apartment.' Merrick is very astute. He told me the theatre was going to change—that it had to open up to people to do their own thing. And he was thinking correctly. So I started working on the show last summer."

"And before *that* started?" we asked.

"I'd say everything all started five or six years ago, when I decided to stay put in New York and pursue writing seriously. Before that, I worked with Marlene Dietrich as her accompanist. I travelled all over with her. Poland. Germany. Italy. Russia. When you went into a country with her, you went in as a conquering army."

"And before that?"

"I've got a great Dad. Bert Bacharach, the columnist. And I've got a great Mom. She has gray hair, too, which she keeps gray. Lovely hair. And she's a lovely lady. I was born in Kansas City, where my Dad was a clothing buyer for the Woolf Brothers department store. In 1932, we moved to Kew Gardens, where I grew up and went to school. When I was fifteen, some of the guys at school and I formed a band. Ten pieces, with myself at the piano. We played at parties and at local dances. I graduated from Forest Hills High School, and then I enrolled at McGill University, in Montreal, where I studied music. I wrote a song there called 'The Night Plane to Heaven,' which was published and then died before it had lived. After college, I was drafted into the Army and toured the First Army area billed as a concert pianist, which I was not. After my Army discharge, I played piano in night clubs, including Nino's Continental, on Fifty-third Street, and the Bayview, on Fire Island. Then I worked as accompanist for Vic Damone, the Ames Brothers, and then Marlene Dietrich. I started writing my own orchestrations as a kind of self-defense. No matter how good the words or the melody of a song, it has got to be showcased properly. And then, you can write a great song, but you need a successful record if you're going to have a hit. You need that certain magic to happen at a recording session. Much of the feeling of a record—my records—comes from the rhythm section. And that's something I'm going to watch carefully in this show. I want to come into that show with the rhythm section steaming. Not steaming in New York. Steaming in *Boston*. I won't be able to do my own orchestrations. I don't think it can be done in a show. You finish writing a song at four in the morning on the road in Boston, say, and then start doing an orchestration, and they'd *carry* you home. We'll have a lot of music rehearsals for this show. I'm so deeply committed to the show I'll pay for the rehearsals myself if necessary. I put such utter heat in myself when I write; I want to work the same way whether it's for this show or anything else. The pressures of success sometimes have a way of turning you around. I'm very concerned about the brevity of all kinds of living. But I don't have a fear of running dry. I just always have the feeling that time is running out on me."

"Have you changed since all this has happened to you?" we asked.

"It's much easier for me to say no to people now," he said. "I get into enough of a pressure cooker all on my own. I'm not concerned about whether I'll be in fashion next year, or whether the bubble bursts a little. Of course, I'm concerned about staying healthy. I'm a great believer in exercise. I play basketball. I swim a lot. I believe in massage. I've got this little girl, and I want to be a good father to her. And I want to be a *live* father. There's that. But every time I get into a recording studio, there's that final moment of truth. The whole life leads into that one evening. It's a highly personal thing. I don't care if thirty-two people tell me it's great. It has to satisfy *me*. You preserve the success in your own mind. My gratification standard is how I personally feel."

A couple of days later, we joined Mr. Bacharach in the lounge of the Royale Theatre. A piano had been set up just outside the Ladies' Room. Mr. Bacharach sat at the piano playing one of the songs for "Promises, Promises." He wore a navy-blue knit shirt, white slacks with dotted blue stripes, white socks, and white, very clean Topsiders. His sunglasses rested on top of his head. On the piano was his sweater, a black cardigan with leather buttons. As he played—with immense concentration and intensity—he kept his Topsiders on the pedals and pumped his legs vigorously. He was rehearsing a song called "Wanting Things" with Ed Winter, a handsome young man who is to play the Fred MacMurray part in the musical. Mr. Winter was wearing black-rimmed glasses (in front of his eyes), dark slacks, loafers, and a blue shirt open at the collar. He was singing, "Tell me why must I keep wanting things,/ Needing things that just can't be mine . . ." Singer and composer went through the song, and parts of the song, a few times, with great concentration.

"I love the two levels of it," Mr. Bacharach said when they took a break. "I love to be able to approach it conversationally and musically."

They were joined by Arthur Rubinstein, another young man with black-rimmed glasses, who will conduct the show's orchestra. Mr. Bacharach told singer and orchestra leader how he wanted to have the song presented, where liberties should not be taken, where he loved to use strings and use them again if they worked, and where he'd like to have the singers try not to breathe. Then he picked up his cardigan with the leather buttons and ushered us upstairs.

"It's a wild experience to go into something as a novice," he said, that puzzled look getting deeper again. "I like to show them what I don't like and what I do like. We'll work from that as a springboard. It's kind of a teamwork thing, but the basis has got to be how *I* feel. You've got to protect your own taste. It doesn't look like any big ego problems, with the music staff. They're all young in spirit and in enthusiasm. We all have great hopes. And we're getting Phil Ramone, the best sound mixer there is, to mix the sound in the theatre for us. We're going to build a different kind of orchestra pit for this show. It will be partially enclosed. And we'll have voices in the pit to reinforce the voices onstage. We'll have an orchestra pit that will travel with us to three different cities."

Then there was the big day of the first full-cast rehearsal. On the sixth floor of the Riverside Plaza Hotel, on West Seventy-third Street. David Merrick was there, pacing up and down, wearing a dapper tan suit with a pink shirt, and no glasses. Neil Simon was there, wearing a dark suit with a cream-colored shirt, and black-rimmed glasses. The choreographer, Michael Bennett, and the director, Robert Moore, were there. And all the actors, singers, and dancers. Mr. Bacharach arrived with his green overnight case and sat down at the piano. A handsome man six and a half feet tall who had a dark mustache and goatee and was in shirtsleeves stood up near the piano, facing everybody. The other people in the room seemed to be tense and somewhat nervous, but he looked cheerful, relaxed, and happy.

"Hi, folks," the tall man began. "I'm Charlie Blackwell, your stage manager. I'm required to read these five Equity rules to you. 'One. You must have signed a contract and have paid current dues before reporting for rehearsal. As an Equity member, you have no right to waive minimum conditions of the contract. No change in the minimum conditions of the contract shall be made by the Actor or Manager except when authorized by counsel or the Executive Secretary in writing, and the company shall be notified of same. Two. Rehearsal hours: Rehearsals prior to the last seven days before the first public performance . . .' "

As Mr. Blackwell read on, Mr. Bacharach quietly and slowly opened the green overnight case. He took out a pile of sheets of music and carefully, without rattling the sheets of paper, set them up in front of him on the piano.

◆ Composer in Tartan Cap

BACK we went last week for another visit with Burt Bacharach, composer of the score for the new musical hit "Promises, Promises." We had seen him in September, when he arrived in New York with the score to start working in rehearsals, to the brink of which we accompanied him, leaving him with his producer, David Merrick; his book writer, Neil Simon; his lyrics writer, Hal David; and all the others. At the time, Mr. Bacharach—talking nostalgically about his wife and little girl back in Beverly Hills, talking affectionately about his parents, talking ambivalently about being stuck in New York and on the road for three months—had a kind of remote, persistently puzzled, and not exactly happy look, almost as though he were about to go to prison. Last week, he had a clearly happy look. He didn't look puzzled; he looked relieved and free.

"It's a wonderful time of one's life," he told us when we met him at his apartment, on East Sixty-first Street. "Four more days in New York, and then I'm going to Palm Springs with my wife and little girl for three and a half weeks. We're recording the score of the show before I leave. I got my Christmas shopping done, and it took me exactly one hour. I went on a rampage in the stores. Then it was done. Gone. Finished. The opposite of the way I work. It was very exciting to see the show evolve. But if someone came to me now and asked me to do a show, I'd say, 'Forget it!' " Mr. Bacharach did a kind of quasi-buck-and-wing and clapped the palms of his hands against each other. "This afternoon, I'm going to tape being on Johnny Carson's 'Tonight Show,' if you'd care to come along The 'Tonight Show' is David Merrick's idea. He called me three times yesterday and said, 'Do me a favor. We've all got to work now. You've got to be on the "Tonight Show." ' He believes in letting the world *know* you've got a smash. It's a very sensible approach. He really believes you should publicize a hit. It's a good thing the show's a hit. I'd hate to toot a horn for a ship in trouble."

"Well, how has it been since we left you on Labor Day, at the Riverside Plaza Hotel, starting your first rehearsal?" we asked.

"I feel it can't possibly have been three months. It feels more like half a year to a year. Just before we opened, I got a present from Neil Simon with a card saying, 'It was a great nine years!' All I know is I'm glad it's over. I got sick on the road with the show, and, of course, getting sick colors everything. The weekend after we opened in Boston, I had the worst sore throat of my life. I called in a strange doctor, which is Mistake No. 1. Never get a strange doctor if you get sick out of town. Call your own doctor and ask him if he knows anyone where you are. Anyway, I wound up with pneumonia in Massachusetts General Hospital, which is a great hospital to be in if you've got to be in one. I hadn't been in one since I was four and had my tonsils out. In the hospital, I knew there was work to be done. There were new songs to be written for the show. But I felt: The *hell* with the show. It's my *life*. I've just got to live and get out of here. Then, as soon as I got out, I wrote a new song for the show —'I'll Never Fall in Love Again,' which just might, by the way, turn out to be the biggest hit of the show. And there I was, getting the new number into the show, working with the people learning it, and everything. And that is not the way to recuperate from pneumonia."

"How do you feel now?" we asked.

"Great," said Mr. Bacharach, clapping his palms together again. "Let's go to the 'Tonight Show.' " He put on a tartan cap, a single-breasted navy cashmere coat, oversized French sunglasses, and a Dior fringed mohair plaid scarf that was twelve feet long. The last, he told us, was a present from Marlene Dietrich, with whom he had worked as accompanist on an international concert tour several years ago. "When I arrived in Poland to meet Marlene, she was waiting for me, in a snowstorm, at the airport with this scarf, so I'd be warm," he said. "I can't wear bizarre clothes. I'd never be able to put on a Nehru jacket. But anything Marlene gave me always felt sensible and right."

"What has happened to the show since Labor Day?" we asked in a taxi going to the "Tonight Show."

"It's tighter, funnier, shorter, and it plays better than it did when we started," Mr. Bacharach said. "In Boston, we were half an hour over what we are now. Neil really knows how to cut. He was great on the cutting."

"What about the music?" we asked.

"One song came out and stayed out," Mr. Bacharach replied. "Five songs came out and were replaced. About a third of the score, I'd say. And one great thing about this show— we all got along fine. There was none of the horror stuff I'd always heard about—about being on the road with the show and everybody hating everybody else. We were a very happy, cohesive company. As for Merrick, he leaves things quite alone. And when he doesn't, it turns out that he's right. He's more than a businessman. He's got good taste."

"Did you like writing songs for the show after getting to know the people who would sing them?" we asked Mr. Bacharach as the two of us went up in an R.C.A. Building elevator to the headquarters of the "Tonight Show."

"It was wholly satisfactory," Mr. Bacharach replied. "As a matter of fact, it's a very interesting thing if you write for one particular person. Once I knew Jill O'Hara, the leading lady—once I knew her face and knew her voice—it became real life. That's the way it works. My song 'The Look of Love' came right off Ursula Andress in 'Casino Royale.' You get the personality and establish the voice, and it helps you."

We stood by as Mr. Bacharach checked in with the receptionist at the windowless inner offices of the "Tonight Show." The show's producer, Rudy Tellez, a young, nervously cheerful man wearing a knit sports shirt, came out and greeted Mr. Bacharach, shaking his hand with fervor. "When I first heard your 'Reach Out' album, I wore out four albums of the album," he told him.

"It keeps selling and selling," Mr. Bacharach said.

"Anything you do has that King Midas touch," said Mr. Tellez. "I turn you over now to John Gilroy, here." He introduced a young, cheerfully nervous man in shirtsleeves. "Thank you, and see you downstairs."

Mr. Gilroy invited us both into his office, where he consulted a number of typewritten notes about Mr. Bacharach.

"We get you into makeup at six and the show goes on at six-thirty, but you come on at seven-fifteen," Mr. Gilroy said. "You talk to Johnny first. When you first come out, Johnny should talk to you some about 'Promises, Promises.' If you want to pay tribute to Merrick, Simon, and the lot, do it up front. Then Johnny talks to you. O.K.?"

"O.K.," said Mr. Bacharach.

"We have Frankie Laine in the show. And George Segal, the actor, playing his banjo," Mr. Gilroy said, and added, "Are you here to stay?"

"Do I look all right?" Mr. Bacharach asked, taking off his scarf, cap, coat, and glasses.

"Fine," said Mr. Gilroy. "What you going to sing? When the orchestra plays 'Bond Street,' you want to sit in at the piano?"

"That might be an idea," Mr. Bacharach said. "I have reservations about singing on the show—singing one of the numbers from 'Promises, Promises,' I mean. The only time I can get away with singing is when it's a song that's already established."

"Anything you want," Mr. Gilroy said. "Now . . ." He consulted his notes. "One question people are asking: Would you change your style for Broadway? Did you think about that?"

"Oh, heavily," said Mr. Bacharach. "I don't think I compromised on anything."

Mr. Gilroy made some notes for Johnny Carson. "I understand you use a chorus in the pit. That's a first, isn't it?"

"Yes, and we've got a lot of electrical equipment in that pit," Mr. Bacharach said.

"Like a recording studio," Mr. Gilroy said. "Do you think that 'Promises, Promises' will have an effect on future Broadway musicals now that the pattern has been broken?"

"Possibly," Mr. Bacharach said. "And I have to praise Merrick for that. He spent a lot of money on the musical effects—on an echo chamber, everything. It was a gamble."

"And he won," said Mr. Gilroy. "Do you think you might do another show? A Burt Bacharach original?"

"Right now, I think I just want to go away for a vacation," said Mr. Bacharach.

"Anything else?" asked Mr. Gilroy.

"The peak thing I might mention," Mr. Bacharach said. "I got a call from Mrs. Samuel Rubin, representing the American Symphony Orchestra. She said that Leopold Stokowski wanted to commission me to write something. I told my mother about it. She cried."

"Anything else?" Mr. Gilroy asked, making some notes.

"I don't think so," Mr. Bacharach said. "I'm very happy. There's *that.*"

◆ The Return of Mr. S.

OUR Mr. *Stanley* is back? True. He dashed in here, wearing Levi's and a bulky Irish sweater, with his every tooth still there, all his old energy and guileless ways intact. He's been lying low in the woods near the Montauk Point lighthouse, he told us, at one with the ocean waves, watching leaves grow, studying snowflakes, and chopping wood. What lured him back to the city, he said, was hearing about the Executive Coach, which makes the New York–to–Boston and Boston–to–New York run daily in four hours each way, door to door. *"If* your doors happen to be the Essex House, on Central Park South, and the Marriott Hotel in Newton, which mine are not," Mr. Stanley added. "But those are minor details. Here. There's hope for us yet." He took off, leaving us with this report:

Have just spent best two-day vacation of past decade. Took in both New York and Boston, without hassle of visiting World Trade Center, Faneuil Hall, or other obligatory shrines. Just got blast out of knowing they were *there,* before cutting back to my grains of sand. Travelled via Executive Coach, new bus service. In operation seven weeks. Shell of vehicle—called MCI-MC 9—made by Motor Coach Industries, which makes same shell for Greyhound. Conventional MCI-MC 9 carries forty-seven passengers. Quota on Executive Coach: sixteen plus driver plus hostess. Way to travel!

Departed city on button as scheduled, at 6:30 P.M., with freezing, teeming rainstorm outside.

Started up Broadway, past Lincoln Plaza Cinema. Moviegoers getting soaked in rain. Inside Executive Coach, all dry, all cozy, all warm. Like nice, homey, oversized, modern-décor living room. Thick beige carpeting. Swivel armchairs in matching leather tip back and further back as well as go around and around. Table in rear to eat, play chess, confer, or whatever at. Large rectangular tank full of tropical fish behind driver. Color television with VCR video-cassette player. Telephone to outside world. Lavatory with real washbasin in middle of counter, plus shelves, carpet, curtains, real soap, real cotton-terry-cloth towels, vase of fresh geraniums. Kitchenette with theatrical-dressing-room-type lights overhead, bar with white Formica top, bright, California-hued dishes and mugs, refrigerator, microwave oven, cushiony bar stools. Non-jarring p.-a. system. Entire works custom-designed for Executive Coach. Jolly sign in rear: "OUR SHIP DOESN'T ALWAYS LOOK LIKE THIS, SOMETIMES IT'S WORSE." Good joke touch. In keeping with mood of club of Boston lady passengers returning from wild weekend in New York. Ladies *very* jolly. Very talky.

"Hi, I'm Irene," club president informed busload. "And this is my friend Margaret. This is my friend Elaine. This is my friend Rebecca. This is my friend Mary Anne. We saw Greta Garbo in Bergdorf's this morning. I said, 'That's Greta Garbo.' I said, 'Let's go where she goes.' We also saw What's-His-Name. We went to the Music Hall. We did everything. We went to Sardi's. That's where we saw What's-His-Name. Wait till we tell our husbands."

Passing Stadium Motor Lodge in Bronx. Drinks served by hostess wearing brown-and-tan skirt-jacket combo in keeping with coach décor. White hair. Steel-rimmed specs. Chubby. Full, friendly face. Red cheeks. Like Mrs. Santa Claus.

"My name is Fran," hostess said, putting glass of cold white wine in wire rack on wall next to my swivel chair, up front. "I'm here to make you comfy. You comfy?"

Complimented Fran on drink holders.

"We try not to let drinks slop," Fran said. "If the road makes the coach shake like rock'n'roll to Dublin, the driver tells me not to serve."

Reached country. Onto Route 684. Very dark outside. No sights. Just road signs illuminated by headlights. White letters on green: "BREWSTER—8 MILES." Tremendous windshield on MCI-MC 9. Like Captain Kirk's in "Star Trek." Windshield wipers as long as golf clubs. Silent. No squeaks. No squoosh-squoosh.

Fran served box suppers. Sandwiches from Kaplan's deli at the Delmonico. Corned beef on rye. Chicken salad on rye. New pickle. Cole slaw. Good stuff. Top quality. Freshly perked hot coffee. No slosh. Great. Irene, Margaret, Elaine, Rebecca, Mary Anne holding off on supper. All of them too busy with second drink of Executive Coach two-drink limit. Too busy smoking. Too busy talking. Too busy ensemble-singing "Down by the Old Mill Stream."

Driver over p.-a.: "Fran, I suggest you not serve for twenty minutes. We're going to be on a rough stretch here."

Irene, Margaret, etc., pretended envy of passengers finished with sandwiches. Pretended to be fainting from hunger. Sang "She'll Be Comin' Round the Mountain."

Driver and Fran discussing Executive Coach problem with reservations. Three passengers didn't show. Plane shuttles cancelled because of weather, so people asking for Executive Coach. Had to be turned down. Three reservations wasted because of no-shows. Driver and Fran very upset. Said E.C. policy of leaving exactly on button still good policy, no matter what.

Outside Hartford, Route 86 smooth. Rest of suppers served. Fran drew dark curtain behind driver. Vote taken among passengers to select movie to be shown on VCR video-cassette player: "All the President's Men" or "Close Encounters of the Third Kind" or "The Godfather" or "Godfather II" or "Love at First Bite" or "10." Irene, Margaret, Elaine, Rebecca, Mary Anne screamed, yelled, campaigning for "Love at First Bite." Strong lobby. Their strategy to get "Love at First Bite": Loud group recitation of entire *plot!* Comprehensive report on what was funny in movie before movie *started!* Coach lights out. Lots of laughing at George Hamilton as Dracula in movie. Dracula-Rumanian accent not too bad. All passengers either liking Dracula stuff or mesmerized by it. Movie over by time we reached Framingham, Mass. Fran, putting coach lights on again, gave lowdown on E.C. movies: usually passengers vote unanimously for "10."

Disembarked right in front of Marriott Hotel in Newton. Pouring rain. Decided against hassle to get downtown. Stayed put. Took eighteen seconds to check in, get key, go up to room. *Quelle service!* On table at picture window with view of Charles River: milk, homemade chocolate-chip cookies. Courtesy management. Bed turned down. Neutrogena soap in bathroom. Sewing kit with thread of six different colors, windshield-ice scraper, lint mitts, pens in fine working order, knitted shoe bags, shower cap, *TV Viewer* magazine—all courtesy management. TV set in fine working order. Hooked up to movie service called Spectradyne Movies, at $5.25 per, charged on bill. Nobody else needed to vote for preference on offerings: "Altered States," "For Your Eyes Only," "Stripes," "Tarzan, the Ape Man." Watched "For Your Eyes Only." Then hit hay.

Ice, sleet, freezing staccato rain roughing up Charles River in A.M. Breakfast via room service: half grapefruit, bran muffins, coffee. Traffic outside bumper-to-bumper on bridge going downtown. Accurate weather forecast on Boston PBS: rain, rain, rain. Don't watch morning TV at home near Montauk, so watched talk shows. Learned lot. Mostly women on shows talking about bad deal given women. Women on shows looking unhappy. Not relaxed. Unhappy-looking woman said men taking advantage of women for five thousand years, so time to change. Men should stay home, take care of babies. Talk extremely belligerent. Switched to woman telling about buying Lincoln rocker for thirty dollars, getting rocker recaned for sixty dollars, so got rocker worth two hundred and fifty dollars for only ninety dollars. Nice to see *happy* woman. Switched. Got free medical info from Dr. Isadore Rosenfeld, apparently very popular doctor on talk shows, very popular doctor with popular people. Learned lot from Dr. Isadore Rosenfeld about how to treat alcoholism. Good free advice: don't drink too much—especially with pills. Switched. Watched man called Jeff, wearing leopard-skin vest, dancing boots, teach dance called The Gigolo. Jeff taught John Travolta, m.c. said. Jeff, with dumbbells, instructed viewers to work out along with him, with dumbbells. Went along with Jeff, pretended to hold dumbbells, went down on one knee to dance The Gigolo. Too hard.

Headed downstairs. To Health Club. Big setup. All free to guests. Saunas. Swimming pool—forty feet long, heated to eighty-three degrees. Gunite hydrotherapy spa heated to hundred and five degrees. Plenty of towels. Exercycles. Rowing machine. Leg press. Dumbbells. Sit-on treadmill. Sit-up board. Curling. Weight lifting. Tried everything. Great workout. Felt shipshape. Tried doing The Gigolo with dumbbells. Too hard. Cute girl named Jennie, wearing Wallabees and maroon warmup pants over black tank suit, in charge. Jennie said she was lifeguard, said pool was neat. Showed off for Jennie. Did thirty-eight laps. Felt swell. Lounge area with Ping-Pong, played Black Knight pinball game, Pac-Man video game, Phoenix video game. Great way to relax. Wished woman accusing men of taking advantage of women for five thousand years could sample spa. Very therapeutic. Wound up three-hour stint in spa with long session in Gunite hydrotherapy and another thirty-eight laps in pool. Tried The Gigolo again. Mastered it. Fulfilling. Still pouring outside. Spent rest of day with Spectradyne Movies in room. And practiced The Gigolo.

Rain letting up at take-off time, 7 A.M. next day, for trip back to New York. Biggest group among passengers—half-dozen men all wearing tweed jackets, flannel trousers, all looking like Secretary of State Alexander Haig, sitting with each other around conference table, discussing plan to attend electronic-typewriter convention in New York. Other passengers—suit-wearing men, suit-wearing women, priest —very quiet. All reading *Wall Street Journal.* Breakfast served by different hostess, young, slim, with long blond hair. Hostess introduced self as Wendy. Tweed-jacketed bunch very loud laughers. Big laughs at what each Haig said to others. Brown-haired Haig said to gray-haired Haig, "This beats driving. Every time my father drives to New York, he gets a ticket." Much loud laughing at this joke.

Wendy served cranberry muffins. Hot coffee. Nice to look out big windows. Farms. Sheep. Tractors. Pickup trucks. Bare-limbed trees. Ski areas getting ready. Nice to read Mass. Turnpike Authority sign, red letters on white: "SEA-SON'S GREETINGS." Took walk to kitchenette for second cranberry muffin. Passed Haigs, all discussing business. "Technologically, you can't beat the electronic concept in Japan." Also, "I still can't accept the concept that Sears satisfies the businessman." Also, "The U.S. office-automation market is growing at breakneck speed, due to expansion of the office-automation concept." Impressive talk.

West on Route 90. Sign: "LIVE WITH 55." Then Route 86 to Hartford. Tried swivel armchair in various positions. Leaned way back, head almost touching floor. Put feet way up to window level. Made several three-hundred-and-sixty-degree turns. Crossed legs. Swung side to side. Fine exercise, almost as good as Marriott spa.

One of Haigs to Wendy: "I guess you spend your afternoons shopping in Saks Fifth Avenue."

Wendy: "My favorite store is Bloomingdale's, but I like to browse in Tiffany's."

Glad to see sign "WELCOME TO NEW YORK THE EMPIRE STATE."

Put feet up again. Took snooze. Last stretch. Counted trucks. United Chrome Tile Corp. AFI Food Service Distributors. North American Van Lines. Michelin. Ripco. West Farms. Pennsylvania House Traditional Furniture. Mayflower Electronic Devices. United Van Lines. United Van Lines truck driver blew kisses to Executive Coach.

"WHITE PLAINS—10 MI."

More trucks. Modern Packaging. Jahn Foundry Corp. American Tourister. Miller Foods. Grand Union. Allied Container Corp. Spring Air Back Mattress. Pallmark Corrugated Containers. Finast. Dellwood. Frito-Lay.

Counted transporters. Horses. Automobiles. Boats. Golf Carts.

Arrived Essex House on button—11 A.M. Over and out.

❖ *Ralph Bunche*

RALPH JOHNSON BUNCHE, who was an Under-Secretary and an Under-Secretary General of the United Nations for the past sixteen years, until shortly before his death last month, was one of the greatest Americans of our clouded and mind-numbing times. Whatever part of his life we look at—and we have looked at quite a bit of it in recent years—we see what we have come to think of as profoundly, almost quintessentially American. What to us is exhilarating about the life of Ralph Bunche is the way it was so marvellously bound up in the fabric of everything we love about this country.

Mr. Bunche was born in Detroit on August 7, 1904. His father, Fred Bunche, was an itinerant barber. His mother, Olive Agnes Johnson Bunche, was an amateur pianist. Both his parents died in Albuquerque in 1917—his father of the flu, his mother of tuberculosis. After that, Mr. Bunche was raised in Los Angeles by his maternal grandmother, Mrs. Lucy Johnson, whose husband, the principal of a Negro elementary school in Waco, Texas, in the eighteen-eighties, had died of malaria, leaving his wife and five children penniless in Indian territory. "My grandmother—I always called her 'Nana'—had ten children, but five died, and one of those who died was named Ralph," Mr. Bunche told us in one of many conversations we were privileged to have with him in

the last few years of his life. "Nana was a matriarch. She
didn't take any foolishness from anybody. She had no education, but she had deep insights. She was very small but
very strong, very wiry, and very outspoken. She looked like
a white, and was often mistaken for one. Once, in Los Angeles, where we lived in a mostly white neighborhood, a
salesman for cemetery plots came by and gave my grandmother a sales pitch, one of his selling points being that they
didn't allow Negroes or Jews in the cemetery. Well, she got
a broom and chased him out of the house. Another time, the
principal of my high school, when I was graduating, said to
her, 'Mrs. Johnson, we're sorry to lose Ralph. We've never
thought of him as a Negro.' My grandmother said to him,
'How dare you insult our race?' She always drilled into me,
'Do the best you can. Maintain your self-respect. Never let
anybody detract from it.' "

When the family still lived in Detroit, Ralph Bunche's
uncles Charlie and Tom worked to support them at the
Diamond Match Company. They worked there for eight
years, ten and a half hours a day, at a daily wage of sixty-
three cents. Then they got jobs at a hotel, as an elevator
operator and a houseman, and eventually as a dance-orches-
tra drummer and a dress-cutter, respectively.

"We all left Detroit in the summer of 1914, just before the
First World War," Mr. Bunche told us. "My mother, my
Uncle Charlie, my grandmother, and I went on the Santa Fe
train. My father, to save money, rode the rods. We went to
Albuquerque, because both my mother and my Uncle
Charlie had t.b. and the climate in New Mexico was supposed to be good for that. Soon after we got there, my
mother took my sister, Grace, and me to the nickelodeon at
the Busy Bee Theatre. She walked us down to a seat in a
middle row. Right after we sat down, an usher came and
asked my mother to move to the rear. My mother told him
very quietly, 'We're staying right here.' And we did. After

that, we went to the Busy Bee regularly, and we sat wherever we pleased."

Mr. Bunche went to high school in Los Angeles, working after school and on Saturdays as a carpet layer for a big rug-cleaning establishment. "The owner got interested in me and offered to send me to Cal Tech or to M.I.T. to study the chemistry of dyes," Mr. Bunche told us. "I consulted with my grandmother, and she was against it. She said it's important to be free. So I went, on my own, to U.C.L.A."

As a sophomore, Ralph Bunche was rejected by the R.O.T.C., because he had a punctured eardrum—the result of two mastoid operations. He hitchhiked to the R.O.T.C. summer camp, in the state of Washington, anyway. We have a snapshot of him taken there. Twenty years old. Tall. Muscular. Handsome. Smiling broadly. Army fatigues. Shirtsleeves rolled up. "I didn't want to be in the R.O.T.C.," he told us. "It was just a good way to spend the summer. They took us on outings. We played baseball. The camp food was good. It was a good way to keep in condition and make some money, too. You could come out after six weeks with a hundred and sixty-five dollars. The commander was very nice to me. He let me stay, and he let me live in the barracks with the other fellows. To get back home, I stowed away on the H. F. Alexander, an Admiral Line ship going to San Francisco. They put me in the galley, shelling peas. I worked on Admiral Line ships the next two summers. I was a terrible sailor. I'd get sick every time we passed the outlet of the Columbia River. But I really enjoyed getting up at five in the morning to the sound of the call boy singing:

"Sleepin' good,
Sleepin' good.
Gimme dem covers,
I wish you would.
I know you's tired

And sleepy, too,
I hates to do it
But I'se got to do,
For you must rise and shine
For dis Admiral Line.

"Then the call boy would yank the blankets off us."

On our desk, under the snapshot of Mr. Bunche at the R.O.T.C. camp, we have assembled a few other scraps and notes from his life. There is a lined composition book with a faded green cardboard cover on which is written, in ink:

Ralph J. Bunche '27
Philosophy 3B
Row I—Seat 1—Sec. C

One of the handwritten compositions (it was graded A), dated April 22, 1925, when he was a sophomore, is entitled "Is Man Naturally Low and Despicable?"

It is difficult for me to accept fully Hobbes' theory of the position of man in society and in nature [Mr. Bunche wrote]. In the first place, it seems to me that Hobbes' conception of man as "naturally self-seeking, vile, brutish and egoistic, and *nothing more*" is quite a pessimistic and unwarranted one. It is true that man has these qualities in him, but I contend that these base characteristics are in part counteracted by good ones. I have a deep-set conviction that man *must* have an inherent notion of right and wrong; a fundamental moral structure and a simple sense of individual obligation, whether he be in a natural state or in society.

"In my senior year at college, I had the highest grades, and I was selected to be the commencement speaker," Mr. Bunche told us. "Dean Charles Rieber took an interest in me. Although he was stiff and formidable, his office was always open. He once said to me, 'You're going to be a lawyer.' Everybody just assumed I was going to be a lawyer. If a Negro was going to be educated and a professional, he became either a doctor, a teacher, a minister, or a lawyer. I walked into Dean Rieber's office and said I had no idea what my commencement speech should be about. He handed me a book of Edna St. Vincent Millay's poems and said, 'Here. Go to the beach, and come back with a philosophical topic.' So I went, and came back with the topic 'The Fourth Dimension of Personality' for my commencement address."

In his commencement address, Mr. Bunche said, in part:

Humanity's problem today is how to be saved from itself. If we are to develop our personalities to their fullest, we must add a fourth dimension to this ordinary self—that we may expand up and out from our narrow, immediate world. This fourth dimension—call it "bigness," soulfulness, spirituality, imagination, altruism, vision, or what you will—is that quality which gives full meaning and true reality to others. In identifying myself with my fellows and seeking to coöperate in hearty good will and understanding with them, I find my life in deed and in truth. My fellow-graduates: We are youth, and have the world yet to face. We are told that we have daring, vigor, and resourcefulness. Then let us *dare* to live as *men* live! Let us dedicate our vigor and our resourcefulness to the cause of human fellowship! I commend to you the lines of Edna St. Vincent Millay:

"The world stands out on either side,
No wider than the heart is wide . . ."

"I guess I was always hardheaded and independent," Mr. Bunche told us. "I always felt I wanted to do what I *wanted* to do. I liked adventure, and I was willing to gamble, to take chances. When I began teaching political science at Howard University, in 1928, Mordecai Johnson, the president of the college, once openly criticized me in a faculty meeting. 'Bunche is going all the way to Africa to find a problem,' he said. Negro colleges are petty places. The horizon is very limited, very narrow. They can be a graveyard. They're diseased. They know they exist as expedients. They're not in the free, competitive market. I had to get out. I've always had faith in the essential goodness of people. I think that basically man is good. He can be misled, but he's *good.* When you believe that, there's a lot you can do in the world. The only limitation in my job at the U.N. is that I can't participate in domestic partisan politics. I draw the line at endorsing any candidate, and I won't sign a petition on a piece of pending legislation. On the other hand, I've never had trouble speaking my mind on the race problem or poverty. At the beginning of the Montgomery, Alabama, bus movement, led by Martin Luther King, I went down there. I like to speak my mind. I've been asked to go into politics, but to be a good politician you've got to tolerate idiots as well as geniuses, and I'm a little impatient with idiocy. And I could never go out and ask anybody to vote for me, and eat pizza pie and bagels and lox, and all that. I've been asked what my main drive has been, and I think one thing: competitiveness. I have the pride of a competitor. I like to win. I think back on my school days, when I was the only Negro in the class, and I was determined to show I was as good as the white kids. In later life, when I worked for the O.S.S. and the State Department, I had pride in the fact that I was the first Negro to be given that kind of job. And I was determined to show them. I'm sentimental. I associate myself with whatever people I'm working with. I like people easily. I haven't seen Noble Sissle three times in the last ten years. One morning, he calls me up to say, 'Luckey Roberts is dead.' As soon as I heard Noble's voice, the picture was right there for me: the gray hair, the thin face, the squint, the wrinkles under his eyes, the sort of impish smile—if a man in his late seventies can have an impish smile—the dimple in his cheek, and the warm eyes."

Almost half a century after Mr. Bunche wrote in his composition book at college that it was difficult for him to accept Hobbes' conception of man, he gave a talk in Honolulu at the East-West Philosophers' Conference. The title of his talk was "Race and Alienation." In it he said:

> In all of his thousands of years here, man has lived in a constant state of alienation, in his relations with nature, with his fellow-men, with younger generations, with himself, his gods, his beliefs, ideas, and values. This, however, is not at all to endorse the Hobbesian view of the natural life of man as poor, nasty, and brutish, or to say that man is innately evil or warlike and that wars are therefore inevitable. I feel sure that man will still be here thousands of years hence. For I believe that despite so much wickedness and evil design in the world, man is essentially good.

In recent years, Mr. Bunche was plagued by all kinds of physical ailments, including trouble with his legs, so that walking was very difficult for him. Stubbornly, he insisted, against his doctor's orders, on marching with Martin Luther King in Selma, Alabama, in 1965, and in Dr. King's funeral procession, three years later. "I had been proud to walk with him," Mr. Bunche told us. "And this was the last walk for him. Probably for me, too. It was a sad occasion, but the trip was personally gratifying to me. In Atlanta, I stayed deliberately at Pascal's, a Negro-owned hotel, because I wanted to be with other Negroes. I wanted to be with those boys in the Mau-Mau jackets, and so on. My daughter Joan might have said that I would be jeered at. But all those boys couldn't have been nicer to me. Even Stokely Carmichael was nice."

Through all the daily pressures of Mr. Bunche's job at the United Nations—working on cables to and from the peace-keeping missions throughout the world; conferring with the Secretary-General and other senior colleagues; meeting ambassadors from the various missions; attending Security

Council and General Assembly meetings; supervising the peace-keeping efforts in the Middle East; seeing countless visitors from all over the world who wanted to talk about their problems—Mr. Bunche never ducked the single big issue of civil rights in the United States. "I'm in the struggle inevitably," he said to us one day. "I'm a member of a minority group." He told us he did not have any respect for what he called the self-appointed leaders of his race who were only "soapbox revolutionaries." "I have respect for the ones who get out in the front lines and march," he said.

Part of Mr. Bunche's own front-line work consisted of setting forth, again and again, his view that the United States needed to fight racism and poverty with the same all-out effort it made in waging any other kind of war. "Nothing is going to change the course of racial deterioration unless this country makes a massive effort to eliminate ghettos and to eliminate slums," he told us. "There are efforts now to improve life in the ghetto, but polishing up the ghetto is not making an assault upon the ghetto itself. We need to look problems straight in the face and put aside halfway measures and rationalizations. I don't want to predict trouble, but I fear it. The troubles we've had so far have been spontaneous and unplanned. However, nothing is more vulnerable than the modern American city. If the thirty billion dollars annually spent by this country on the war in Vietnam were channelled into an all-out effort, at all levels of our government, to mobilize the war on the ghettos, we'd make a good start in the war on racism."

Mr. Bunche was married on June 23, 1930, to Ruth Ethel Harris, who was born in Montgomery, Alabama, and was then a first-grade schoolteacher in Washington. He told us one day that his children—Ralph, Jr., Joan, and Jane (who died in an accident in 1966)—had been sheltered for the most part from direct experiences with racism. Joan, who is now in her early thirties and works for the United Nations

Development Program, made her first trip to the Deep South about eight years ago, to take part in a voter-registration drive in Louisiana. With considerable pride, Mr. Bunche gave us a copy of a letter she had written to her parents. We quote from it:

DEAR MAMA AND DADDY,

As I mentioned on the phone, the trip down was exceedingly pleasant. We drove in an open convertible, and I was the only Negro—there was a white man and a white girl. Although people occasionally looked, they never said anything, and we were served everywhere. We finally decided, after we were served in a Georgia diner on the highway which was filled with rednecks, that they probably thought that we had been on a Florida vacation, since we were all quite tanned, including my natural tan.

But when we arrived in Plaquemine, the vacation was over. It is about the ugliest town I've ever seen, except for White Castle, where I am now. I was so depressed when I got here I was ready to come home. I stayed in Plaquemine two days before I was assigned here. They put me in the nicest Negro home in town, which was the home of a local ex-madam. She was quite old and batty, and stayed in bed all day, as she has arthritis. There are no professional people in these small Negro communities, and the people are very poor—most of them work on the plantations, of which there are many around here. So that usually the best homes where they house the task force in the different towns are either with retired or aging madams, preachers, who are practically illiterate themselves, or maids who work for white families. This is an extremely poor community. The whites are almost as bad off as the Negroes. The population is about 1,500, about 50% of which is Negro. There are no sewers in the entire town—everyone has open drainage ditches in front of their houses—and the gnats and mosquitoes swarm all over the place. My legs are literally bitten all over. I now don't leave the house without rubbing mosquito repellent all over me.

The Negroes here live in utter poverty, and I am amazed how they manage to survive. The houses can best be described as wooden shacks. The women have many children. We visited one home, to teach the mother how to register, and she is 32 years old, with 17 children, and the house was so tiny, I couldn't imagine where she put them all. Many farm the children out to relatives and friends. The babies are poorly clothed and badly fed, and many of the children don't go to school at all. Our meals were horrible at first—pigtails, etc. I couldn't eat a thing, and I have lost a lot of weight. The diet here is perfectly awful —the people eat almost no meat, except for pork. I really feel sorry for the children—they are so undernourished, and many have that disease that forms scabs on their skin, due to lack of protein.

As for the whites in this town, they are perfectly horrible. They seem to all wear mean expressions on their faces—very tight-lipped, with wrinkled faces from the sun. Evidently they think nothing of calling the Negroes who live here "niggers" to their faces. Of course they don't like Alice and myself, and are rather unfriendly in the stores, since they all know who we are and what we are doing. An outsider stands out like a sore thumb in this town, since it is so very small. The police follow us around all day, and drive around our house, and our clinic. We see them so much that we are beginning to wave at them—there are only three police in the entire city, and they seem to patrol only the Negro areas. Our day begins by visiting the Negro homes in the area, asking them to come to a clinic that we have set up in an old abandoned wooden house. Alice and I always go together, and we often take some of the local teen-agers with us, since they know the people. Alice is a quiet Negro girl from New Orleans, who has worked with the civil rights movements all over the South. She is rather nice, and is a student at a Negro college in New Orleans. Mimi Feingold, the white girl from Swarthmore, was with us for a while, but they have sent her to another small town to organize a voter registration drive there. The Negroes seem to like us very much, and everyone is extremely friendly. They all say that we are helping them gain their freedom, and so they go out of their way to drive us anywhere, and are willing to do almost anything. You learn to wave at and speak to all the Negroes on the street, no matter who they are, and they all wave back. Even the toughest Negroes treat us politely, so that I'm not too afraid anymore working in the Negro neighborhoods. It is really amazing and inspiring to see how interested the Negroes are in learning how to register, despite their lack of education and poverty in their lives. A very poor woman of 31 here has nine children and recently suffered a heart attack, and I taught her every night until she learned to fill out the forms. When I took her to the registrar's office, she passed the first time—I was really thrilled.

Wherever Mr. Bunche's work took him, he made friends, and he seemed to stay in touch with everybody who had ever come into his life—from elementary school; from U.C.L.A.; from Harvard, where he obtained his Ph.D. in government and international relations in 1934; from the London School of Economics and the University of Cape Town, in South Africa, where he did additional graduate work; from Howard University, where he was head of the Department of Political Science for many years; from a two-year collaboration with Gunnar Myrdal in the study of the Negro in America; from the Second World War years, when he was Senior Social Science Analyst on Africa and the Far East in the Office of the Coordinator of Information, and, later, in the Africa section of the Office of Strategic Services; from the State Department, where he worked in many jobs and was a member of the United States delegations to all the conferences that worked on founding the United Nations; and, after 1947, from the United Nations Secretariat.

"I have the heaviest personal correspondence of anybody in the place," Mr. Bunche told us during one of our talks in his office at the U.N. His tone was one of very subdued pride —almost matter-of-fact. "I get thousands of letters. I read them all. I have a lot of pen pals, too. There's one lady, an invalid, who lives in England. She writes beautifully. I like her handwriting and the way she often starts out a letter with 'Hello, there!' or 'I take my pen in hand.' I've never met her. I once sent her some flowers on her birthday. We've been on a first-name basis for two years—at my suggestion."

Here are a few samples of Mr. Bunche's extraordinary correspondence.

From Dr. Cecilia Irvine, one of his teachers at Jefferson High School in Los Angeles (1959):

DEAR RALPH:
You were extremely kind and gracious to write a letter to me on the occasion of my retirement.

Many times during the years I have wanted to write you to express my great admiration, not only of your achievements, but of the spirit in which you are leading your life.

I would like to picture to you the boy you were. You were distinctly a thorough-bred who walked with a springy step, always you seemed completely at ease with the world and always looked up. I think, more than anything, I remember you with your head held high. I remember your grandmother. I met her just once. She was dressed in black with a Queen Mary black hat, and I have never forgotten the emanation of power from that tiny figure.

You were much too kind and generous to me. I always had sense enough to know that in my classes were boys and girls of ability and quality far above those possessed by myself. I consider it a great privilege to have invested my life in teaching, and I wish all teachers could be as happy as I am looking back over the years which seem so short.

Thank you for your part in making this occasion happy and may God bless you and strengthen you as you go on in the great service you are gifted to make to humanity.

To Miss Gwen Phillips, editor-in-chief of the 1961 *Spartan*, Scituate Junior-Senior High School, Scituate, Rhode Island (1960):

DEAR MISS PHILLIPS:

I am happy to respond to your request for a brief comment on the theme you have chosen for the 1961 *Spartan:* "The Place of the Aspiring Individual in a Despairing World." Why "despairing world"? Are you certain of that? I am not. It is a troubled world, to be sure, full of disturbed, possibly fearful people. But I do not believe that the peoples of the world are despairing, without hope, or resigned to disaster. Not at all. I think the world's people, rather, or at least that vast majority of them who inhabit the underdeveloped areas, nurture greater aspiration for a vastly better world in freedom and in their standard of living than ever before in human history. And I believe those aspirations will be progressively realized. We live in an exciting and dynamic world, which must go forward, and I am confident will go forward despite all present dangers.

From and to Sheryl Donaldson, sixth grade, Kavanaugh School, Palo Alto, California (1963):

What is the single most important ideal a child must learn to practice in order to accept the responsibility of adulthood?

DEAR SHERYL:

I would say that in my view integrity is the most important ideal a child must learn to practice in order to accept successfully the responsibility of adulthood.

To the boys of Den 3, Pack 35, of the Cub Scouts of Parkesburg, Pennsylvania, in response to a request from the Den Mother of "the only colored Den in town" (1958):

It seems to me that the way to be a good American is do the best you can on everything you are called upon to do. When you have done your best you can always feel satisfied and no one can ever justly criticize you for not having done better. Try hard and work hard, always. There is a lot of fun and satisfaction in achievement, in doing things right and doing things well.

I must admit that at times, only because of my race, I have worked a little harder just to prove that race has nothing to do with ability or achievement.

From and to Morton C. Haight, Fort Lauderdale, Florida (1968):

DEAR MR. BUNCHE:

I am a retired member of the New Jersey Bar (after a practice of 40 years), a taxpayer who is vitally concerned and interested in the welfare of this Country and its people.

I am an ardent believer in equal rights and responsibilities for all of our citizens irrespective of race, color, or creed.

I am satisfied (as I believe you must be) that no advantages of any kind or character can be secured by any minority groups by violence, unlawful acts and the destruction of life and property.

Why wouldn't it be possible (and an extremely commendable gesture) for you and a representative group of your race (as listed below) to organize and by speeches, writings and other methods impress upon the illiterate and underprivileged peoples in our Country that unprovoked and spontaneous acts of violence and destruction would not accomplish their desired results and an improvement in their social welfare.

DEAR MR. HAIGHT:

I thank you for your letter of 5 February which I have read with much interest. Indeed, I might say that I have read it with sympathetic interest because of my impression that you are entirely sincere in what you have written.

I do, of course, agree with what you have to say about the futility of violence and unlawful acts, but I do not at all agree with your assumption that speeches of any kind by anyone in our country today can have much impact, or do very much to prevent a recurrence of the tragic disorders in many of our urban centres in recent years. To assume otherwise is to misjudge seriously the cause of these disorders and the temper of the Negro in the ghettos today.

You see, Mr. Haight, the ghetto dweller in the American cities today (and this is where most American Negroes are now found) has reached a stage of frustration, despair and bitterness verging on desperation. He finds himself firmly segregated in black ghettos despite all that has been said and done about achieving equality of opportunity and citizenship for the black American, and despite the fact that there are very many white Americans, like yourself, who really believe in equal rights and opportunities for all Americans irrespective of race, color or creed. Nevertheless, the hard fact is that the ghetto dwellers have seen little or no improvement in their lots. Indeed, their existence is more segregated now than ever. In Harlem, for example, everybody, every activity, everything is black except the police, the landlords and the shopkeepers. Inevitably, the Negro confined to the black ghetto by economic and social forces as strong as any law comes to the conclusion that he is there because he is not acceptable to or wanted by the white society outside of the ghetto. He comes to feel that outside is a hostile white society and he in turn develops a hostility toward it. In time, because of this, a vicious circle is created, and the Negro, instead of seeking escape from the ghetto, finds a haven in it because he feels safer there and not unwanted. This is the inevitable pathology and psychology of the black ghettos and this, in my view, is the basic cause of the riots. I frankly fear that unless some massive efforts are made to change radically the lot and status of the Negro in the ghetto there can be no change in his psychology or outlook and, therefore, there will be an intensification of the racial troubles which the country has so sadly suffered.

In other words, I believe that the only way to change the direction of the disastrous racial course now being followed in the U.S. is for the society, its Government at all levels and all of its people, to face up to the fact that in order to avoid the ultimate catastrophe of virtual racial guerrilla warfare in our cities, heroic efforts have to be exerted now to eliminate the black ghettos by a full integration of the Negro American into the society. The indispensable first step for this is the will and the determination on the part of the white society to accept the

Negro on the basis of equality so that every Negro can find his
level in the society solely on the basis of his individual merit
without any handicap of racial prejudice.

At the United Nations Secretariat one day, while we were
waiting to see Mr. Bunche, one of his close colleagues, Brian
Urquhart, Director of the Office of the Under-Secretaries for
Special Political Affairs, said to us that he thought that what
Mr. Bunche was proudest of was his role in building up the
peace-keeping capacity of the U.N. We asked Mr. Urquhart
to tell us something of the way Mr. Bunche worked. "First
of all, he doesn't discourage easily, and he's always full of
ideas," Mr. Urquhart said. "I've known him and worked
with him since 1946, and his devotion to the U.N.—I must
say, greatly to his own cost—has been absolutely single-
minded. He's usually the first into a dangerous situation and
the last out. He regards life with the calm and compassion
of a selfless man devoted to a great task. He's a most tremendously unsanctimonious man, and a very unusual man in
public life. After a while, most public figures begin to show
certain idiosyncrasies. You get used to the idea of *being*
someone. Very few politicians, for example, are capable of
being self-critical. Ralph may not have any great opinion of
himself, but he has a tremendous opinion of the organization he works for and the job he's trying to do. He has a very,
very tough, analytical mind. He's very uncompromising
about anything he thinks is right or wrong. He's anxious to
get the thing right, and that's *it.* He cannot be pushed off a
position by any amount of arguing or by a desire to be
popular..He's always been meaning to go back into academic
life. Thank goodness, he hasn't done it. His loyalty to the
U.N. is total."

"I got a lot of notoriety during the Palestine mediation
work and when I was awarded the Nobel Prize," Mr. Bunche
said to us at the U.N. one day. "But I'm much more proud

of what I've been doing here since 1950."

It was a lifelong practice of Mr. Bunche's to write notes about his thoughts and observations and put them away in desk drawers, books, cardboard boxes, and, occasionally, filing cabinets. He gave us a number of samples of his "notes," including the following:

I have come in contact with a good many celebrated and occasionally great people. But as one comes to know them, they all have surprisingly apparent frailties and quite frequently serious flaws of character and personality. Greatness, more often than not, is the product of a combination of ability and the accidents of time and circumstance.

Foundation [the Rockefeller Foundation] started 50 years ago with less than $250 million. It has since given away approximately $1 billion. Nevertheless, its holdings today amount to $770 million (5 or 6 years ago it was $550 million).

Moral: It pays to give!

As a youth in Los Angeles, I began to develop real racial consciousness for the first time. I had had some racial experiences before, but it was in Los Angeles that my thinking about race began. I recall some inner feeling of resentment about not being "Negro" enough, as compared with my Negro chums. I envied Chuck Matthews for his ability to play the sax and the ukulele and to whistle jazz tunes so much better than I could. And dance better, too. I felt the same about Charlie Sanders. I saw their musical ability and sense of rhythm as "Negro" traits. Similarly, I envied George Duncan's ability at buffoonery. Sometimes sly, sometimes uproarious, but always, as I thought, distinctly Negro. By contrast, I felt something like the interlocutor in a minstrel show and somehow racially short-changed.

Now, more than
ever, I seem to regret·
that I lost my

mother when both
she and I were so
young. I feel
cheated to have been
deprived of her.
I have retained
an image of her
as a pretty, very
sweet and romantic
lady, a dreamer,
accomplished in
music and poetry,
and always an
invalid.
    I can never
get it out of my
mind that on that
night of her death
in Albuquerque
she had asked
for milk and there
was none in
the house because
because I had
drunk it up.

One day, while we were chatting with Mr. Bunche in his
office, he handed us a copy of a letter that his mother had
written to her brother and sister about a year before she
died. Like Ralph Bunche's life, it tells us something about
what America, at its best, can be, and what the human race,
at its best, can be. We quote from it:

ALBUQUERQUE, N. MEX.
JUNE 5, 1916

DEAREST TOM AND NELL:
    It seems a long time Nell, since we had fare well glimpses of
each other on the Depot platform that morning,—and when I

reflect that I haven't written to you in all that time, it seems even longer. You know tho' that it isn't because I havn't thot of you. I have thot of you and Tom often, and some very dear thots too. I was just out on the front porch, looking at the small green fruit on the plum trees;—and I was just thinking—about how we used to get up in the mornings to pick the plums from the "Eating Tree." (you remember the "Eating Tree"—don't you?) It was this pleasant remembrance that sent me in to write you. I wish Tom shared it with us,—don't you? You know this is "San Felipe Day" Nell, with celebrations in Old Town, and many "Mexicans,"—and I'm not there! Dosn't that seem— queer to you? I might say that I don't go because I have no comfortable shoes, but that would be only part of the truth. The greater part of the truth is this; that I am beginning to be more like you, to care more for the things that build real character, —and less for the frivolous things. Since I've been reading and studying more,—and consequently freeing my mind of much silliness, vanity and other un-necessary things; I've often re- flected, (not without a sense of humor) on the tortures you must have endured, through my superficiality,—at the circus grounds,—and other places of amusement? we attended. I didn't realize, then, why you couldn't enjoy the noise and sights fully—as much as I; but I do begin now, to catch the smallest inkling of the truth—and this, I think is it, that I lived only on the surface of things, never having thought deeply enough to recognize anything but the surface. I'm still largely superficial Nell, but I'm learning a little bit every day; how to be happy, contented, how to supersede hate with love, and best of all, how to live more in the Reality of things, nearer to God. I'm still grumbling a little, still complaining of my health at times, but I have high hope and strong conviction that health and happi- ness are for me. I'm even beginning to get back snatches of long forgotten ambitions, Nell, such as I had when I went to school, wrote crude verses, and dreamed of being a poetess. What won- derful things God performs in our lives, when earnestly sought, he gives us back the high ideals of our childhood, and glimpses of untold love, in beautiful thoughts. I'm sure that until now,

I have never even half dreamed the great meaning and purpose of life. I don't think any of us can regret our experiences, good or bad, if they lead us at last to something permanent in goodness and beauty. You see, I have a tendency for preaching, but I also realize that practicing is worth more to me, at present. I'm so glad that Tom has had such splendid luck; I love his optimistic out look, and yours too, Nell; God surely want us to be optimistic, through thick and thin, and you two have proven your selves good soldiers. Ralph has done fine in school this year, in study and application, and I know you will be glad to know that his temper is improved. You see, what benefits me, also benefits the children, and for this I am especially thankful. We have relapses into old ways, but they are less frequent. Fred is working steadily as usual, and we're continuing to make ends meet, and combining contentment with it, which has been a revelation to me as a remover of worry. The roses were beautiful in our yard Nell, they are almost all gone, but the fragrance was lovely while it lasted. We're all glad that Tom sent the Piano, I wish we had had it, when you were here. It's just as calm and beautiful, this eve. here, as you can imagine, you know Nell, one of our typical New Mexico sunsets. We have a little Mission Church across from us, in that vacant store building, now, so Ralph & Grace go there to church and Sunday School. It's convenient. I don't want to close this letter with out thanking you for all your little deeds of kindness and love, while here, Nell, and for which I didn't seem to have the grace, or the thoughtfulness, to show real appreciation; but "better late than never" and the memory holds the kind and lovely things, when the harsh ones are long forgotten. Tom knows, that I'm grateful to him too, not only for help received, but for the spirit in which it was given. Some day, (and this is *not* a daydream,) you shall have some recompense, equally as substantial as hearty, real, gratitude. Eff is the same dear girl, always doing some thing for our benefit and happiness. I thing Charl is liable to develope into a Socialist; He has a brake man friend who loans him literature on the subject. If women were allowed to vote in this state, I would vote the Socialist ticket. I wish Tom would vote it. Well, dear ones, I think I must say adios now, so Mama's letter and mine can be mailed to you. I'm not sticking so close to my Spanish at present; I came to the conclusion that the study of building a better mentality would be more profitable. I may take it up again later on. I'm a regular Subscriber to the Nautilus magazine now, and if you all would like to read it some time, I will send you some of my copies. I think the Band Concerts will soon begin now; Grace is the only one who manifests much of a desire to attend. I think we'll all enjoy going tho', because it's in the open air. I'm glad you're learning to be such a good cook Nell; you were a mighty good cook in embryo, when you were here. Well, if I write any more, my letter will exceed two cents, so here's yours for Love, happiness, and good will. —Oll.

"It's the only letter of my mother's I've ever had," Mr. Bunche told us. She didn't need to write another.

◆ Popov

WE tried to have some cultural exchange last week with Oleg Popov, the clown and star of the Moscow Circus, now at Madison Square Garden. Popov is a charming clown, whose name many circus buffs have recently begun to mention along with the names of Chaplin and Cantinflas. He comes on, in the one-ring, one-clown circus, in between such acts as the trained bears riding bikes, scooters, and motorcycles and the wild Cossack horsemen doing crazy, wild things with their horses. He juggles, performs some mighty beautiful footwork on the slack wire, and dances around, wearing a large, floppy black-and-white checked cap and a black velvet jacket, in little acts of innocent humor that recall simpler and easier times and places, far removed from the Brothers Ringling. All of which we wanted to talk with him about. So we went to lunch, at the Penn Plaza Club at the Garden, with Popov and, of course, with his interpreter, a crisp, slim, authoritative, attractive blonde named Nina Morozova, who is assigned by the Russian government to make conversation possible with the performers of the circus. Popov is round and chubby, with a classic round Russian face, a round nose, round blue eyes, full cheeks, and short, wispy blond hair, which he covers, in his act, with a full reddish-blond wig. He was wearing a Cardinlike chocolate-brown suit, a brown-and-white checked shirt with a fashionably large and pointed collar, and a wide purple tie. Mrs. Morozova had on black slacks and a grayish-blue turtleneck sweater. We all ate the same lunch: hot onion soup, grilled Cheddar-cheese sandwiches, and coffee. With us, also eating onion soup and a grilled cheese sandwich, was the great Bill Doll, who does publicity for the Moscow Circus. He regarded everybody with an expression of pride and happiness, and didn't talk.

We looked Popov straight in the eye and asked, to establish a connection, "Would you try to explain how, in your work, you are different from other clowns?"

Mrs. Morozova translated our question swiftly.

Popov looked us straight in the eye and replied, not very energetically, in a quick burst of Russian, then subsided, looking, we thought, a little weary and sad, and resumed eating his soup.

"Clowns all over world are almost same," Mrs. Morozova said immediately, in that peculiarly urgent yet impersonal tone of the interpreter. "In Soviet Union, our clowns are different. In Soviet Union, clowns put on not too much makeup. Here in America, clowns perform just to make you laugh. Each skit of Russian clown has *idea* behind it."

"Do you think you have had some influence on clowning over here?" we asked.

Popov listened deadpan to the translation of the question, and then answered it.

"Clowns here have started putting less makeup on," Mrs. Morozova said. "All clowns come to see him. In 1963, when he came here for first time, one famous clown waited one and half hours to see him and talk to him. One of Ringling Brothers saw Russian program and said to Popov, 'My clowns will repeat your act.' "

"Do you like that?" we asked. "Others imitating you?"

"He believes in exchange of art," Mrs. Morozova translated. "Otherwise, it would not be profession. Exchange is very good thing."

We all finished our onion soup.

"Can you characterize what *you* do as a clown?" we asked.

"You can make people laugh in various ways," Mrs. Morozova said, interpreting. "Three hundred times, box across cheek. Four hundred times, make someone's face soapy. Two hundred times, kick person. Three hundred times, throw water. In Western Germany, critic once said of him, 'Popov makes laughter without hitting or humiliation.' Popov believes that sums it up."

"Do you like being a clown?" we asked.

"In any profession, it is necessary to *love* your profession," Mrs. Morozova translated, not quite communicating the strong passion Popov got into his own statement in Russian.

"But why do you like it?" we asked.

Again, Popov got considerable feeling into his reply.

"Clowning is unlimited genre of art," Mrs. Morozova said. "It is an art without limits. There are many possibilities in it, and so it is very gay. All other arts in circus—juggling, acrobatics, animal acts—have limits. But there are no limits on clowns. It is not easy to make person laugh. It is easier to make person cry than it is to make person laugh."

Popov had given a small smile after he stopped talking, but Mrs. Morozova gave quite a generous burst of laughter before translating what he said. "He believes good mood prolongs life. If he makes life longer for people, it gives him pleasure."

Everybody around the table smiled and started eating a grilled Cheddar-cheese sandwich.

We asked Popov to tell us how he happened to become a clown.

Showing some uneasiness at talking about his personal life, he told us the following: He was born in Moscow in 1930, an only child. His father worked in a machinery plant, his mother as a retoucher of photographs. He was nine at the start of the Second World War. His father was killed at the front. He attended school until he was twelve, when a number of schools were closed because of the war. He then went to work repairing machinery in the printing plant of the newspaper *Pravda.* He worked there for about a year and a half. Then:

"We had bombings," Mrs. Morozova translated. "We had death in the streets. We had hunger. When children are deprived of gaiety, they still seek gaiety. All over Russia, we have amateur-club circles. For singing, for dance, for music. He belonged to one of these circles, and it was there he met schoolboys from State School of Circus and Variety Show Arts. They told him about their school. He applied, took examination, and he was accepted. He went to school six days a week for five years. He studied dancing, juggling, acrobatics, gymnastics, balancing, music, history of Western theatre, history of Russian theatre, history of circus. He was best in acrobatics. So after graduation he became acrobat, on slack wire."

"Did you look pretty much the way you do now?" we asked.

At last, Popov gave a genuine laugh, and then he gave his answer.

"He was very thin, and he had long hair," Mrs. Morozova translated.

Popov did a little act at the table, in pantomime, demonstrating that he had a very good heart and was very nice, and then he spoke a few more words in Russian.

Again, Mrs. Morozova burst into a big laugh. "He says he is very kind man, and kind men are stout, so he is stout."

"How about your mother?" we asked. "What did she say about your wanting to be in the circus?"

"He did not tell her," the interpreter said. "She wanted him to be doctor or pilot. She found out after one year. And then she scolded him. But after he became famous clown, she came to watch him in circus. And he looked out and saw her. Hers was brightest face in whole audience."

Popov told us a few more facts: After graduating from the circus school, in 1950, he travelled all over the Soviet Union with a company of other young circus artists. He visited all the circuses in the country for five years, performing in them and seeing all the Russian clowns. In 1955, he was sent to perform at the International Youth Festival in Warsaw, and there impresarios from Belgium, England, and France saw the Russians and invited them to appear in their countries. He was mainly an acrobat and juggler until one day, on tour, a clown became ill and Popov went on in his place. Up to fifty years ago, Russian circus artists used to take foreign names for themselves, but then a family of animal trainers named Durov started using their own Russian name. A juggler named Nikitin followed their example. Today, all Russian circus performers have Russian names.

We asked Popov for the names of comic artists he admires. He seemed to rouse himself to a new level of enthusiasm and energy, and said "Charles Chaplin."

"Charles Chaplin is greatest," Mrs. Morozova translated.

"In what way?" we asked.

Popov looked at us as though he thought we were nuts, and muttered something.

"Humanity," Mrs. Morozova translated.

Popov muttered a few additional statements.

"It is an art, like any other art, to be clown," Mrs. Morozova translated. "You cannot learn it. You have to *have* it."

Popov muttered some more.

"He says you have to be a decent person," the interpreter said. "Then you see everything in another light."

Popov made one more terse statement.

The interpreter said, "He says he tries to do everything with love."

❖ *Aboard*

THE other evening, we went to a formal dinner aboard the M.S. Sea Venture, a brand-new twenty-thousand-ton cruise ship, after she arrived here from Oslo, Norway, and before she left on her maiden voyage to Hamilton, Bermuda. We were invited by a couple of Norwegian shipping companies—Oivind Lorentzen and Fearnley & Eger, both of Oslo—and by Flagship Cruises, Inc., of Bermuda, a hands-across-the-sea owner-builder-operator partnership that has supplied the Sea Venture with Norwegian deck and engineering officers, a Norwegian, Italian, and Australian medical staff, an English-speaking Italian cabin, kitchen, and dining-room staff, and American hostesses and an American cruise director. The dinner was preceded by an inspection of the ship. We were led around by a lot of uniformed, pleasant, guttural, refreshing Norwegians, including the captain of the Sea Venture, Erik Bjurstedt, who is six feet three, who has the kind of solid Scandinavian maritime background that makes people feel like plunging confidently into the cold waters of the fjords, and who has a staff with names like Hauge, Vaage, Larsen, Nilsen, Hansen, Arnesen, and Knutzon. Our companion guests included a large number of pasty-faced, beleaguered New Yorkers like us—Comptroller and Mrs. Abraham Beame, Deputy Mayor and Mrs. Timothy Costello, Police

Commissioner and Mrs. Patrick Murphy, and people in the travel or tourist or tugboat business. Everybody was in formal dress—in a bedraggled way. We found ourself alongside Comptroller and Mrs. Beame, he in a small dinner jacket with a bow tie at a tilt, and she in a spangly, sparkly light-blue sleeveless silk gown. Mrs. Beame, whose eyelashes are very long and very black, was cheerful as we all examined the equipment described to us in a press handout as designed for "modern, luxurious American living at sea." Mr. Beame looked as though he might be considering how much it all had cost: the boat-deck staterooms with full tub baths, showers, refrigerators, and television sets; the two outdoor heated swimming pools, one with a sun deck for all-weather use and a retractable glass Solardome; the eleven lounges, four bars, and four dance floors; the sauna baths, the beauty parlor, and the barbershop; and the twelve lifeboats, four of them ninety-passenger canopied launches.

"Do you like ships?" we asked Mr. Beame.

"When they're standing still," Mr. Beame said.

"The only time we went on a ship, he got a hundred-and-two-degree fever the first night out," Mrs. Beame said to us. "We'll never forget it."

"Well . . ." Mr. Beame said.

"And I got sun poisoning on my lips," Mrs. Beame said. "Everybody said to us—it was a cruise to Nassau—'You're going in April. You're lucky. It'll be marvellous.' "

"It was so rough," Mr. Beame said mildly.

"He couldn't leave before April 15th," Mrs. Beame said. "He was Budget Director at that time. We left after the budget was submitted."

"Everybody was seasick," Mr. Beame said.

"Do you go to many parties on ships?" we asked.

"I urge him to go," Mrs. Beame said. "I like meeting people. We always enjoy these parties on ships."

"When they stand still," Mr. Beame said, with a tiny smile.

"They're better for him than a lot of the things he has to go to," Mrs. Beame said. "He doesn't know how to say no."

"Well . . ." Mr. Beame said.

"He's very civic-minded," Mrs. Beame said.

We all paused to admire the ship's bulbous bow and swing-out gyro-fin stabilizers for smooth sailing; the all-weather air-conditioning and heating system, with special dehumidification capacity; the twin propellers; and various pollution-control features.

One of the Norwegians said that the Sea Venture was built for the New York market. "New York is the best port in the world, and this ship is going to the best island in the world," he said. "Until November, this ship will go back and forth between New York and Bermuda."

"What are some of the other standstill ship parties you have gone to?" we asked Mrs. Beame.

"We went to the Rotterdam one," she said. "That was just before my son Buddy was married. It was very exhilarating. We went to the Andrea Doria one. When that ship sank, it broke my heart. I'll never forget those staterooms! Every one lined in silk!"

"I'm all for the cruise business—don't misunderstand," Mr. Beame said to us. "I was all for the big new passenger-ship terminal that has just been approved by the Board of Estimate. Its purpose is to hold the cruise business being lost to the City of New York, and attract more. It will be between Forty-eighth and Fifty-second Streets, and it will be the kind of terminal that will enable the ships to dock more easily. Adjoining the terminal will be a convention center. It will all cost about twenty-five million dollars, which is high, but we will substantially get that back in the form of rents."

We wound up in the Bermuda Lounge, where waiters

were passing around trays of highballs and canapés. There was a six-piece orchestra playing a kind of tarantella rock. Couples were dancing on a marble dance floor. We hung around Captain Bjurstedt, and he told us he was born in 1932 in the coastal town of Lillestrom, went to school in Oslo, and now lives in Aalbaek, Denmark, with his wife and four small children, who will, courtesy of Oivind Lorentzen, Fearnley & Eger, and Flagship Cruises, accompany him from time to time on the Sea Venture.

We were approached by a man who was raising his high-ball glass high to the Captain. *"Skoal!* I'm Arthur Christy, and I want to ask you just one question," the man said.

"I will do my best to answer," the Captain replied.

"What is the thing called the bow thruster?" Mr. Christy asked. "I had my own ship in the Navy in the Second World War, and I've sailed in the Bermuda races. Sailed in every race from 1946 to 1954. But I can't figure out the bow thruster."

"It is the forward propeller, operating in a tunnel in the bow, which can push the ship and make it possible to dock easily in any port," the Captain said.

Mr. Christy sipped his drink and looked happy. "So if you're docking, you just push the buttons operating the bow thruster," he said. "I'm fascinated by all your push buttons. We never had anything like that on *my* ship."

Captain Bjurstedt looked as though he were concentrating very hard. "They are very nice, these push buttons," he said.

"Yeah," said Mr. Christy. "Tell me, Captain, you use a sextant on the ship?"

"Of course," said the Captain. "Three times a day. It is the rule."

"Well, *skoal* again," said Mr. Christy.

We were soon seated in the dining room. On the dinner menu were Iranian Beluga Malossol Caviar on Iced Throne with Blinis, Clear Turtle Soup, Vol au Vent of Fresh Crevettes à la Newburg, Tenderloin of Prime Beef Wellington, and other delicacies. Our table companions included Mr. Christy, who told us he was a lawyer, and a Mr. and Mrs. John Bull, who said they were going on the maiden voyage to Bermuda.

"Not me," said Mr. Christy. "I've never gone on a cruise. I'd climb the wall after a few days. I'm basically a fisherman, but I like to fish when *I* like to fish. I go to the Canadian North Woods by myself. I do a lot of things. I scrimshaw whales' teeth." He put a lot of caviar on a piece of toast, ate it with zest, and washed it down with a gulp of vodka.

Mr. and Mrs. Bull smiled graciously. Mr. Bull said he was the president of the Moran Towing & Transportation Company. Mrs. Bull is a painter.

"I've been in the shipping business thirty-odd years and I've never been on a cruise," Mr. Bull said. "It will be very nice to relax, for a change, on a ship."

"Wow! Not me," Mr. Christy said. "Give me the Canadian North Woods."

"Do you like to scrimshaw?" we asked Mr. Christy, getting into the cruise spirit.

"For my friends only," Mr. Christy said. "I refuse to do it commercially."

"How's the tugboat business?" we asked Mr. Bull. We were on the turtle soup, and we had a vague feeling that we were approaching Bermuda.

Mr. Bull grinned good-naturedly and shrugged a little. "The number of ships coming into New York has been greatly reduced," he said. "New York as a port has been dying out. We have been diversifying ocean towing. We now tow drydocks from here to Vietnam."

"John Bull," Mr. Christy said. "Wow! I'll bet you get a lot of kidding, with that name."

Mrs. Bull smiled graciously. "He's used to the name," she said.

"When I went to P.S. 127, in Brooklyn, I was in a play," Mr. Bull said, with another good-natured grin. "The program said 'Uncle Sam, played by John Bull.' "

"Wow!" said Mr. Christy.

In the middle of the dinner, someone clanked silver against a glass, and everyone stopped talking and turned to the dais, where a tall, distinguished-looking man wearing a maroon dinner jacket was starting the mid-meal speeches.

"That's Horace Craddock, of Flagship Cruises," Mr. Christy said.

Mr. Craddock told a joke about a Christian in Roman times who was thrown to the lions; the lions refused to eat him, and when the Christian was asked later why the lions refused to eat him, he explained that he had told the lion, "If you eat me now, you'll have to make an after-dinner speech."

There was some nice, prolonged laughter, and then Mr. Craddock told a little bit about the building of the Sea Venture. "I don't know how much this ship cost, and nobody's telling me," Mr. Craddock said. "Some of our people tell me it cost twenty million dollars, and occasionally we say it cost thirty million dollars, because we want to discourage our competitors from building a ship." More nice, prolonged laughter.

Then Mr. Craddock introduced a handsome, tall Norwegian—Oivind Lorentzen, Jr., son of the head of the Oivind Lorentzen shipping company. Mr. Lorentzen had an old-fashioned prophet's beard and old-fashioned twinkling eyes. "We believe this ship will get fantastic business," he said seriously. "This ship is manned by Norwegians and Italians—both great participants in the tradition of this country."

Mr. Lorentzen introduced Deputy Mayor Costello, who looked euphoric and rhapsodic as he got up to speak. "Tonight somehow captures everything," Mr. Costello said.

"Mayor Lindsay sends warmest regards, and regrets that he cannot be here tonight. He doesn't really realize how *much* he should regret not being here. But he is busy guiding *another* ship through very troubled waters." Mr. Costello then raised his glass in a toast. "May the one-thousandth passage of this ship be as smooth, her dining room as crowded, and her women as beautiful as they are tonight. *Skoal!*"

"Skoal!" Arthur Christy called out, standing up. Everybody else stood up and said *"Skoal!"*

We turned around to the table adjoining ours. *"Skoal!"* we said to Police Commissioner and Mrs. Murphy, who were holding hands and looking very happy.

"Skoal! I sort of feel I'm on a cruise," Mrs. Murphy said. "I can't wait for the ship to pull out."

"We're really going someday," Mr. Murphy said. "We haven't settled in our minds when or where or on which ship. But we're going."

"And we're leaving the kids at home," Mrs. Murphy said, with a laugh. "All eight of them."

"When I was fifteen, I sailed to Ireland and back, on a visit to relatives in County Cork," Mr. Murphy said. "Except for the time I was in the Navy, in the Second World War, I haven't been on a ship since. We lived in Brooklyn for most of our married lives, and for about thirty years we've been driving on the West Side Highway and looking at, and daydreaming about, those ships, and talking about going on a cruise."

"Well, here we are!" Mrs. Murphy said. "I feel we're doing it right *now.*"

We went over to Mr. and Mrs. Beame and said *"Skoal!"* to them.

"Skoal yourself!" Mr. Beame said. "Great trip."

❖ *Sermon*

MOORHEAD KENNEDY, the hostage in Iran freed six months ago with fifty-one other American hostages, turned up the other Sunday as guest speaker at St. Ann's Episcopal Church on Main Street in Bridgehampton, Long Island (year-round population 950)—between Southampton, to the west, and East Hampton, to the east. The theme of his sermon was "Risk-Taking."

St. Ann's, a tiny, spireless church of white stucco, has pews accommodating seventy people. On this Sunday, the fifth after Pentecost, at a few minutes before 9:30 A.M.—an early hour designed to accommodate parishioners who might want to get on to the beach, to golf, to sailing, to tennis—we saw few signs on Main Street of partying or beautiful-people-ing. Except for one middle-aged man wearing Levi's cut-offs, a bright-red tank top, and leather sandals, carrying the Sunday papers, and ambling past the hardware store and the delicatessen across the street from St. Ann's, everybody in sight seemed to be heading for the little church: a few families with young children; many elderly couples; many elderly singles; many women in print dresses and white tie shoes; many men in seersucker suits and bow ties; several men and women struggling valiantly with walkers; about a dozen under-thirties; and only here and there a facial complexion attesting to wholly concentrated time in the sun. The pews were filled when we arrived; forty extra chairs set up in the nave were being taken fast. Everything was ready; an immaculate red carpet led down the aisle from the entrance and up a few steps to the chancel, where stood the American flag on one side and the Episcopal flag on the other. There was a two-manual pipe organ to the right of the pulpit. On the opposite side, on the wall, were posted hymn numbers:

513

537

347

An eleven-year-old acolyte, with long, straight blond hair, wearing a white cotta over a red cassock, and sandals on her bare feet, entered from the sacristy holding a candle-lighter. She bowed her head before the altar and lighted two standing candles on either side of the altar. Also from the sacristy came a crucifer, fourteen years old, wearing a white alb that partly covered plaid pants of many colors, and he bowed his head, picked up the brass processional cross from the chancel, and returned to the sacristy. The organist, a young man with steel-rimmed glasses and a small bald spot on top of his head, who was smiling very cheerfully, and who was also wearing a white cotta over a red cassock, took his place and started playing the prelude "May God Smile on You" from a cantata by J. S. Bach. Then everybody stood and sang Hymn 513 as the processional came down the aisle: the crucifer, holding the brass cross; the women of the choir, and then the men, both the men and the women wearing white cottas over red cassocks; the acolyte, carrying St. Ann's banner (silver lilies on a blue field); a lay reader, wearing a white alb; the Reverend Mr. Frederick W. Rapp, tall, gray-haired, solemn, and imposing, wearing a white alb and a red stole; and, walking alongside the rector, Moorhead Kennedy, wearing a gray-blue summer worsted suit with the State Department Award for Valor pin in his lapel, a

blue-and-white striped shirt with a button-down collar, and
a maroon tie embroidered with little blue sailboats. Mr.
Kennedy's hair looked almost all white—whiter than we
had remembered from our glimpses of him on our television
screen last January—and he seemed to have put on a bit of
weight. Like most of the others in the processional, he was
carrying a hymnal and singing, along with the congregation:

> Almighty Father, strong to save,
>   Whose arm hath bound the restless wave,
> Who bidd'st the mighty ocean deep
> Its own appointed limits keep:
>   O hear us when we cry to thee
>   For those in peril on the sea. . . .

The service that followed was quick, smooth, business-
like, to the point, and musical. Then Mr. Kennedy, standing
in the pulpit, gave the sermon.

"I feel like beginning 'Fellow-Hostages,' because every
one of us is a hostage to our life styles, to prejudice, to the
opinions of our peer groups," he said. "I, for example, am a
hostage to getting my children through college." He paused,
smiling, as the congregation gave him sustained and understanding laughter. Mr. Kennedy then told the story, from
the Gospel of St. Luke, of a man of position and means who
came to Jesus and asked, "Good Teacher, what shall I do to
inherit eternal life?"

"Jesus saw that this man was just the right person to work
with him, but when he asked the man to sell all his possessions and distribute them to the poor, and then to follow
him, the man was very sorrowful," Mr. Kennedy said. "And
Jesus said that it was difficult for those with riches to enter
the kingdom of God. 'It is easier for a camel to go through
the eye of a needle, than for a rich man to enter the kingdom
of God.' Jesus could see that the man *might* have been just

the right person for him, but a total *commitment* was required. The man was a hostage to his possessions. The man was unable to take the *risk* of giving up what he had in order to do something new and exciting, whatever it might lead to."

There was complete silence in the church, and a certain amount of tension, along with wariness.

"Of course, to take a risk just to prove something to yourself is very wrong," Mr. Kennedy continued. "A room I was held hostage in at the Embassy had a window, a balcony, and an awning. Like so many others, I was strongly affected by those World War II movies about the heroics of Americans in tight situations, and so I briefly considered trying to escape. It was a long run, however, from the residence to the compound wall. I was pushing fifty, and I had never been much of an athlete to begin with. Those twenty-year-old student guards could outrun me. Also, on the other side of the wall were the mobs. Then, I had been in the country only a few weeks and didn't know the city, so where would I go? I remember the deep feeling of relief when I was moved to another room, from which there was no way of escape." Mr. Kennedy smiled reassuringly, and the congregation responded with mild laughter and mutterings of empathy.

Mr. Kennedy went on to say that shortly after his release he had been offered good jobs if he continued in the Foreign Service. He had talked things over with his wife, Louisa, who had been a founder and spokesman of the hostages' Family Liaison Action Group, and then, Mr. Kennedy said, he had decided to retire from the Foreign Service and to join the Cathedral of St. John the Divine, in New York, in two main capacities: as director of the Cathedral's Peace Institute and as co-chairman, together with Louisa, of the effort to raise thirty-five million dollars for the completion and endowment of the Cathedral, including the Peace Institute. "I had to face the question that many of us face in life," Mr.

Kennedy said as the congregation looked at him intently. "It was 'Are you so locked in that you can't break away?' "

"I think it would not be out of order if we express our appreciation to Mr. Kennedy by clapping," the Reverend Mr. Rapp said when the sermon was over. Everybody in the church clapped enthusiastically for a very long time.

After the service, everybody lined up to shake hands with the guest speaker on the way out. As last in line, we retreated with Mr. Kennedy to a shady spot under a nearby maple tree and asked him to tell us a bit more about his plans.

"All right," Mr. Kennedy said. "I feel such a sense of *liberation* now. I don't say this with arrogance. Because I've been very, very scared, a lot of other fears don't seem very important to me now. This was *my* chance to break away, to do something different. It's a little scary to uproot the family. Leaving Washington is a kind of wrench, too. Leaving my home, my garden. We've rented two floors of a brownstone in the East Eighties, not far from the East River, and we've got a garden there, too. I don't know whether I'd have had the courage to do it if it hadn't been for my pension and health-care plan, after twenty years in the Foreign Service. My friends said, 'He's lost his mind. His career was right back on the tracks. He's been offered good jobs, and he's going to work for a *cathedral.*' But I felt, This is the moment to do it. One of the clergy had suggested that I might study for holy orders, and I think I could have done it in two or three years. But Louisa said, 'You put on the round collar, and out I go!' I think Louisa suddenly had this picture of herself passing out cookies after church, which isn't exactly her style." Mr. Kennedy laughed softly. "When the Presiding Bishop heard about it, he said, 'God is speaking through Louisa.' He said I'd be more useful to the Church as a layman."

The fourteen-year-old boy who had carried the cross at

the service passed by and waved to Mr. Kennedy, who smiled and waved back.

"Well, what is the Peace Institute?" we asked.

"You're looking at it," Mr. Kennedy said. "I happen to be very conservative. I'm a Republican. It may be premature at this stage to pass judgment on what the Reagan Administration is doing in foreign policy, but it seems to me that our government is not taking a sufficiently long view of things. What's happened in Iran since January is very important—much more important than what happened with the hostages. The Peace Institute will run seminars on religion and violence, on religion and economic development, and on American foreign policy. We need more continuity. President Carter, as part of his human-rights policy, made Chile our whipping boy, but President Reagan takes a very different view. There is very great bitterness in Iran about the United States. We not only intervened in 1953 to bring the Shah back—we *boasted* about it. We didn't consider how intervention would someday backfire, and also whether we demand too much of some countries. We encouraged the Shah to purchase American war planes to help our balance of payments. And there was the Shah putting in a vast American telecommunications system, because he wanted to be able to say you could have direct dialling from Isfahan to Chicago. This misallocation of resources by the Shah, with which we were identified, took place at a time when many villages did not have roads. All that backfired. The Peace Institute will study questions of that kind. I had this terrible shock of recognition when Vice-President Bush gave complete endorsement to President Marcos of the Philippines. Our government says we're protecting our investments and insuring our bases. That's exactly what was said about Iran. But what happens when Marcos falls? If we continue to support the Shahs and the Marcoses, what happens? The Peace Institute will study ways of our having a more flexible foreign policy. Why do we get into bed with dictators? Thomas Jefferson and John Adams dealt with dictators, but we didn't get entrapped by them. The Peace Institute will study all these things."

The morning sun was hot now, and it was growing warm under the maple tree. Mr. Kennedy loosened his necktie ever so slightly. "We missed the point badly in not understanding the revolution in Iran," he said. "Religion is very much a part of life in the country, and one area that people feel very threatened in is in what's happening with the women in the country. There's some parallel in this country in the way Jerry Falwell is appealing to the feelings of insecurity about women. I was shaken when I learned that the nomination of Judge O'Connor for the Supreme Court was being referred for approval to certain religious leaders. Our Founding Fathers made it clear that this country was not beholden to any one religion. There is a void today, which Jerry Falwell is filling. I'll want the Peace Institute to study all that."

"How do you think it will go?" we asked.

"There's a lot of preaching about foreign affairs, but the Holy Spirit isn't enough—a preacher needs to have *facts,*" Mr. Kennedy said. "After twenty years in government, when I'm answering a question I sometimes find myself asking, 'What's the *policy?*' Then I say to myself, 'My God, Kennedy, relax! You're a free man now.' When I catch myself framing answers to say what's expected of me, I immediately realize how wonderful it feels to air my own views. And the Cathedral is such a dynamic place after one has been in a structured institution. We're like a medieval cathedral, with arts, crafts, drama, and music. The Cathedral has always had an international character. In 1925, Franklin D. Roosevelt had the fund-raising job that Louisa and I have taken. Roosevelt sent people all over the world and filled the Cathedral with Shinto vases, a menorah, Persian carpets leading up to the altar—things like that. He did a bang-up job; then he ran for governor of New York. The Cathedral is not just a church in New York. It's the world's largest cathedral. People in the neighborhood love it. On one of the brutally hot nights early this summer, I stayed at the Union Theological Seminary, because Louisa and I still hadn't moved to New York. Late at night, I walked over to Grant's Tomb, where a jazz concert was in progress. And I was *recognized*. One of the people there called out to me, 'Hey, man! You're the cat who's raising thirty-five million dollars for our Cathedral!' "

❖ Narrator

MAYOR KOCH didn't have time to come to the piano for the first *Sitzprobe* of Sergei Prokofieff's "Peter and the Wolf" with the Mayor as Narrator—a performance of which with the Greenwich House Orchestra, celebrating the seventy-fifth anniversary of the Greenwich House Music School, was scheduled for the afternoon of Saturday, May 2nd, at Town Hall—so Edward Houser, the conductor of the Greenwich House Orchestra, arranged to have the *Sitzprobe* take place in the Mayor's car, early one morning last week, en route from Gracie Mansion to City Hall, and we were invited to ride along.

Houser, who is twenty-six years old and has bright-red curly hair, a matching beard, and the classic look of joyous innocence somehow characteristic of dedicated musicians, had with him the score for "Peter and the Wolf" and a pocket-sized tape recorder. The morning was one of the sunniest so far this spring, and the Mayor, as he emerged from Gracie Mansion, was in comparable form, having, he reported to us, got up at six, when he was awakened, as usual, by his "internal time machine"; jogged for a mile along the East River Drive; and—after putting on a Brooks Brothers olive-green gabardine suit, a maroon-and-white striped shirt, and a navy-blue necktie decorated with green maple leaves (a New York City tie, designed by Gordon

Davis, the Commissioner of Parks)—met over breakfast with Deputy Mayors and other staff members. He greeted us cordially and arranged where everybody should sit in his car, a dark-blue 1979 Chrysler sedan: himself, Houser, and us, in that order, in the rear, and, in front, a hulk of a police-officer-driver named William Kraus and a hulk of a detective named Dennis Martin, with Tom Goldstein, the Mayor's press secretary, squooshed in between them. The Mayor assured Houser that a quick run-through in the car was all he needed in the way of preparation for his début as Narrator of "Peter and the Wolf."

"I'm a fast learner," the Mayor said as we started downtown in the car.

"It's very important to cue these things in—" Houser began, deferentially.

"Of *course,*" the Mayor said seriously. "I can't sing or dance, but I do have timing."

In the front seat, William Kraus and Dennis Martin exchanged knowing looks over the head of Tom Goldstein.

"I've done four Inner Circle shows, you know," the Mayor said. "Those annual shows put on by the reporters in Room Nine at City Hall. The Mayor is always required to do a reprise at those shows. I was terribly frightened when my turn came to do it. Lindsay was a good song-and-dance man. Beame did it, too. But I *did* it. Four times. If I can do that, I can do anything."

In the front seat, Tom Goldstein, who had been listening to a beeping portable push-button telephone, turned around and reminded the Mayor that there would be a brief stop at the Hilton, where the Mayor was supposed to welcome delegates to a convention of the National Catholic Educational Association at nine o'clock, and that he had the meeting on his budget at ten.

"Fine," the Mayor said crisply. "Shall we start?" he said to Houser.

"This is the Introduction," Houser said, handing the Mayor a separate sheet of paper. "You read from the top. And I'll play—"

"Got it," the Mayor said, pointing a finger at Houser's tape recorder. Then he read, "I'm going to tell you the story of Peter and the *Wolf,* and I've asked the instruments of the *orchestra* to *help* me," and he pointed again at Houser's tape machine.

Houser pressed the "On" button on the machine.

"Peter's tune is played by the *stringed* instruments," the Mayor read, his cadence leaving nothing to be desired and his projection exemplary. There was much appreciative nodding in the front seat as the stringed instruments played Peter's tune.

"His friend the *bird* is represented by the *flute,"* the Mayor read, and then he paused.

The flute was heard.

"There is a *duck,* too, and his quacking song is played by the *oboe."* Pause. Oboe. "The *clarinet* plays the sound of the *cat."* Pause. Clarinet.

The Mayor seemed to have fine control of his performance. "The grumpy grandfather is played by the bassoon, which is a very *grumpy instrument,"* the Mayor read. Bassoon. "The wolf is played by *three French horns."* French horns. We were going down Second Avenue in heavy traffic, passing the Roosevelt Island Tramway. Grumpy drivers around us indicated a few times that we seemed to be moving too slowly, but William Kraus didn't seem to notice them. Bicycle riders came alongside our car, but none looked in.

"And the *hunters,"* the Mayor read, "are played by the kettledrums and the *bass* drum." As Houser's machine emitted the sounds of the kettledrums and the bass drum, we reached East Fifty-seventh Street. There was a bus between the Mayor's car and the right turn. Our driver missed the turn, shrugged, and went on listening to the performance.

"I'm quite amazed," Houser said, looking amazed and handing the Mayor the full script of "Peter and the Wolf."

"Shall I start?" the Mayor asked, and he started. "Early one morning, Peter opened the gate and went out into the *big green meadow,*" he read, and the piano music on Houser's machine came in as we worked our way west on East Fifty-third Street. "On the branch of a *big tree* sat a *little bird,* Peter's *friend.* 'All is *quiet,*' chirped the bird gaily." Again, the music came in on cue.

"I'm quite amazed," Houser said again. "Everything is completely synchronized."

The Mayor made a sign for silence and read on: "Soon a *duck* came waddling around. She was *glad* that Peter had not closed the gate, and decided to take a *nice swim* in the deep pond in the *meadow.*"

In the front seat, the hulks pursed their lips in what looked, in the rearview mirror, like complete mesmerization. The traffic was heavier than before, but the Mayor ignored it. His concentration on his role was total. His reading became more and more dramatic.

"Just then the *hunters* came out of the *woods,*" he was reading when his press secretary turned around and pointed out that we were a couple of blocks from the Hilton.

"Shall we pause?" asked Houser.

"No, let's go on," the Mayor said, and he read on: ". . . following the *wolf's trail* and *shooting* as they went."

The Mayor put his script down reluctantly as we reached the Hilton.

"I've heard Tom Seaver do it," Houser told the Mayor while we were all walking inside. "Boris Karloff did it. David Bowie did it. Eleanor Roosevelt did it. But this will be the first authentic New York version. Do you have experience in reading to kids, Mr. Mayor?"

"No, it just comes natural," the Mayor said. "As a child,

I used to listen on Sunday to fairy tales on the radio told by the Singing Lady, Ireene Wicker. She was *wonderful.* "

"I can't get over how synchronized you are with the music," Houser said.

"I took lessons at your Greenwich House Music School," the Mayor said. "When I first moved to the Village, as a young man, I lived at Bedford and Barrow, and down the block was this settlement house, with its school. So I decided to learn to play the guitar. But I made a mistake. I wanted a guitar for folk music, and they gave me a *Spanish* guitar. But I struggled through, learning chords. At about three dollars an hour."

"Now the lessons are about sixteen for adults, fourteen for children," Houser said.

"You know the way they have an annual concert? Every December?" the Mayor said. "When everybody gets up and does his thing in the music? I was all ready, with my Spanish guitar and my *chords,* but the part they gave me in the program was the checking of coats and hats. I didn't care. I was part of the program. We'll finish the rest before the budget meeting, O.K.?"

"Yes," Houser said. "And it's going great."

"My feeling is, *whatever* you do, throw yourself *into* it," the Mayor said. "Very important. I'm not afraid of it now."

❧ The Shave

WHAT has happened to the shave in barbershops? We looked into the question last week. In a random canvass of barbershops, we found that roughly one out of three still offers the shave to customers, and at the following representative prices:

James, Hairstylist to Men, at the Plaza—$8.

Paul Molé's, 1021 Lexington Avenue—$6.

Jerry, Hairstylist to Men, at Bergdorf—$5.

Monique of the Waldorf—$5.

Johnny's Barber Shop, 2 Park Avenue—$3.25; $3.75 with tonics.

Ritz-Carlton Barber Shop, Boston—$5.

Arcade Hair Stylists, 25 West Forty-third Street—$4.50.

Many barbershops started putting out "NO SHAVE" signs about twenty years ago, for reasons that, according to the barbers we consulted, included the arrival of the chromium blade; the arrival of the electric razor; the arrival of long-hair styles and the beard; the popularization of unisex barbershops and beauty parlors; the large number of men who were in the armed forces in the Second World War and had to start shaving themselves and then, it turned out, didn't give up shaving themselves; too much trouble; very little profit. In the barbershops where shaves are still given, some are given by barbers who use the old-fashioned straight steel razor, which is known in the profession as the "cut-throat" razor. Most of the shaves are given with a razor that looks like the old-fashioned straight razor but has a disposable chromium blade. For customers who request shaves with a genuine old-fashioned straight razor, about half the shops that give shaves have barbers who know how to hone the razor on a stone, smooth it on a two-piece canvas-and-leather strop, and then give the shave. A few barbershops, like Jerry at Bergdorf, refuse to give a shave with anything but the straight razor. "We have Ambassador Frederic Mann and Selig Burrows and Jule Styne, and they want the real thing," Miss Katherine King, the manager of Jerry, told us. "We do at least six shaves a day. We're doing more now than we did ten years ago. The shave is coming back. We give the closest shave in town."

At James at the Plaza, Mrs. Marie Dussol, the manager, told us that ten per cent of her customers get shaves but that only one of them, a businessman named Charles Beer, insists on being shaved with the old-fashioned straight razor. "He can *feel* the difference," Mrs. Dussol told us.

In order to give shaves in this city, a barber must have a Master Barber license issued by the State of New York. Requirements for the license are: attending a barber school for six months and working as an apprentice in a barbershop for eighteen months, *or* working as an apprentice in a barbershop for twenty-four months—and then taking and passing an examination given by the Division of Licensing of New York's State Department. This examination consists of a practical demonstration and an oral test, and includes a section on the shave: applying the lather, sharpening the razor with the strop, and shaving with the straight razor. Applying hot towels is not included. Most people who cut hair don't need a Master Barber license. They go to a beauty school for a thousand hours, pass a hairdressing test, and get a Cosmetology license. But Cosmetology graduates are not allowed to do shaves. (The New York State Department of Education, which supervises and licenses beauty schools, informed us that "beauty school" is "the generic term" for "cosmetology school," and that the shave is not part of the cosmetology-school curriculum.) At the Atlas Barber School, at 44 Third Avenue, which is the only classic, shave-teaching barber school left in the city, Matthew Raguso, the director and co-owner, told us that at the moment he has forty-five students, all of whom are studying, among other things, the shave. Mr. Raguso told us that he has been in charge of the school since 1957. Tuition is $1,935 for a thousand hours of instruction, of which three hundred are devoted to teaching the shave. Upon enrollment, each student gets a kit of tools. Along with a pair of scissors, two combs, two kinds of clippers, and a textbook, the kit holds a straight razor, a hone, and a strop. Mr. Raguso told us that he is a faithful devotee of the old-fashioned shave. "Here we teach, The customer can feel the shave," Mr. Raguso told us. "We teach, It is very important to get the right lather, very important to get a lather machine that gives the right lather. Very important, because we don't use brushes anymore. We teach, It is very important to tell whether a beard is a soft beard or a tough beard. Very important how to use the hot towels to soften the tough beard. Then we teach how to strop on canvas, how to strop on leather—five strokes on each side. We teach, The shave is *artistic.* With a straight razor."

"What about disposable blades in the imitation straight razor?" we asked.

"Garbage!" Mr. Raguso said.

We called up Jerry Spallina, who started Jerry at Bergdorf, and who now has a shop in Fort Lauderdale, Florida, at Le Club International, and he told us that nobody in Fort Lauderdale ever asks for a shave. "I'm now in this beautiful place. It used to be owned by John Brown, of Kentucky Fried

Chicken, who just married Phyllis George, and now he's the governor of Kentucky, so he can't own this place anymore," Jerry explained to us on the phone. "When I had my shop in the Squibb Building, at 745 Fifth Avenue, and then my shop at Fifty-fourth and Madison, I always used to send a barber up to shave old Mr. Goodman at Bergdorf Goodman. Now the shave is gone with the horse and buggy."

"We used to soap up the outside of balloons and make our students shave *them*," Paul Ferrara, who runs the Robert Fiance Hair Design Institute, at 405 Fifth Avenue, told us. "But shaving is no longer a part of our repertoire."

Paul Molé's barbershop, now seventy-five years old, is co-owned by an Englishman named Adrian Wood, and Mr. Wood told us he still gives shaves, but not many. "The clean look is in again, but our clientele, mostly bankers and stockbrokers, never abandoned the clean look in the first place," Mr. Wood said. "But these are people who like to shave themselves. They don't come to the barber for a hot towel. They're smart. They know they can go home and get the same result with a hot shower."

Monique of the Waldorf told us that her shop still gives shaves, with the old-fashioned straight razor, but not so often these days. "Customers who used to live in the Towers would come in here daily for a shave," she said. "James Farley. For over thirty years, he came in every morning at eight o'clock. Now the shave is almost extinct."

We wanted to know how the shave stood in Boston. "Thirty-four years ago, we used to do seventy-five shaves a day," Ralph De Stefano, manager of the Ritz-Carlton Barber Shop, told us over the telephone. "Now we average four, maybe five a day. It has always been a ritual with executives, the type that has more time. The late James N. B. Hill, grandson of the railroad tycoon. People like that. Once, I had three kings in here at the same moment—Peter of Yugoslavia, Michael of Rumania, and Leopold of the Belgians, all chatting together while sitting in the barber chairs."

"Only one," Benny Monticciolo, the owner of the Arcade Hair Stylists, downstairs in our building, said when we asked him how many regular customers he had for shaves. "He's Larry Stevens, of Stevens Personnel, on Fifth Avenue. He comes every Friday. We use the chromium blade. He rests. Otherwise, it's a dead item."

We told Kenneth, of Kenneth's, at 19 East Fifty-fourth Street, which was one of the first of the glamorous beauty salons to open its doors to unisex, about our study. Ten per cent of his clients now are men, he told us, but not one of them, in three years, has ever asked for a shave.

The hotbed of old-fashioned shaves seems, from our quick survey, to be Johnny's, at 2 Park Avenue. There we talked to a master barber named Vito Moles, who used to have his own shop, around the corner at 152 Madison Avenue, and who has been a barber for fifty-two years. When we arrived, we found a young man wearing bluejeans lying in one of the shop's eight barber chairs and getting shaved. A splendid-looking copper-and-chromium towel sterilizer stood off to one side. The name "Bramhall Deane Co." was engraved on the cover in script. "It's sixty years old," Mr. Moles told us. "Good as new. Nothing like a nice hot towel over the face to give you relaxation. First I give the hot towel, then the lather, then another hot towel, then the shave, then the hot towel again. The men who come here as regulars know what's good for them. Every morning at seven-thirty, I shave Louis Helpern, in the underwear business. At eight, I shave Moe Mitchell, also in the underwear business. I've shaved four *generations* of Mitchells. Every afternoon at three, I shave Murray Singer, of the piece-goods business. Our manager, Joe Chiusano, shaves Harold Sachs, of the handbags business. Martin Fein, the auctioneer. Sidney Blaine, sportswear. These men don't know how to shave themselves. Every time they try it, they need a doctor. When they come in on Monday, after being on their own, they look like a porcupine. The sideburns are cockeyed. The hair is left on. They look terrible."

Jack Hausman, the vice-chairman of the board of Belding Heminway (threads, literally), is one of the Johnny's regulars. We telephoned him at a hotel in Palm Springs, where he was taking a little vacation.

"Vito has been shaving me for years and years, and I've never got nicked," he said. "Here, I miss Vito. It's restful to get a shave. I take a little nap. The hot towel is comforting, especially in winter. I started working at the age of fourteen, for my father, M. Hausman, at 110 Grand Street. The barber was a block away. I went there for a shave, because my father and my older brother went there for a shave. I followed the same procedure. When we moved uptown to East Thirty-second Street, we all started going to Vito, around the corner. I always go at nine-thirty in the morning. I'm not happy doing it any other way. I have breakfast every morning with my wife, Ethel, in Peacock Alley, at the Waldorf, and I walk every morning to work on East Thirty-second Street. I've been doing *that* for years and years, too. I don't like change. Here, I really miss Vito. I'm not getting shaved here. I look like a porcupine. I look terrible."

❖ Rehearsal

LAST week, we hung around a bit with George Abbott, the actor-writer-producer-director, during a rehearsal of "Winning Isn't Everything," which was written by Lee Kalcheim, was being directed by Mr. Abbott, was being produced by the Hudson Guild Theatre, and is scheduled to open on November 8th. The play is No. 119 in a long line of shows that Mr. Abbott has been involved in: a line that started in 1913, with "The Misleading Lady," and has included, among others, "Three Men on a Horse," "On Your Toes," "The Boys from Syracuse," "Best Foot Forward," "The Pajama Game," "Damn Yankees," and "New Girl in Town" (all of which he directed and either wrote or helped to write), as well as, among others, "Boy Meets Girl," "Brother Rat," "Room Service," "Pal Joey," "On the Town," "Billion Dollar Baby," "Call Me Madam," "Wonderful Town," "Never Too Late," and "A Funny Thing Happened on the Way to the Forum" (all of which he also directed). Because many people, not including Mr. Abbott, make a fuss about his age, we might as well mention that he was born, in Forestville, New York, on June 25, 1887. We met Mr. Abbott last week, at his suggestion, in front of his hotel, in the Fifties just west of Fifth Avenue, at nine o'clock in the morning of what turned out to be the first really cold day of the new fall. We were about a minute late, and found him standing and waiting—six feet one and three-quarters, with the posture of a West Point cadet. He was wearing, against the cold day, only a small, rakish-looking beige English cap, a bright-yellow turtleneck shirt, a Brooks Brothers tweed suit, brown socks, and brown loafers. He greeted us with a friendly grin, but he was clearly impatient to get moving.

"I hope you like to walk," he said, briskly starting off westward, with long strides. "The theatre is on West Twenty-sixth. In Chelsea. Sometimes I walk all the way. Other times, I walk part of the way and then jump on a bus. Our rehearsal starts at ten and goes to three. I don't like to be late. Maybe this morning we'll just nab a taxi." At the Ninth Avenue intersection, he grabbed us by the arm, saving us from being run over by a delivery cart, and firmly guided us through some heavy traffic. It was rush hour, and taxis seemed unavailable. Suddenly, though, he whistled through his teeth, pointed a commanding finger at a taxi with its "Taxi" light on, and nabbed it.

"The theatre is between Ninth and Tenth," he told us as the taxi headed south. "We're not only Off Broadway but *Off* Off. It's a little theatre. The theatre is so small, in fact, that we can't have all the critics come at once. We have to spread them out over three performances. The play is a farce, and it needs an audience reacting, along with the critics. The theatre is little, but it does such good things. 'Da' opened down there, and now it's a hit on Broadway. The place is run by a young man named Craig Anderson. Very smart. He's going to be a power in the theatre."

"How old is he?" we asked.

"Gosh, thirty, I guess," Mr. Abbott said. "He runs a terrific organization. It's quite a complex down there. The theatre is only part of many things that the Hudson Guild does. Child care. Classes in this and classes in that. You can see that it's all an influence for good. It's very exciting down there. It's all very much the heart of New York." Mr. Abbott gave us his grin again, and looked us straight in the eye. "Do you like New York?" he asked us.

"Love it," we said.

"Same here," Mr. Abbott said, still fixing us with a keen gaze, and, inescapably, making us notice that the color of his eyes was deep blue. "Technically, my home now is in Miami Beach. I decided to award myself Florida temperature for the rest of my life. But I don't *stay* there. I come here in the spring and in the fall and live in the hotel. I spend my summers in the Catskills, about a hundred miles from New York, at the Merriewold Club, where I play a lot of golf, but I keep driving my car back and forth between there and here."

"When did you last direct a show here, before this one?" we asked.

"Two years ago," Mr. Abbott said. "It was called 'Music Is,' and it was a failure. It got good reviews out of town, but when we brought it to New York it got panned. I can generally see what's wrong with my failures, but this one was a disappointment. I thought the costumes were good, and *they* got panned. It's easy to have a blind spot, but after that failure I was unhappy about the theatre. So I started reading novels. I read a ton of novels, and I began to get a feeling for the novel, so I wrote one. It's called 'Try-Out.' It's being published in the spring, by Playboy Press. Well, here you are. In Chelsea. You can see how good-looking this place is."

Mr. Abbott charged out of the taxi, and we followed him at a fast clip into a modern brick-and-glass building identified over the entrance as "HUDSON GUILD." Inside, he sprinted up a metal stairway to the second floor and led us to a large rehearsal hall, very light, with a lot of windows, and containing the props of the rehearsal: tapes affixed to the lino-leum-tile floor to show positions onstage; a few tables and folding chairs in the stage area; more tables and folding chairs offstage; a large coffee urn and a stack of disposable cups along the wall opposite the windows; above the coffee urn, a bulletin board holding the four-week rehearsal schedule for the play and a sketch of the play's single set—a room in a somewhat seedy hotel in an unnamed medium-sized American city. Mr. Abbott told us that "Winning Isn't Everything" was about a political campaign. All the members of the cast were on hand, together with Mr. Abbott's assistant, Judith Clark, who is his daughter. A thin blonde wearing black pants and a royal-blue turtleneck, Mrs. Clark clearly resembles her father—especially in posture. Also present was Mr. Kalcheim, the playwright, who has a brown mustache and is somewhat bald, and who was wearing aviator sunglasses, gray cords, and a black turtleneck. He was smoking a thin cigar. Everybody present said "Good morning, Mr. Abbott" except Mrs. Clark, who said, "Good morning, George."

"We'll start with the first act," Mr. Abbott said politely, sitting down on a folding chair facing the actors, and inviting us to sit alongside him. Mrs. Clark sat on his other side, at a table, on which she had the script of the play.

Most of the actors and actresses seemed to be in their twenties or thirties, except for the man who played a middle-aged campaign chief—one of the leads. As Mr. Kalcheim joined us, we asked Mr. Abbott how he had come to take on the play, and he said that Audrey Wood, the agent, had sent it to him to read, and he had liked it.

"It's Mr. Abbott's kind of play," Mr. Kalcheim said happily. "There's nothing like working in the theatre," he went on. "I live in Connecticut, with an apartment in New York, and I have to go to California a lot, where the television work is, but for me there's nothing like the theatre. In films or in television, the whole process takes place in the head of the director. But in the theatre you have the interrelationships of the actors. You hear the audience reaction. And you can change it. You work with it a little at a time, layer by layer, like a piece of sculpture."

Mr. Abbott looked at the actors. "Let's see if they know the lines," he said, again very politely.

"George, they want to go without the book," Mrs. Clark said.

Mr. Abbott nodded in approval, and the rehearsal began.

At the start, Mr. Abbott remained seated, his arms folded across his chest, his posture just as upright as when he was standing. His concentration on the actors was total. Not a syllable got past him. He made terse comments. Very instructive. It all made us long to be on the stage. "Hold your line, please," he would say. "Let the phone ring before you say that." Or "Say the line first, *then* cross." Or "Move over to the other side of the table when you take the thing." Or "Let's say the line standing up, then collapse after the line." Or "Have your back to them when you yell 'Oh, no!' " Or "Excuse me, we'll have an extra yellow pad, so that's your motive for going over there." Or "If you don't say 'freshman' and make it stand out, you don't have anything." Or "You could move upstage a little bit, Kathy." (This was addressed to the ingénue, and he used the character's name, as he does with all the actresses and actors.) Or "You're *bored* with her; sit down." Or "Get up on 'I don't want to.' Up. Up. To *her,* to *her.* " Or "Keep that up, *up.* 'Law and *or*-der!' " Or "Don't drop the end of your sentence." Or "Try it again, please." Or "Kathy, don't jump that cue." Or "Let's change it. Say 'Hello,' then walk forward on your line." Or "When you first start, don't face dead out." Or "Your tone is placating. You're like a salesman. A *Buick* salesman." Or "Wait till he shakes his head, then sit on it. Let's get the *sarcasm* in it." Or "Let it hit you a beat before you reply to her announcement."

When it was necessary, Mr. Abbott would change his position. He would jump up to demonstrate a posture, a gesture, a walk, a way of avoiding a collision between actors. Occasionally, he would stand, hands folded behind his back, and lean forward watching intently. Then he would hitch up his pants and sit down. He would laugh with true enjoyment at some of the jokes. Once in a while, he would tell the actors, with great courtesy, that their delivery of a supposedly funny line was not making him laugh, and would suggest a way of making it work.

"Pick it up, Kathy," he said at one point to the ingénue, and he clapped his hands three times.

"Don't I have to stop and think about it?" Kathy asked.

"No, you think about it and you're dead," Mr. Abbott said.

Everybody at the rehearsal responded to Mr. Abbott with his own kind of complete concentration. Nobody was superficial or just going through the motions. Everybody seemed to be giving everything to the effort. Some of the actors seemed to tire. The men took off their jackets. Not Mr. Abbott. He kept his jacket on, and buttoned.

"Do you want to go back, George, or go on?" his daughter asked him at one point in the first run-through.

"Go on," Mr. Abbott said.

Later, a young production assistant took orders for lunch. Mr. Abbott ordered a ham sandwich on rye toast.

"Milk?" asked the assistant.

"Coffee," Mr. Abbott said.

The actors were not afraid to question Mr. Abbott's decisions.

"Somehow, the blocking in this scene—I don't feel like going to the places I have to go to," said the actor playing the middle-aged campaign manager, whose name was Duffy.

"Yeah, sure, this is only a rough draft," Mr. Abbott said reassuringly. "It's not set in my mind."

Or Mr. Abbott would question his own decisions. "That move I gave you is not good," he said later on to Duffy. "Let's do something else."

During the break for lunch, we noticed that the rehearsal schedule had earlier provided for a day off, and Mr. Abbott told us he had used the time to go to see Woody Allen's movie "Interiors" and had liked it very much. "Wonderful acting," he said, taking a big bite of his ham sandwich.

"So *talky*, though," Mr. Kalcheim said, puffing on his cigar.

"I just saw an even more talky one—that new Swedish one, Ingmar Bergman's 'Autumn Sonata'—and I liked that one even better," Mr. Abbott said, with another of his grins.

"I was surprised to learn the other day that you wrote the screenplay for 'All Quiet on the Western Front,' " Mr. Kalcheim said.

"Oh, I was *one* of the writers on it," Mr. Abbott said, with a laugh. "I directed one pretty good picture—'Manslaughter,' with Claudette Colbert and Freddie March. And the picture versions of 'Damn Yankees' and 'Pajama Game.' But I didn't have the patience for movies. All that sitting around. What we've accomplished so far this morning—that time we would have spent just waiting to set the lights for a movie, and waiting for the actors to come out of their little coops. It always bothered me, spending the company's money in the way they do to make movies. One thing about my pictures, I always had a strict schedule."

As the rehearsal got going again, we were joined by Craig Anderson, the young man who runs the Hudson Guild Theatre. He was looking pleased. "Isn't it refreshing to watch Mr. Abbott work?" he said to us. "To see him give that vitality, that understanding to the actors? His energy, his *talent* is so contagious. He makes people listen to each other. He makes them respond on their feet, the way an actor should. I don't know what's happened, but we don't *have* people like him anymore. Most people even in their fifties are so tired, so uncaring, compared to him. Maybe, if we get people in their twenties and in their thirties to learn from him, we'll save what he represents. That's what Off Off Broadway is all about. Strong, sturdy, dedicated people working with the younger ones. I find myself saying to myself, 'My God, this man is sixty-one years older than I am, but this man is just my age.' "

◆ *Adlai Stevenson*

ONE of the big "if"s in recent history is what our country might have become and how the world at large might have been affected if Adlai Ewing Stevenson had been elected President of the United States thirteen years ago. Some months back, talking about this "if" and about the various blows Mr. Stevenson had had to take, we asked one of his closest friends, Mrs. Edison Dick, who had known him for forty years, whether she felt sorry for him. "Not at all," she said. "I can feel sorry for a person who hasn't prevailed against fate, but I think he has prevailed." Over the past year, we had the deep pleasure of seeing quite a bit of Mr. Stevenson, with the intention of writing about him in these pages, and the more we saw of him, the surer we were she was right. Of course, every time we listened to him speak, and every time we read his prose, we regretted that he wasn't doing some writing in these pages himself. "I had a taste for literature and for the academic," he said to us last winter, early on a Sunday morning—a corner of time he had reserved in his back-breaking schedule for one of his talks with us—and he went on, "It's been part of the luggage I've carried in public life which doesn't yield public dividends." As always when he talked about himself, there was a lightness in the texture of his voice, and now its tone conveyed a detached, wry enjoyment of his own plight.

That morning was two days after his sixty-fifth birthday, and he had been awakened at his apartment in the Waldorf Towers—his official residence as United States Ambassador to the United Nations—at one in the morning by a caller from the State Department who wanted to tell him about the country's first major air strike in Vietnam. When we arrived for our appointment, around eight o'clock, we learned that Mr. Stevenson had been on the telephone with government officials intermittently throughout the rest of the night. Nevertheless, he looked fresh and alert, and he was newly shaven and pink-cheeked, dressed in pin-striped navy trousers, a brown tweed jacket, a blue shirt open at the neck, and well-worn bedroom slippers. He had a new crisis on his hands, he told us. Also, he was wondering what to do about a number of house guests—friends who had come from far points to help him celebrate his birthday. They would be getting up soon, and meanwhile he had arranged for several meetings, on the crisis, to be held later that morning at his office at the United States Mission to the United Nations. He expected to attend a hastily called meeting of the Security Council in the afternoon or evening. Notwithstanding this program, Mr. Stevenson showed no inclination to call off our talk. At the time, we were preoccupied with the broad question of what *might* have been, for him, and, as a result of having already spent a good many hours watching him and listening to him, with the further question of what might still *be.* We asked him, after one jangling telephone call, what he would like above all else to be doing at that moment. "I'd like to be out on my farm, in Libertyville, pruning trees," he said, and then, with that delightful, friendly Stevenson laugh, he added, "And I'd like an opportunity to get some rest. I've had about eleven days' vacation all told since I went into this job, four years ago. I'd like to do some reflecting and reading. I have an enormous accumulation of books I'd like to read. I'd like to be able to spend some time with my children and my grandchildren. And I'd like to travel, in a leisurely way, when I wouldn't be on exhibition and wouldn't have to perform. In the past twenty-four years—ever since I went to Washington during the war—I haven't had an opportunity to travel without having the travel coupled with ceremonies or the writing of articles or the taking of notes. But my first responsibility is to the President and to this job. I'd like to be useful as long as I can be. I've been so involved with affairs of my own generation I'd feel a little bereft if I were *not* involved. It's tempting sometimes to dream about a tranquil old age, but I think I'd be a little restive."

In the past four and a half years, in addition to attending sessions with President Kennedy's Cabinet, and then with President Johnson's, and attending meetings of the Security Council and the General Assembly and endless United Nations commissions, Mr. Stevenson had several speaking engagements a week, usually at luncheons or at dinners. (When he was not attending breakfasts, luncheons, cocktail parties, dinners, cookouts, and suppers given by other people, at least half of which were connected in one way or another with the United Nations, he usually played host at two or three of them a week himself.) One of his extracurricular appearances last August, shortly before the Democratic Convention, was at the final dinner of the annual meeting of the American Bar Association, held in the Grand Ballroom of the Waldorf-Astoria, where he was to make a speech. We met Mr. Stevenson at his apartment a few minutes before he was due at the dinner, and accompanied him to the Grand Ballroom, marvelling as we went at his fantastic energy. He appeared to be wholly absorbed in what he was about to do; there was no sign that he had walked into hundreds of other ballrooms set up for two or three thousand chicken dinners to be eaten by uncomfortably dinner-jacketed or strenuously gowned goers and doers—lawyers, engineers, actors, opera lovers, zoologists, and all the others. From the Bar Association dais, he looked into thousands of unanimated faces without mirroring anything of what he saw; his expression remained lively. An audience of lawyers, Mr. Stevenson had warned us, was by nature extremely conservative, and it seemed to us that he was relishing the challenge. The usual string orchestra, in red-and-gold uniforms, played "Some Enchanted Evening" from a balcony, and Mr. Stevenson, looking up, gave the musicians a nod. He remarked to one of the lawyers on the dais that a pre-dinner highball might be a good idea, and the lawyer offered him what he described as his own "slightly used bourbon." Mr. Stevenson smiled gratefully and took it. Then, as his custom was at dinners of this kind, he put on his horn-rimmed glasses and started studying the speech he had written and making improvements in it. As usual, there were interruptions for autographs, for the introduction of wives, and for announcements from citizens that they had voted for him in 1952 and/or 1956—information that was frequently offered in a near-recriminatory key, because, in a success-happy age, he had not won.

In addressing the A.B.A., Mr. Stevenson tried to make his gray, largely humorless audience laugh, and he succeeded. "I've been paying dues to the A.B.A. for forty years," he began, before starting to read his prepared speech. "Now I have the privilege of making a speech. Without compensation, of course. [Laughter] There's something about a Presidential election year that makes even retired politicians restless. [Laughter] At the United Nations, I sometimes yearn for the peace and tranquillity of a political campaign. Everybody wants to talk to me about politics, evidently forgetting that I am now a statesman. [Laughter]" With his audience warmed up and at least somewhat relaxed, Mr. Stevenson said what he had come to say. The pronouncements of Barry Goldwater were much in the minds of Americans that August, and Mr. Stevenson made it clear that he, too, was thinking about them. "I have thought that the strength of the American political system lay precisely in its lack of extreme contrasts, in its rejection of dogma, in the fact that rigid ideology really has no relevance to our great political parties," he said. "And this system has remained intact for more than a century—the most stable, durable, and adaptable system the world has ever seen. But now, as society and the world become more complex, some people want to repeal the whole thing. They seem to yearn for the old simplicity, for the shorthand analysis, for the black-and-white choice, for the cheap-and-easy answer, for the child's guide to good and evil. The very color and diversity of our pluralistic society seem to confuse them; they want it plain and unitary." The lawyers sat there. Quite evidently, they were not on fire. But Mr. Stevenson wound up with undiminished passion and undiminished devotion to what he wanted to tell them. "The greatness of the issues calls out for greatness in ourselves, to vindicate democracy, to speak for freedom, and to make our profoundest affirmation of faith in the American way of life," he concluded. The applause was dutiful. However, Mr. Stevenson didn't seem disappointed as the thousands of lawyers began to plod out of the ballroom. One of them, a chubby man, rather pale and ill at ease, came over to Mr. Stevenson and, after telling him that he had voted for him in 1952 and again in 1956, said, "I remember 1960 in Los Angeles. That was quite a demonstration they put on for you." "They raise more hell when I'm *not* a candidate than when I am," Mr. Stevenson said, with his laugh.

Later on, in reply to a question, Mr. Stevenson told us that he thought he could speak fairly easily now, although it had taken him many years to reach that point. "I had a terrible time as a young man," he explained. "I was very self-conscious, and I could never speak in public without getting paralyzed with fright." He said that his eldest son, Adlai E. Stevenson III, who is a lawyer and a member of the Illinois House of Representatives, was developing into a good speaker. "He's a very thoughtful student of public life," Mr. Stevenson said. "He has a natural dignity about him, yet he has a wonderful sense of humor. I don't know whether he's got the stomach for the crudities of politics. I don't think he'd ever be any good as a demagogue."

At the Democratic Convention, a week or so afterward, Mr. Stevenson, who was a delegate from Illinois, seemed to enjoy himself. He particularly enjoyed the fact that with him in Atlantic City were his three sons—John Fell and Borden in addition to Adlai III—and John's wife, Natalie, and Adlai III's wife, Nancy, both of whom were delegates, the former from California and the latter from Illinois. Mr. Stevenson joked with the boys about the Convention activities of the two young women, who, he said, had a natural talent for politics. "Natalie is so damn important I want to follow her around and pick up crumbs of wisdom," he said. Later he told us, "I've been going to Conventions since 1948, and this is the first time that I've been able to get to the *Convention.* Heretofore, I've always been locked up in an icebox. When you're being nominated, you can never get out of your hotel room. You eat sandwiches. You walk from microphone to microphone. You put your head out the door and look up and down the hall. Then you settle in to write a speech, and furtive characters peer in at you from time to time. And out of all this comes imperishable American political prose."

In Atlantic City, Mr. Stevenson was again besieged by people who wanted to tell him that they had voted for him. Hotel doormen, addressing him as "Adlai," told him that he should be the Presidential nominee, and Mr. Stevenson courteously thanked them. A woman came over to him and said, "You have such a nice warm face," and Mr. Stevenson courteously thanked *her.* A couple of women, both wearing plaid Bermuda shorts, told him that their names were Rhoda and Sally, that they taught second grade somewhere out West, and that he was their "favorite candidate." "We ought to go back to school," Mr. Stevenson said gallantly. "Things have improved."

In the course of some Convention high jinks, Mr. Stevenson said to us, "They used to call me aloof. Actually, I love to be with people. I *enjoy* them. But you can't have things both ways, and when you have to work on a speech, you can't be shut up in your room working and out with people at the same time. However, I've never been able to go for the smash-and-grab kind of person in politics, and, for some reason, that made a certain number of people say I wasn't being practical. It's entirely possible, I think, to be a responsible and completely effective public official without being a smasher-grabber."

One question we'd wondered about for some time was how the legend had arisen about Mr. Stevenson's being "indecisive," and we asked for his explanation of it. "It arose largely from one fact, and that was that when President Truman asked me to be the Presidential candidate in April of 1952, I declined," he told us. "I declined for two reasons. One, I was already an avowed candidate for reëlection as Governor of Illinois. I didn't see, in justice to the people of Illinois, how I could be a candidate for two offices at the same time. And, two, I didn't *want* to run for President. I had no such ambition. I wanted to finish the job I'd started in Illinois. For the ensuing six months, I was beset right and left by individuals and delegations from all over the United States putting pressure on me to announce that I was a candidate and to enter the primaries and compete for the nomination. When I refused to do so and never wavered and was very decisive, and then was subsequently nominated at the Convention and accepted, I was told, 'You're indecisive.'

Nobody can believe you when you say you're not a candidate. It's a curious thing. The more decisive you are in not seeking an exalted office, the more they say you're indecisive. My very decisiveness was attributed to what they call indecision. Sometimes you look back at it all and it seems almost comic. I don't have any feeling of bitterness. Both times I ran, it was obviously hopeless. To run as a Democrat in 1952 was hopeless, let alone run against the No. 1 War Hero. Even so, if it hadn't been for that going-to-Korea business, I might have beaten him." There was no sound of regret or vanity in Mr. Stevenson's voice; he spoke with as much enthusiasm for the subject, and as much appreciation of its inherent interest, as if he had been discussing some episode in history that he just happened to know something about.

The talk turned to Washington, D.C., and we asked Mr. Stevenson whether he liked the place.

"I've lived so much of my life there and know it so well it's difficult not to like it," he said. "Washington was different in the thirties, when I first went there. My feelings are bound up with the way it used to feel during the long evenings—sitting in the gardens of those Georgetown houses in the hot summers, perspiring, with our visions and with our dreams. When I was there during the war, we didn't have much time for fun, but the work itself was fun. In those days, we were interested in ideas. Now it's all so much personality talk, gossip, and rumor—who's up and who's down. The criticism is sort of brittle now, and there's a lot of malice and mischief."

On the first day in Atlantic City, a television interviewer asked Mr. Stevenson, "Governor, how do you feel about the Convention? Are you *sad?*" (He was always addressed as Governor, even though his last title was Ambassador.)

Mr. Stevenson looked far from sad, and he told the television commentator that he wasn't sad. "I'm hoping to see all the many old friends who fought and bled for me in hopeless causes," he said.

In the raucous, emblazoned Convention Hall, he was presented on the stage in the customary man-who fashion ("the man who was twice given the nomination for President by his party"), and the audience received him with a boisterous ovation. It was Mr. Stevenson's mission in Atlantic City to deliver a tribute to Eleanor Roosevelt. Again, he had worked hard, and had come up with a memorable piece of writing to present as a speech. "Thank you, my dear friends, for your welcome—and for all your loyalty and comfort to me in years past when our party's fortunes were not as bright as they are tonight" was his beginning. He continued, "For what I have done and sought to do for our country and our party, I have been repaid a thousandfold by the kindness of my fellow-citizens—and by none more than you, the leaders of the Democratic Party." The audience now seemed politely patient. "It is of another noble American that I am commissioned to speak to you tonight," Mr. Stevenson said, projecting his intimate words into the echoing vastness of the Hall. "She has passed beyond these voices, but our memory and her meaning have not—Eleanor Roosevelt. She was a lady—a lady for all seasons. And, like her husband, she left 'a name to shine on the entablatures of truth—forever.' There is, I believe, a legend in the Talmud which tells us that in any period of man's history the heavens themselves are held in place by the virtue, love, and shining integrity of twelve just men. They are completely unaware of this function. They go about their daily work, their humble chores—doctors, teachers, workers, farmers (never, alas, lawyers, so I understand), just ordinary, devoted citizens—and meanwhile the rooftree of creation is supported by them alone. There are times when nations or movements or great political parties are similarly sustained in their purposes and being by the pervasive, unconscious influence of a few great men and women. Can we doubt that Eleanor Roosevelt had in some measure the keeping of the Party's conscience in her special care?" It seemed to us, at that moment in Convention Hall, that almost nobody wanted to think about the question he had just asked or the answer to it; now that the nominations were in, the audience's mind was on who else was going to get what. The delegates adjusted their paper campaign hats and shifted in their seats, and many of them looked as though they were now having some difficulty tolerating their former candidate. Nevertheless, he went the course with what he had come to say: "She thought of herself as an ugly duckling, but she walked in beauty in the ghettos of the world, bringing with her the reminder of her beloved St. Francis, 'It is in the giving that we receive.' And wherever she walked beauty was forever there." The delegates gave Mr. Stevenson's speech a nice hand, and the name of Eleanor Roosevelt was not mentioned at the Convention again.

About a month later, on September 22nd, it was Illinois Day at the World's Fair, and who but Adlai Ewing Stevenson, of Illinois, was tapped for the Day. "I've been promising Bob Moses I'd come, and I'm glad I finally made it," Mr. Stevenson said to us as we joined him in one of those Greyhound motorized chairs. He looked expectant, and threw us a Stevenson smile. "Illinois Day gave me the day off from the war in Cyprus," he added, with satisfaction. It was about ten o'clock in the morning, a time that is very popular for ceremonies, and Mr. Stevenson was one of the first of the invited guests to arrive at the Illinois Pavilion for the Day. Among those who turned up later were Benny Goodman, Cab Calloway, Governor Otto Kerner, and Robert Lincoln Beckwith, a great-grandson of Abraham Lincoln and one of the sixteenth President's three surviving direct descendants. A press agent handed out a release stating that none of the descendants have children and that "it is expected the Lincoln blood will discontinue with them." Mr. Stevenson read the release with what seemed to be respectful interest. He looked with pride at the sayings of Lincoln's inscribed on the outside of the Pavilion, among them "WHILE MAN EXISTS IT IS HIS DUTY TO IMPROVE NOT ONLY HIS OWN CONDITION BUT TO ASSIST IN AMELIORATING MANKIND." Then he was ushered into the darkened theatre of the Pavilion, where about three hundred devotees of Illinois were assembled and where the sensational attraction was the six-foot-four-inch mechanical figure of Lincoln, which was to sit, stand, and speak Lincoln's speeches. But first Mr. Stevenson had the privilege of sitting through an hour-and-a-quarter Illinois Day program that included the dedication of a memorial to the late Illinois Secretary of State Charles F. Carpentier; a kind of pageant about the history of the State of Illinois; some folk songs by students at the Old Town School of Folk Music, in Chicago; a short speech by Mr. Beckwith; a somewhat longer speech by Governor Kerner; and the bestowal of prizes on winners of the Chicagoland Music Festival. Then Mr. Stevenson was introduced. He was brief in his remarks. He said, "Governor Kerner, Mr. Beckwith, Mr. Moses, distinguished guests, sons and daughters of Illinois: We meet here in the midst of the American quadrennial political Olympics, at a time when the air is both figuratively and literally filled with the spoken word. Any man of conscience and sensitivity should exercise particular care in anything he says in public (or, for that matter, anywhere). I am conscious of the remarks of Illinois's greatest son, Mr. Beckwith's great-grandfather, and an intimate friend of my own great-grandfather Jesse W. Fell, of Bloomington. In his message to the Congress in December, 1862, he addressed himself to political leaders of his own and future generations. In the midst of a bitter fratricidal struggle, where tempers and factionalism colored the judgments of many men, Lincoln warned, 'If there ever should be a time for mere catch arguments, that time surely is not now. In times like the present, no man should utter anything for which he would not willingly be responsible through time and in eternity.' " The devotees of Illinois looked blank. The words of Lincoln as Mr. Stevenson spoke them did not appear to make much of an impression. The audience was evidently waiting for the mechanical Lincoln to speak. This Lincoln—a Walt Disney creation, manufactured at a cost, the Illinois press agent told us, of ninety thousand dollars—followed Mr. Stevenson, and its speech was billed as "Great Moments with Mr. Lincoln." Mr. Stevenson listened to it in apparent fascination. The mechanical Lincoln really did sit, stand up, and make a speech—by means of a recording by an actor—in a very deep, melancholy, Lincolnesque voice. We thought the robot was creepy, but Mr. Stevenson admired it. "It's a marvel," he told us. "In one speech, the quotes put together ran all the way from 1838 to 1864."

At the United Nations one afternoon last January, we waited at the entrance to the General Assembly Building for Mr. Stevenson, who was scheduled to deliver a major address before the Plenary Session in General Debate. "The U.N. is finished," the uniformed guard at the entrance where we stood stated to us in a highly certain tone. He was an American, and he knew what he was talking about. "Next year it won't be here," he went on. "Look at the faces of the delegates, especially the Africans. They don't want the U.N. in America. Look at the Ambassador from Hungary. Ice-cold. He doesn't talk to nobody. We're through here. Red China wants to start its own U.N. Who wants this one?"

The session was called to order by the chairman, His Excellency Mr. Alex Quaison-Sackey, of Ghana, at three-thirty. The gallery was packed. With Mr. Quaison-Sackey on the dais sat U Thant. The United States delegation sat with delegates from Upper Volta on its right, delegates from Belgium and Austria behind it, delegates from Thailand and

Syria in front of it, and delegates from the United Republic of Tanzania on its left. Mr. Stevenson—his glasses on, the plastic earphone for translations over one ear, a lumpy brief-case open on the floor at his side—sat putting a few more touches on his speech. Then he seemed to listen intently as the first speaker, the distinguished representative of Mali, talked for quite a while, in French, about being "non-aligned but not for imperialist aggression." There was perfunctory applause. A young man introduced as the Foreign Minister of Morocco made a halting address, also in French, on what we gathered was his interest in peace. There was no applause. Then the Foreign Minister of Pakistan took the floor to discuss, in English, the "crude, absurd, and mischievous" remarks of the distinguished representative of India dealing with what he charged was a fraud that had been perpetrated by India upon the five million people of Kashmir. "They are the ones whose right to self-determination has been denied," he said. "They have the right to be free. Justice must be done!" There was perfunctory applause. The next speaker was the distinguished representative of Afghanistan, who said in a speech in English, which took thirty-five minutes, that Afghanistan was following a policy of friendship with her neighboring African nations; that the United Nations was the only place of hope for saving the world from destruction; that the United Nations' financial crisis, with other crises, was deepening anxiety; but that the Afghanistan delegation was not getting discouraged. There was mild applause. Mr. Stevenson didn't seem to be missing a word. We were sitting on the sidelines, behind some observers who kept calling out friendly remarks in Portuguese to the delegation from Brazil, which was seated nearby. We assumed that the observers were also from Brazil. The noisiest observer was a middle-aged lady who had several rings on her fingers; one ring was set with a pearl the size of a lima bean, which was surrounded by a big cluster of diamonds.

She held a mink coat in her lap, and stroked it nervously, without letup. She didn't close her mouth for more than two minutes at a time throughout the address delivered by the distinguished representative of Afghanistan. A number of the delegates looked asleep, or half asleep. Mr. Stevenson glanced occasionally at the text of his speech. Otherwise, he was wholly attentive. At 4:59 P.M., he was called. "The last speaker is the distinguished representative of the United States," the chairman said.

Mr. Stevenson started by saying that it was his first opportunity to extend congratulations to the chairman for the way he had conducted that session of the General Assembly. Then he said, "I have asked to speak at this late date so I can share with all delegations, in a spirit of openness, my government's views on the state of affairs at these United Nations as our annual general debate comes to its conclusion. Certain things which I shall say here today have to do with law, with procedures, with technical and administrative matters. So I want to emphasize in advance that these are but manifestations of much deeper concerns about peace and world order, about the welfare of human society and the prospects of our peoples for rewarding lives."

The group of Brazilians in front of us, including the noisy bejewelled lady, were quiet for the first time. They were paying attention. Everybody in the hall seemed to be awake and listening. What Mr. Stevenson was talking about was the U.N.'s financial crisis, which was mainly the result of more than a hundred and thirty million dollars in overdue assessments owed by Russia, by eight other Communist nations, and by France, Belgium, Paraguay, South Africa, and Yemen. Under Article 19 of the U.N. Charter, any nation that is two years in arrears automatically loses its vote in the General Assembly. It was one of Mr. Stevenson's chores to express the opinion of our government (which happens to carry the largest part of the United Nations expenses) that there should be no voting in the General Assembly until Russia paid at least one-third of its overdue assessments. And so Mr. Stevenson, in his speech, was going to warn the General Assembly against the notion of a "double standard" of assessments for United Nations peace-keeping operations. "We cannot have two rules for paying assessments for the expenses of the organization—one rule for most of the members, and another rule for a few," he said. But before he reached that point in his speech he made some remarks about the United Nations as a whole. "I speak to you as one who participated in the formulation of the Charter of this organization, in both the Preparatory Commission, in London, and the Charter Conference, in San Francisco," he said. "I recall vividly the fears and hopes which filled and inspired us as a second world war ended— fears and hopes which brought us together in an attempt to insure that such a world catastrophe would never again occur. At those conferences we labored long and diligently, we tried to take into account the interest of all states, we attempted to subordinate narrow national interests to the broad common good. This time we would create something better than static conference machinery—something solid enough to withstand the winds of controversy blowing outside and inside its halls. This time we would create workable. machinery for keeping the peace and for settling disputes by non-violent means—and endow it with a capacity to act."

The speech had about five thousand words, which he had checked for policy with the State Department, as he always did in his job, but which he had put together himself, in his own remarkable way. It took him about forty-five minutes to deliver. He wound up saying, "I, for one, cannot escape the deep sense that the peoples of the world are looking over our shoulder—waiting to see whether we can overcome our present problem and take up with fresh vigor and renewed resolution the great unfinished business of peace—which

President Johnson has called 'the assignment of the century.' " The hall was full of delegates who were supposedly divided, but the applause for Mr. Stevenson was immediate and strong.

For most men, delivering a five-thousand-word speech might constitute a week's, or even a month's, work. For Mr. Stevenson, it was a small and routine part of a twenty-four-hour schedule. The very next morning, he was speaking in the General Assembly again—this time paying tribute to Sir Winston Churchill, who had died three days earlier. Afterward, he conferred with his associates, and then went to a meeting with U Thant, and on to a luncheon for twenty-four people being given by Liu Chieh, the Chinese Ambassador to the U.N. From the luncheon he rushed back to his office to meet with a couple of congressmen from Florida who were en route to Churchill's funeral, and then to confer with Norway's Ambassador to the U.N., who had some ideas about a compromise plan for the countries owing assessments. After that, the new Ambassador from Malta to the U.N. paid a courtesy call on Mr. Stevenson, and for half an hour Mr. Stevenson listened intently to a discussion of the people of Malta (there are three hundred thousand of them), and of the fact that during the sixteenth century, when Malta fell under the rule of the Knights of Malta, no Maltese were members of the Knighthood, and of the possibility of setting up a Malta office in Washington. Having also seen eight other callers, Mr. Stevenson went off to a cocktail reception being given by the American-Arab Association, and after half an hour there he made for a party launching an Indian exhibit at the Union Carbide Building, where he found a mob of celebrated public figures, looking freshly bathed, rested, and barbered, and dressed to the teeth in formal clothes. Mr. Stevenson was wearing the same pin-striped blue suit, by now wrinkled and limp, that he had started the day in at 7 A.M. Vice-President Humphrey was at the party, tall and ruddy-faced and glowing, and was reminiscing about the Inaugural festivities, which had taken place a week earlier. There was a lot of kidding about the big hand Mr. Stevenson had got when he arrived at the Inaugural Ball. Everyone had flocked around *him*. "I never get anywhere, but I get all the applause," Mr. Stevenson said, making Vice-President Humphrey and several other guests laugh. He looked at the exhibit for about an hour, and then made for his apartment at the Waldorf. He had to change to black tie and attend the Diamond Ball for the benefit of the Institute of International Education, in the Grand Ballroom of the Plaza Hotel. His housekeeper, Mrs. Viola Reardy, told him she couldn't find his formal silk shirt and shoes. Mr. Stevenson worried about the possibility of having lost these articles, which were new. "You probably left them at the Inauguration," Mrs. Reardy told him, and Mr. Stevenson put on a regular shirt with his dinner jacket and wore his daytime shoes.

At eight o'clock the next morning, Mr. Stevenson was on a shuttle plane to Washington, where, at the request of the British Ambassador, he was to give the memorial address at the National Cathedral service for Sir Winston Churchill. When he had found time to write the tribute was something we couldn't figure out. It ran to about thirteen hundred words. "Sir Winston Churchill is dead," Mr. Stevenson said at the Cathedral. "The voice that led nations, raised armies, inspired victories, and blew fresh courage into the hearts of men is silenced. We shall hear no longer the remembered eloquence and wit, the old courage and defiance, the robust serenity of indomitable faith. Our world is thus poorer, our political dialogue is diminished, and the sources of public inspiration run more thinly for all of us. There is a lonesome place against the sky. So we are right to mourn." For Sir Winston Churchill the love of freedom was "not an abstract thing but a deep conviction that the uniqueness of man demands a society that gives his capacities full scope," Mr. Stevenson continued. "It was, if you like, an aristocratic sense of the fullness and value of life. But he was a profound democrat, and the cornerstone of his political faith, inherited from a beloved father, was the simple maxim 'Trust the people.' " Near the close of his tribute Mr. Stevenson had a sentence describing Churchill: "The great aristocrat, the beloved leader, the profound historian, the gifted painter, the superb politician, the lord of language, the orator, the wit— yes, and the dedicated bricklayer—behind all of them was the man of simple faith, steadfast in defeat, generous in victory, resigned in age, trusting in a loving providence, and committing his achievements and his triumphs to a higher power."

From the Cathedral, Mr. Stevenson went to the British Embassy for lunch and a reception. Then he went to the State Department for conferences on half a dozen pressing problems of foreign relations. He caught the three o'clock shuttle plane back to New York, and at four-thirty, in his U.S. Mission office, he started a series of meetings with members of his staff. At six, he attended a cocktail party given for U.N. delegates from the African nations, in the U.S. Mission building, by the Harlem Lawyers Association and Ambassador Franklin F. Williams, the U.S. representative on the U.N. Economic and Social Council. There an editor of the *Amsterdam News* named James Hicks told Mr. Stevenson he'd had trouble getting an advance copy of his speech about Churchill, and added that, come to think of it, during his Presidential campaigns it had always been difficult to get copies of his speeches in advance. "I'm afraid I sit up scribbling until the last minute," Mr. Stevenson told him. "Churchill was always rewriting his speeches until he had to give them." And then he had one of those characteristic funny afterthoughts that constantly bubbled up in him: "But that's where my similarity to Churchill ends."

Mr. Stevenson was due at eight-thirty that evening, in dinner clothes, at a concert of the New York Philharmonic, but when he was about to go home to dress, his secretary sent word to him that a group of educators working for UNESCO were gathered in the Savoy Hilton apartment of his old friend William Benton, the former Senator from Connecticut, who was now the U.S. representative to UNESCO, and that Senator Benton had been stricken suddenly with pneumonia and had to go to the hospital, so there was nobody to speak to the group of people in his apartment. The educators from UNESCO wanted to hear all about the history of the U.N. situation in reference to Article 19, and the problems arising from it. In a manner in which there appeared to us to be no hesitation, no doubt, no resentment, no self-pity, Mr. Stevenson immediately headed for Senator Benton's apartment. Ambassador Marietta Tree, the U.S. representative to the U.N. Trusteeship Council, who was present at the cocktail party, rode up in the car with him; she was on her way to a dinner being given by the Pakistani Ambassador to the U.N., she said.

"I went *last* week," Mr. Stevenson told her playfully. "You'll be offered a hookah. I smoked a hookah last week. Watch your step with that hookah, my girl. Ambassador de Beus, of the Netherlands, smoked the hookah with me last week and then told me, 'My public vice is women. My private vice is the hookah.' "

Mrs. Tree said that she would watch her step.

"And don't eat too much," Mr. Stevenson said. "The food is delicious, but you'll find that nothing is green or ever has been."

"Long time no see!" the Savoy Hilton doorman called out to Mr. Stevenson as he got out of the car.

On the sidewalk, Mr. Stevenson almost collided with a jaunty young man carrying a briefcase. The young man halted and gave Mr. Stevenson an admiring little bow. "My pleasure!" the young man said, yielding the right of way to Mr. Stevenson.

"Why, thank you," Mr. Stevenson said, graciously bowing back.

He had less than an hour in which to go home, dress, and keep his date for the Philharmonic, but he walked into Senator Benton's apartment and shook hands, greeting each of a couple of dozen educators as though he had done nothing else that day and had nothing else to do.

A very serious woman there reminded him that they had met some years ago on a houseboat in the Vale of Kashmir. "I believe you said it was the nearest to Heaven you'd ever come," the woman said. "I'm so sorry I wasn't here in this country to cast my vote for you."

"And we couldn't spare it," Mr. Stevenson said.

Mr. Stevenson, rushing no one, held a conversation with everybody in the room. Then the educators sat down, and Mr. Stevenson, taking a chair in a corner of the room, started talking to them. Even here, he began by making his listeners laugh. "I don't often get a captive audience," he said, and everything in his expression signified that he was appreciating the fact that he had one now. They laughed. "It's not often that I get the opportunity to talk to such a literate and cultivated audience," he went on. Again they laughed. He added, "There were times, as a Democratic politician, when I never expected that at all." In the next thirty minutes, speaking quickly, he gave a brilliantly clear, concise, and orderly history, description, and explanation of the events leading up to the current difficulty with the back assessments, of Article 19, of the significance of the deadlock, and of the reluctance of any of the countries—even the Soviet Union—to have an out-and-out confrontation with the United States, because they couldn't be sure they would win. Then Mr. Stevenson allowed time for questions. One man asked him if he thought the Russians wanted to break up the U.N., and Mr. Stevenson said no, he thought they would like only to convert the General Assembly into a static debating forum. As he came to a close, he again, irrepressibly, said something to make his listeners laugh: "I remember my father telling me the story of the preacher delivering an exhortation to his flock, and as he reached the climax of his exhortation, a man in the front row got up and said, 'O Lord, use me. Use me, O Lord—in an advisory capacity!' "

As we were leaving Senator Benton's apartment, we asked Mr. Stevenson how in the world he had the strength and the interest, after the day he had put in—a day that was still far from over—to give that much concentrated attention to this small group of workers for UNESCO. His answer had no note of martyrdom in it but was casual and matter-of-fact. He told us, "You don't like to come in and say, 'What the hell, it's useless to try to explain, it's too complicated.' So you try to tell them the score. They should be informed."

The party given for Mr. Stevenson on his sixty-fifth birthday was held at the River Club, and was attended by a couple of dozen of his close friends, who had started the tradition of giving him such a party fifteen years earlier in the Executive Mansion in Springfield. During the evening, Mr. Stevenson happened to say that he thought "the fifteenth running of this classic should be the last." He also said, "I've heard that a woman's best years are between thirty-nine and forty. My best years have been the past fifteen. For tomorrow is today, and I shall never be any older than I am now." He had been listening for a couple of hours to funny, nostalgic, and loving remarks about himself, including the reading of "A Composite Portrait of Adlai by His Friends on His Sixty-fifth Birthday," in verse, each stanza having been composed by one of his friends. Mr. Stevenson laughed and cried at his party, and scribbled notes of things he wanted to tell his friends at the end. "The best of one's life is one's friends," he said to them. "I've never thought it necessary to be serious about serious things. It takes only a pin to prick the biggest balloon. Horace Walpole said, 'Old age is no uncomfortable thing if one gives up to it with good grace and doesn't drag it about.' I feel there's so much to do, so much to make up, and I do believe that nothing succeeds like excess. My dearest friends, forgive me my excesses, and I'll forgive you your successes. Give me the benefit of your candor and your criticism, but please keep your doubts to yourself, because I have enough of those of my own."

On the winter morning of the first major air strike in Vietnam, we asked Mr. Stevenson some questions about past Presidents of the United States, and in spite of the crisis of the moment, he replied as though our questions were timely and in order. "I think great Presidents are usually the product of their times," he said at one point. "Abraham Lincoln has always been my hero, as he is the hero of most Americans. As President, he contributed to the world the end of slavery, which was an enormous leap forward in history, but then he was assassinated and he didn't have to live through the Reconstruction and the bitterness that followed the war. No one can say what he might have been had he not been assassinated. Bear in mind, however, that I was raised in Lincoln country. My great-grandfather was Lincoln's friend and the first to propose him for the Presidency. It was to him that Lincoln addressed his autobiography. So I was naturally saturated with Lincoln from infancy. The other figure who is very important to me is Woodrow Wilson. He showed us, on the world scene, an extension of what Lincoln preached; namely, that freedom isn't a limited—a parochial—matter but a universal matter. Also, Wilson was the first President I ever met. When I was a boy of twelve, my father took me to visit President Wilson, then Governor of New Jersey, at his summer house in Sea Girt, New Jersey.

It was a hot day in August, 1912, and he was running for President. I mounted the stairs of that large frame house alongside my father, and Governor Wilson came out and met us on the porch. He shook hands with me in a formal, courteous way. I was paralyzed with awe. The conversation related mostly to the campaign and how things would go in Illinois. There was a lot of talk about the Democratic Party and the state of mind of people in the Middle West. My father was confident about everything, because of the Bull Moose split. Governor Wilson was extremely courteous to me. He asked me in a friendly, fatherly way if I was interested in politics or in public affairs, and he expressed the hope that I was. You know the way older people often get humble with younger people, and in somewhat that spirit, I think, he made a casual remark about Princeton, and about his having been president of Princeton before becoming Governor of New Jersey. That's what decided me on going to Princeton, right then and there. I came away with the feeling: I'm his deathless friend. His supporter. His admirer. That's my man." There was affection but no sentimentality in Mr. Stevenson's manner as he talked about Wilson. "And another great President was, of course, Franklin Roosevelt," he went on. "Here, again, there were many contributing factors. The historical ones are obvious. He showed us the way to so many social transformations, bloodlessly. He died in office, from his labors, which always dramatizes and adds an emotional factor to the life of a man." Mr. Stevenson talked for some time about President Truman, saying he would be entitled to a high mark in history for the way he dealt with the postwar period. Then he went on to talk about John F. Kennedy's extraordinary mind and spirit and promise. "When President Kennedy was assassinated," he said, "we were all left with a sense of incompleteness."

There was one hot, muggy night last summer, during the political campaign, when we rode back with Mr. Stevenson on a shuttle plane at the end of one of his incredibly full working days in Washington. It was late when we landed at LaGuardia Airport. The city was steaming. Mr. Stevenson was greeted by his driver, who handed him a portfolio of emergency cables and messages to be studied. He did the work in the car as he was riding toward his apartment, and then he remembered that Mayor Wagner had wanted to talk to him about some local aspects of the election campaign, so he asked the driver to stop at Gracie Mansion. It was around ten-thirty when we got there, and we ran into the fading moments of what had been a Young Citizens for Johnson Barbecue, with food prepared by President Johnson's own caterer, imported from Texas. The barbecue seemed to be under the supervision of Lynda Bird Johnson, Robert F. Wagner, Jr., and other very young, very attractive, very recently well-fed Democrats, and they all greeted Mr. Stevenson cordially. It happened that he hadn't had anything to eat since lunch, which he had eaten at the State Department with Dean Rusk. The Gracie Mansion lawn, under festive garden lighting, was strewn with delicious-looking and aromatic-smelling remnants of what had clearly been a great party. Robert Wagner, Jr., said that his father was upstairs, and quickly led Mr. Stevenson up to see the Mayor. Half an hour later, Mr. Stevenson came down. To us, he looked a little hungry but not a bit tired. The party was petering out by then, and the Mayor's guards, who did look tired, were encouraging the young guests to leave. Everybody assumed—wrongly, we thought—that Mr. Stevenson wanted to get away as fast as possible. We thought we saw Mr. Stevenson peering wistfully at the Gracie Mansion lawn. It looked inviting, that hot, humid, misty night, with paper picnic plates dotted about, and with suntanned, laughing young men and women standing around in clusters, talking, presumably, about the campaign, and with President Johnson's caterer—fat and jolly, wrapped in a huge white apron, and wearing a chef's tall white hat—still overseeing a long table laden with steaks, sweet corn, and spareribs. But the party was technically over, and a solicitous guard was ushering Mr. Stevenson out to his car. He went. The guard saluted and left him. Mr. Stevenson's driver opened the car door. Just then, a young couple, both tall and skinny and both wearing sandals and blue jeans, the girl with long blond hair falling loosely over the collar of a shirtwaist blouse and the boy with a cultivated fringe of beard, strolled over to Mr. Stevenson, holding hands. They smiled at him and coolly asked him what was going on at Gracie Mansion. A party, he told them. They looked happy and lazy and not impressed, and strolled away, still holding hands. Mr. Stevenson stood there a moment or two, looking down the street after them, and as he got into his car he said, "Summer in New York is pretty wonderful, isn't it?"

❖ *Arrival*

WE went out to Kennedy International Airport last week to greet Federico Fellini, who was flying in from Rome for his first visit here in several years. Fellini's new movie, "Amarcord," an episodic look back at his youth in his home town in the nineteen-thirties, is a big hit. The lines of people waiting to get into the Plaza Theatre to see the movie are long. The critics have been pouring on praise. And Fellini, after a decade or so of being "out," is "in" again—even more so than when some of his earlier "successful" movies, like "La Dolce Vita," "8½," and "La Strada," were first seen. We went out to the airport in a chauffeur-driven limousine—one of a group of limousines going to meet Fellini—with:

ARTHUR RUBINE, press agent for "Amarcord." A tense and obliging young man wearing a red turtleneck shirt and almost matching pointed red beard.

WALTER MANLEY, a movie producer-distributor representing the producers of "Amarcord." A worried-looking and gracious man with an expression on his face of pure aggravation.

MARIO DE VECCHI, Fellini's personal representative, assistant, and occasional interpreter in New York. A very suave, somewhat jaded middle-aged man with a fading Venetian sunburn on his face, a small brown mustache, a dramatic manner, and a dashing chocolate-brown corduroy sports coat flung over his shoulders.

THE DRIVER, an earnest young man, wearing steel-rimmed glasses, who had a textbook on economics on the seat next to him.

As is usual with Fellini (and as is usual with a few other powerhouse directors of movies), all sights, sounds, and actions relating to the man immediately came into sharp focus, arranging themselves at his service. The afternoon was sunny on the drive out. The sky was a perfectly Roman bright blue. As we neared the airport, a large jet took off in the sky ahead of us, with a long black stream of smoke trailing behind it, dirtying the blue sky and gradually obliterating an early-rising half-moon. The traffic was unusually heavy. The young driver seemed to steer the car into the slowest, most nerve-racking traffic lanes. Walter Manley said that he hoped we would not miss the arrival of Fellini's plane. Arthur Rubine said that he had missed meeting a plane only once, and that once was enough. Mario de Vecchi, sitting between the two other men, leaned back against the seat, holding a thin Toscano cigar, and, in between giving backseat advice to the young driver, talked at length, with relish, and with many gestures, about some of the Fellini wonders that occurred in the course of filming "Amarcord." De Vecchi had been present throughout the making of the movie. He spoke English in a sophisticated international way, displaying an impressive familiarity with American slang. "Nobody believed Fellini would get the shot in one take," de Vecchi said in describing the filming of the scene in which the townspeople go out to sea in small boats to watch the sailing of a big ocean liner. "We had this incredible movement of people, of props. All the extras. All the boats. Et cetera. Et cetera. David Lean said, 'The guy is crazy. He'll never get it.' "

"David Lean?" we asked.

"David Lean," de Vecchi said. "David Lean lives in Rome. He came to watch. Everybody came to watch. So there we are. Two hundred extras. All the little boats. Fellini says, 'Lights. Action. Camera.' Bam! He gets it! Just like that!" De Vecchi held on to his cigar with his teeth and slapped the palms of his hands together. "Beautiful!" he added. He gave a long laugh of enjoyment at his tale. "Then. Listen to this. You wouldn't believe it. He with his eye. His eye for detail. Incredible! He notices." De Vecchi pointed up at some imaginary height. "He saw, way up, on the top deck, they forgot to swing the string of lights! So he does a retake. David Lean says, 'He'll never get it.' But he does it again, and this time, with the string of lights swinging on the top deck, again he gets it! Like that!" Once more, de Vecchi slapped his hands together and laughed appreciatively.

"This damn traffic!" Manley said.

At the International Arrivals Building, de Vecchi held his corduroy coat around his shoulders and quickly made his way through the customs area to find Fellini. The plane had just landed. Manley and Rubine looked relieved but still anxious. Rubine gave Manley a quick rundown of the publicity work schedule he had planned for Fellini: "Interviews with the *Times,* the *News,* the *Christian Science Monitor, Newsday,* Reuters. He's not doing any live television. He's not doing any radio. He's doing a 'Today' interview with Gene Shalit. He's doing an interview for WCBS news with Pat Collins. It's a rather slow schedule. Only three things a day. Usually, I set up *twelve* a day."

Rubine and Manley kept their gaze fastened on the customs doors. Passengers streamed through, followed by porters pushing their luggage carts. Big, emotional reunions of relatives. Little children carried by returning fathers, hanging on for dear life to the fathers' necks. Lots of rabbis in black robes and black hats came through the doors in pairs and trios, apparently travelling from Israel via Rome. Then, walking as though to the accompaniment of a jaunty, bitter-sweet Nino Rota score, Fellini and the Fellini group:

FEDERICO FELLINI, the one and only, wearing a beige Italian suit, with a white shirt and a light-green necktie (askew), and carrying a black raincoat. No hat. His hair a little thinner, a little grayer than it was during his last visit. Fellini otherwise looking ageless.

GIULIETTA MASINA, Fellini's wife, slightly built and wistful, yet very strong-willed, and a marvellous actress, who would just as soon take care of her garden in the country as act. She was wearing a black dress and a brown wool cardigan sweater, and she had on gold-rimmed overlarge spectacles.

FRANCO CRISTALDI, a sharp, well-tanned, small man, who is the producer of "Amarcord." He looked on top of the world.

MRS. FRANCESCO ROSI, a very chic, young, and attractive blond businesswoman, who seemed glad to be here.

TONINO GUERRA, fiftyish, a writer who worked on the script for "Amarcord" with Fellini. He had on a blue denim-type shirt, and he had the vaguely detached look of writers everywhere.

Fellini gave his greeters nice, enthusiastic hugs, and, prompted in whispers by de Vecchi, seemed to know exactly who was who. All the greeters asked the same questions: How was the flight? Were they tired? How was Rome? Did they like our beautiful weather? Was it sunny in Rome when they left? Were they glad to be here? Answers to all questions: Yes. Yes. Yes. Yes. Yes. Yes.

"We look like immigrants," Fellini said as everybody stood around at the curb outside the Arrivals Building, waiting for the luggage. He gave a slow little smile, looking about at the frenzy of all the people getting sorted out and distributed into waiting cars and taxis. For the Fellini group, de Vecchi took charge of who was to ride in which limousine for the trip to Manhattan. He did it with dispatch, the corduroy coat never for an instant slipping off his shoulders.

Fellini stood back, watching members of his entourage getting into limousines on their own and then being maneuvered out by de Vecchi, until everything was arranged to de Vecchi's satisfaction. We wound up in the front seat of the car we had driven out in, with the same young driver. In the back seat were Fellini and his wife, with de Vecchi between them.

"The Sherry-Netherland Hotel," de Vecchi said crisply to the driver, and off we went as de Vecchi pulled out a copy of *Newsweek* and started reading aloud from the magazine's review of "Amarcord": " 'Sometimes roughedged, occasionally untidy, "Amarcord" is the most beautiful movie Fellini has ever made and a landmark in the history of film.' "

Fellini listened, looking interested. Then he gave a sigh.

"We should go to the Plaza, where 'Amarcord' is playing," de Vecchi said.

Fellini's face took on an expression of distaste. "To go to the theatre where my picture is playing would make me feel I am like a spy," he said. "When you see a picture with an audience, it changes the picture according to the audience. Each time, with a different audience, in a different country, it makes it different."

As the car came to a standstill in the heaviest traffic yet, we asked Fellini how he had happened to make this visit.

He gave another sigh. "To come out for a week, as I am doing, is a disaster," he said. "I came because friends insisted. I came just like a bag."

"A suitcase," de Vecchi said.

"A suit-*case,*" Fellini said, looking amused, and making a production of each syllable. "I am not a private person. I am a piece of the picture. I do it if I can help. I am the author of the picture, not a salesman. When I finish a picture, I want to get away from it. I prefer to start another picture. But I am asked to help, so I try to help."

We were continuing at a standstill in the traffic. Lots of

horn-blowing. Lots of carbon-monoxide fumes. Giulietta Masina lighted a cigarette. Fellini opened a window of the car. Everybody coughed. De Vecchi said the driver should have headed for the Queensboro Bridge. The driver said it was too late. He was already on his way to the Queens Midtown Tunnel, and it was too late to change. We started moving again. Giulietta Masina stared out at the two-family houses lining the streets running parallel to the Long Island Expressway.

We asked Fellini if he had seen any movies lately that he liked, and he said yes, he'd seen "That's Entertainment!" "It's an American 'Amarcord,' " he said. "It's cruel. It shows how stupid we were in those days. That's good. Now I have something to say to the interviewers. 'It's an American "Amarcord." ' I will repeat it in the interviews." Everybody laughed.

We headed into the tunnel, with its green, creepy-looking lighting and its white tile walls. We emerged in Manhattan. Fellini said the streets were bumpy. De Vecchi informed him that the city was disintegrating.

We asked Fellini what he wanted to do in New York, and he said, "I want to find the books of the great American writers—the ones who write 'Dick Tracy' and 'Popeye.' They are fabulous. They are the real writers about America."

Giulietta Masina said something quickly in Italian.

"Yes, after we arrive at the hotel, we go out to a good Chinese restaurant," Fellini said, pronouncing each word very, very slowly. "And then we have a good Chinese dinner."

"Beautiful!" de Vecchi said, with one of those claps of his hands.

"Bee-yoo-ti-*ful!*" Fellini repeated carefully, savoring the word. He laughed, and gave a long sigh.

♦ On the Great Lawn

ON the mornin' of Simon and
    Garfunkel on the Great Lawn,
Tommy Punch, age thirty-four,
    lookin' weary, lookin' wistful,
    staked out his place on a blanket,
    on the Great Lawn,
Katie Simmons was with him, and
    some other friends.
They were feelin' sad, feelin' over
    thirty.
Lookin' for somethin', lookin' for
    nothin', but feelin' glad to have
    Paul and Artie.
They waited all day, until there were
    half a million on the Great Lawn.
Tommy Punch was comfortable,
    wearin' bluejeans, and a sweater,
    and glasses that he said were "sort
    of Diane Keaton–style."
Strangers half his age or twice his age
    stepped over his body on the Great
    Lawn.
Tommy Punch didn't like havin'
    them there
They stepped on his beer and

crushed his Fig Newtons on the
Great Lawn,
But it was worth it to Tommy Punch
and his friends.
Simon and Garfunkel sang twenty
songs on the Great Lawn and gave
ninety minutes on the Great Lawn.
Twice as many minutes as Sinatra
ever gave, some folks claimed, or
Four times as many minutes as the
Beatles ever gave in a concert.
The biggest show-business event in
history, folks said,
And Mayor Koch, at the concert, said,
Gee, I wish I could sing.
Tommy and Katie knew all the words
of all twenty of the songs,
And they sang along, in "Mrs.
Robinson," "Little Susie," and
"Scarborough Fair," on the Great
Lawn.
Strangers got mud on Tommy's
blanket and kicked Katie in the
shoulder,
But they sang along, in "Late in the
Evening," "Bridge Over Troubled
Water,"
"Still Crazy After All These Years,"
and "50 Ways to Leave Your
Lover," on the Great Lawn.
Around them, strangers, knapsacks by
their side, smoked a little pot, drank
a little beer, and listened to "Old
Friends" on the Great Lawn.
Strangers brought their dogs,
strangers brought their babies,
listened to "Feelin' Groovy" on
the Great Lawn.

Smilin' at each other and lovin', on the
  Great Lawn.
Some folks even stood in the lake to
  listen to the sweet music.
They couldn't get on the Great Lawn.
The whole program was videotaped.
Half a million were very quiet.
Very peaceful.
Very good.
Feelin' sad, but feelin' glad to have
  Paul and Artie.
And Mrs. Robinson.
The next day, the New York
  Times printed a picture of Simon
  and Garfunkel on the front page.
The New York *Times* printed a
  picture of some of the half mil-
  lion.
The bulldozers came at dawn, to turn
  it all over.
The Parks Department set up a
  Mobile Operations truck on the
  Great Lawn.
The Parks Commissioner said, Be
  careful not to hurt these last
  holdouts—the hard-core fans still
  on the Great Lawn.
Some of the kids with knapsacks were
  still sleepin' on the Great Lawn.
Trucks came and took away the snow
  fences and the *po*lice barricades.
Forklifts came and knocked down the
  aluminum scaffoldin' and the stage
  set of the New York skyline.
Garbage trucks moved quickly to pick
  up the litter and the garbage on
  Fifth Avenue and on Central Park
  West.

Garbage trucks moved inside the Park
to pick up the soda cans.
Football players came out to the Great
Lawn.
Soccer players came out to the Great
Lawn.
Frisbee throwers came out to the
Great Lawn, because it was Sunday
mornin'.
Fiorucci and Hirsh, of Fiorucci &
Hirsh Enterprises, were happy.
They had put up the money for the
concert on the Great Lawn.
Half a million people had seen
"Fiorucci" and they had seen
"Hirsh" on the smokestack of the
set at the concert.
The men drivin' the forklifts didn't
care.
The drivers knocked down "Fiorucci"
on the Great Lawn.
The drivers knocked down "Hirsh"
on the Great Lawn.
By noon, a little garbage was still left
on the Great Lawn.
Some knapsacks were still around.
The bulldozers had turned up a lot of
dirt to make a new Great Lawn.
Tommy Punch, feelin' sad, came out
to the Great Lawn.
Lookin' for somethin', lookin' for
nothin', lookin' for lost glasses.
I left my glasses last night, he said
to a Parks Department man.
Go to the *po*lice, the man said.
My generation, Tommy said, thought
we'd change the world,

And we didn't mind.
Lookin' for somethin',
We couldn't find it.
I was at Woodstock. I'm comfortable
   with the masses.
Lookin' lost, soundin' plaintive,
   Tommy said, I left my glasses on
   the Great Lawn.
I thought I'd just come out and see
   if I could find my glasses.

❖ *Quick*

WE have just received this communiqué from a reckless lady we know who travelled to Europe this summer with her twelve-year-old son, missed their prearranged plane connection home, and decided to go all out and fly back to New York from London via the Concorde:

I feel *touched* at last by the space age. No more of this old business of standing by and waiting, waiting, waiting for someone to make room for *us.* We have new horizons. Literally and figuratively, ha-ha! I'll try to sort them out, even though I'm still reeling from the overwhelming fact that we raced the sun back to this side of the Atlantic and won—or more or less won.

We were in a rush to come home, a rush being one of the main reasons people take the Concorde. What the rush was with us was simply that we were wounded in Paris, in Geneva, and in London by an unpleasant and basically all-pervasive preoccupation with money on the part of the natives, and an undisguised interest in us based solely on how much of it we were going to give to *them.* One of the minor blows, among the major ones, for example, was the discovery that the French tradition of including breakfast with a hotel room had been abandoned—at least, in our case. Our hotel sent us the classic croissants, hot chocolate, and fruit, but at an extra charge of fourteen dollars per person. We began to feel comforted, however, on the day of our departure. We found great solace in London in the realization that we were going to have practically an entire day there, with takeoff time at 5:30 P.M. We began to feel more and more elated in the hour-to-hour buildup of the day. There was no last-day pressure. No rush now. The relief from *that* burden all by itself was dramatic. We had a leisurely breakfast in our hotel room (classic croissants, hot chocolate, and fruit, at only eleven dollars per person). My son and I congratulated each other on everything we were going to fit into the next six hours, before we were to set out for Heathrow Airport, and we decided not to eat lunch, in preparation for all the caviar-level delicacies the Concorde promised. We meandered along the waterways in St. James's Park, tossing bits of croissants (heretofore saved for ourselves) to the ducks, geese, swans, and pelicans. We had five long rides on the double-deckers. We walked back and forth across Westminster Bridge and stood around in the Abbey. We took in everything in the fossil galleries in the British Museum (Natural History). We took in everything in the Science Museum—every automobile, train, ship, plane, and space vehicle, as well as the exhibits on climate and the solar system. We bought a Harrods raincoat (for him) and a Burberry (for me). We arrived at Heathrow refreshed, relaxed, pleased with ourselves, and hungry, and we still had almost an hour before flight time.

Our pace, along with the pace of everything else around us, seemed to pick up speed as soon as we presented ourselves, with our luggage, at the British Airways counter. Our tickets were examined faster, our passports returned faster, our luggage taken from us faster than at any other counter during four weeks of travel in Europe. We stood on no lines. The B.A. personnel smiled affectionately at us and showed concern for our comfort, for our thirst, for our film—whether exposed or still in our camera, and how much X-ray it had been subjected to by those security-examination machines. The smiles were fast. The concern was quick. We were directed to wait in the Monarch Lounge, the waiting room for first-class B.A. passengers. We were eligible, because *all* passengers on the Concorde are in first class. "We invite passengers to help themselves to drinks and other refreshments" was the message on a sign posted at a console that offered us our choice of Indian tonic water, Pepsi, tea, or coffee, along with pretzel sticks, cheese puffs, and McVitie's Chocolate Digestive Biscuits. One cheese puff, a sip of Pepsi, and we were immediately asked to zip along to the Concorde lounge, identified at the entrance by a sign saying "Concorde Passengers Only," which adjoined the passenger gate leading to the Concorde. We had a vague sense of being rushed.

"We keep the passengers close to the plane," a young steward wearing a light-gray jacket said to us with a quick smile, and efficiently, with one hand, he offered a tray of filled champagne glasses. He held the bottle in his other hand (Moët & Chandon '71). I took a glass and got our first look at our fellow-passengers—about fifteen of them so far, and every one a male, average age forty-seven, wearing a business suit and either making a free, international telephone call or hovering around the half-dozen telephones available to all Concordeans as part of the eight-hundred-and-thirty-three-dollar one-way fare. (Round trip, sixteen hundred and sixty-six dollars. No reduced fares for anybody on the Concorde.) Not a bluejean or a backpack—the two invariables we'd seen wherever we went in Europe—in sight. The informal dressers were limited to gray slacks, Navy-blue blazers with brass buttons, Gucci loafers, and unlighted pipes in the mouth. Lots of suntans. Lots of Rolex watches. Lots of Omega watches. Lots of Hermès belts. One Ultrasuede safari-type beige jacket with pocketless khaki pants worn by a gentleman with a receding hairline and brown horn-rimmed glasses. Another woman turned up. Very classy. A two-piece Ungaro cotton dress, flower-patterned in rust, yellow, and beige, and, over the dress, a beige cashmere Valerie Louthan kimono-style cardigan. She also had on sling-pump Magli shoes. My son and I were wearing jogging suits and sneakers. We stationed ourselves near a business-suiter with a heavy cold who made three quick international telephone calls in a row: to his secretary, asking her to reserve a table for lunch the next day; to a friend, reporting that he had gone to David Niven's son's restaurant, on Pont Street, near Beauchamp Place, and informing the friend that "Beauchamp" was pronounced as though it were spelled "Beacham"; and to another businessman, advising him that the dollar was really *down* in London. My son got to the international telephone before I did, dialled 01-01 plus the area code and number, reached a friend, and made a date to play tennis in Central Park late that afternoon. While my son was impressing his friend with the fact that the call was free, I was offered a tray of hors d'oeuvres by an elderly gentleman wearing steel-rimmed spectacles, who had on a butler's uniform, with black-and-white pinstriped pants. Ham, asparagus, egg, cottage-cheese, white-meat-chicken, sardine, and Scottish-salmon sandwiches.

"Is Scottish salmon better than Norwegian salmon?" I asked the gentleman.

"Without question, Madam," he said solicitously. "Scottish salmon has a unique taste, which derives from its curing process."

When I finally got to dial my first free transatlantic call, the early-boarding calls were announced, for rows one through six. We were slotted for Row 16, Seats A and B. I got no answer to my first call, to friends in Malibu. No answer to San Francisco. Oh, boy. No answer to Oslo, Norway. A busy signal at my hairdresser's, in New York. No answer from my brother, in Amagansett. My son tugged impatiently at my arm, even though Row 16 hadn't been called yet. In desperation, I called my office. An answer. Hooray! Natasha, our receptionist, told me that the weather in New York was hot and humid.

"I'll be in a little later today," I began.

"O.K.," she said, and hung up before I could tell her where I was.

One fast, bite-sized Scottish-salmon sandwich and into the approach to the plane: the shortest one—about five steps —I'd ever been through. It was called the "jetway." Behind us, a gentleman over the intercom announced that two items had been left behind in the lounge: a cigarette lighter and a bottle of duty-free gin. He added that he hoped the passengers had taken the free newspapers from the lounge, because there wouldn't be any given out on the Concorde. We entered the Concorde, just to the right of the nose to the playing, over the plane's intercom, of "Raindrops Keep Fallin' on My Head." The galley was straight ahead. Smiling stewardesses quickly grabbed our hand luggage and again I had the vague feeling of being rushed as they urged us to take our seats. Their costumes looked very much like those worn by stewardesses on Eastern Airlines shuttle flights: cool-looking, Weatherall shirtwaist dresses (with the red-and-blue British Airways logo on a white background), coverall aprons of blue poplin, and patent-leather Navy-blue moccasin-type pumps with sensible heels. The interior of the main cabin was disappointing. Ordinary. Out of sync with the supersonic technology of the Concorde: conventional seats, paired on each side, with a narrow aisle in between. Little windows. Brown-and-beige carpeting. Orange-and-white vinyl wall coverings. Ordinary seat belts, royal blue in color. Seating capacity of the plane: one hundred passengers. Plus three in the pilot's cabin, plus seven stewards and stewardesses. As we made our way to our seats, we passed the classy lady in the two-piece Ungaro. She was sitting in 3-C.

"The first three rows are the best," she was saying to her seat companion, the wearer of the Ultrasuede safari jacket. "It's quieter up front, and it doesn't shake as much."

Seat belts on, I checked my watch. We were already fifteen minutes beyond the takeoff time.

"It's like your Cape Kennedy," a stewardess explained. "You know, these last-minute adjustments."

"Raindrops" stopped playing, and a stewardess spoke: "Good evening, ladies and gentlemen. Captain Morris and his crew welcome you aboard this British Airways Concorde, the world's first supersonic passenger aircraft. We are now departing for New York. Our estimated flight time today is three hours and ten minutes, a time saving of approximately a half over subsonic jets. Our cruising speed will be 1,350 miles, or 2,000 kilometres, per hour, over twice the speed of sound, and we will reach a maximum altitude of 58,000 feet, or 17,678 metres. The local time in New York is now 1 P.M., and we expect to land shortly after 4 P.M. Machmeters at the front of each cabin show our speed, Mach 2 being twice the speed of sound. . . ." The rest of the talk was the usual stuff: call buttons in a panel over your head, together with reading-light switch and ventilator control; Concorde flight wallet in seat pocket in front of you; five channels of stereophonic sound. Safety instructions were the same—place seat backs in upright position, etc. Disposal bags were the same. Washrooms were the same, except that they had carpets on the floors. My son and I were disappointed. We wanted things to be more space-agey, like the "Mission to Mars" attraction at Walt Disney World. We hadn't even taken *off* yet. No explanations.

My son had opened his Concorde flight wallet: headsets for the "supersonic stereo programmes"; free slipper socks; free postcards picturing the Concorde—"The British Airways Concorde, powered by four Rolls-Royce SNECMA Olympus 593 turbojets, produced by British Aircraft Corporation and Aerospatiale-France"; free stationery pads embossed with "British Airways Concorde," in gold letters, the capital "C" enclosing a little gold crown. The supersonic stereo programs were short.

"There's no time for anything on this plane," my son said. "We don't even get a movie."

At last, some action. The Captain's voice: "Will the crew position the doors, please?"

The Concorde, like any other plane, moved slowly to the runway.

And then: "Will the crew be seated for takeoff, please?"

We took off at six-thirty. The takeoff was sudden, and a bit bumpy. Otherwise, no big difference from other takeoffs. What *was* different was our heightened awareness of space and size. The aisles were too narrow for the full skirts worn by the stewardesses; every time they passed by, the skirts brushed my arm. The stewards' ties looked more suitable: unusually narrow.

The Captain's voice: "We've just heard, as expected, our takeoff time was 6:30 P.M. We'll be in New York at ten minutes to 5 P.M., hopefully." The projected flight time had increased by ten minutes. Bad news and good news—no explanations.

The stewardesses passed out free decks of blue-and-white playing cards embossed with the Concorde logo in gold, but nobody had time to play cards. Champagne was served quickly, with canapés of smoked salmon (Scottish) and foie gras. Then came a nice, fast dinner: chilled Iranian caviar; sirloin steak marchand de vin; garden peas, baby marrow Provençale, and amandine potatoes; palm-heart salad with vinaigrette dressing; fresh strawberries with cream; coffee; brandy; Drambuie; Cointreau; Jamaica Macanudo cigars. Served on Royal Doulton bone *china.* Concorde-blue tablecloths. Great dinner. But no dawdling. By the time the chocolate mints were served, and the coffee, we were going twice the speed of sound. The only sign of it was on the Machmeter: M 2.00. Through the tiny windows, I could see blue sky and a few white clouds.

An opportunity to stretch and talk to a few of the other passengers. A serious young man in Row 17: first flight on the Concorde. A construction engineer on leave from his job in Saudi Arabia. No complaints. A tall, handsome gentleman from Pound Ridge, New York, returning from a visit to his factory in Scotland. First flight. He thought he'd give it a try. A cranky young man in Row 18. He was going to fire his secretary, because she had booked his flight and had not found out about the first three rows of the plane, so that he could have sat in one of them. Complaints about noise, about bumping into people in the aisle. An athletic-looking gentleman with a deep suntan. His complaint: "I usually run about two miles on a flight on a 747. I can't *run* in this aisle." His wife, one of the few other women aboard, had an enormous tote bag, in which she was carrying an accumulation of all the publications she wanted to read. They included *Foreign Affairs, Commentary, Human Nature, New Age, Atlas, The Economist,* and *Barron's.* She usually got through all that and more on 747s while her husband was jogging on them, she said, but so far she had read only one article in *Foreign Affairs.*

At 55,000 feet, and the Concorde going at 1,340 miles an hour, my son informed me that the outside skin of the Concorde was now very hot. He urged me to touch the window. I did. It felt warm. Very different from subsonic planes, which always have drafts around the windows. Every once in a while, the Captain of our Concorde, introducing himself each time as Captain Morris, made some quick announcements about our acceleration and speed. Early on, for example, he said, "In a couple of minutes, we'll be starting our climb using our reheats, or afterburners, as you call them in America, and this provides us with a sudden thrust, in case you detect a bit of a jolt." Another time, as we were cruising at 28,000 feet, we were going at ninety-five per cent of the speed of sound, and Captain Morris told us to watch the Machmeter while he again turned on the re-heats. "We keep the reheats on until one point seven," he said, "and this occurs at 45,000 feet." My son said he under-stood everything the Captain told us. I understood nothing. I didn't even feel the jolt. My son said he definitely felt the jolt. "We're flying on these Rolls-Royce Olympus engines, and we've got two-spool turbojets fitted with the afterburn-ers for takeoff and transonic acceleration," my son said. "The plane has a droop nose. It's partly drooped for takeoff, and when we land it will be fully drooped, but right now it's straight." So much for the space-age babies.

I had set my watch back to New York time. At 3:30 P.M., dinner being over, we were invited to pay a visit to the pilot's cabin. We were escorted up front by a steward, who gave us a few more facts about people who fly on the Con-corde: sixty per cent of the passengers on the London to New York flights are Americans; eighty per cent are business people; forty per cent have been on the aircraft before. There were three officers in the pilot's cabin: Captain Colin Morris, First Officer John White, and Third Officer Peter Phillips. All of them, in white shirts with blue-and-gold epaulets on the shoulders, looked like Basil Rathbone. They were also full of jokes. The cabin looked cramped to me—almost like the space modules I've seen on television—with a breathtaking array of push buttons on control panels. The usual kind of intimidating labels: "Equipment Bay Cooling," "Stand-by Valves," "Master Valve," "Engine On," "O/Full," "U/Full," "Ditching," "Air Bleed Control."

"We take a bit of exercise," Captain Morris said when I asked about the cramped space. "We walk three steps out and three steps back."

"We're fit, virile young men," First Officer White said.

"Let us say everything here is accessible," Captain Morris said. "We can reach everything without having to stretch."

They said they had all worked on different kinds of aircraft before taking the five-month course on how to fly the Concorde. Impression of great reliability.

On our way back to our seats, we passed the lady with the tote bag full of reading material. She was still on *Foreign Affairs.* Her husband looked stationary and grim.

By the time we sat down and I had filled out my customs declaration, Captain Morris announced that we were de-accelerating, and we were over Nantucket, and that the temperature in New York was "a hazy eighty-one degrees." We were down to M .85 when he announced that there would be a ten-to-fifteen-minute landing delay. At M .56, and 15,000 feet, fifty miles from New York, he said, "Mysteriously, ladies and gentlemen, the holding times have increased from ten or fifteen minutes to forty minutes. It will now be *fifty* minutes till arrival."

New York time was 4:50 P.M. With the fifty-minute delay, we'd still be beating the sun by fifty minutes.

At 5:15 P.M., Captain Morris, in a happy voice, announced that we were flying at 8,000 feet. "Good signs," he said. "We can expect to be landing in *fifteen* minutes' time."

All the passengers around us looked bleak.

"The nose down creates a drag and allows the pilots to have a better view of the runway," my son said. "We'll be landing like any other plane but at a greater angle to the landing strip. There are no flaps on the Concorde wings to slow the plane down while landing, so the entire body of the aircraft acts as a flap."

The "No Smoking" and "Fasten Seat Belts" signs flashed on. At M .44, it felt to me as though the plane were going uphill. At M .35, "Raindrops" started playing again.

"Officers and crew take seats for landing, please."

We came down at 5:35 P.M. We *had* beaten the sun. By fifty-*five* minutes. Flight time: four hours and five minutes.

"Raindrops" went off.

"This is Captain Morris. I would like to apologize for the delay. I do hope it hasn't spoiled the flight, and we hope to see you again in the near future. Will the cabin crews please disarm the doors?"

Everybody seemed to get off the plane very quickly. My son and I got off sort of reluctantly, now that the race was over. As we settled in for what turned out to be a half hour's wait for our luggage, I noticed Captain Morris, First Officer White, and Third Officer Phillips walking very briskly toward the exits. They were rushing to get somewhere.

❖ *Albee*

EDWARD ALBEE's newest play, "The Lady from Dubuque," which opened a few weeks ago and closed after twelve performances, reminded us that it was time to have another talk with the author, who had remarked the last time we saw him, in 1974, that he believed it was the responsibility of a serious playwright "to instruct." "The Lady from Dubuque"—and what it had to say instructively about illness, dying, and death (of an individual and/or of our present society) and the attempts of the dying to find a way to die while surrounded by those who resist their death—was received by most of the critics with what seemed to us to be considerable weariness. We therefore felt reassured last week, when we met Mr. Albee for lunch at the Algonquin, to see *him* looking energetic and practically ebullient, and also exceedingly trim, in a Harris-tweed jacket over a navy-blue wool sweater over a Marimekko shirt of dark-blue and light-blue pin checks, with gray corduroy trousers and dark-brown ankle-high shoes. He still had the same kind of full, free black mustache he was wearing six years ago.

"Well, how's the instruction business?" we asked as soon as he had given the waiter his order—fresh fruit and cottage cheese.

"Very good," Albee said, firmly and cheerfully. "Excellent. I just got back from a lecture tour. Four days at universities in Tucson and in Portland, Oregon, and then two days in Seattle, one of them resting and one at the Northwest Theatre Conference. The week before, I flew out to Kalamazoo to talk to students. I do between twenty and thirty appearances a year, all around the country. Over the years, I've become less awkward and less shy. I used to be taciturn. Now you can't get me to shut up."

"What, exactly, do you do out there?" we asked. "And why?"

"I do a lecture or a reading from my plays, with a question-and-answer period," he said. "I also do two workshops, one with students of acting or directing and one with students of creative writing. I talk a lot about the relationship between what drama tries to do and what people *want* you to do. I fly in and rent a car, because I love to drive around and get to know the country. And I love to walk around a town or a campus until it's time for me to go where I'm supposed to go. This last time out, I read from 'The Zoo Story,' 'A Delicate Balance,' and 'Counting the Ways,' and read one entire short play, 'Box.' Most of my characters are fond of the sound of their own voices." He grinned, and dug into his fruit and cottage cheese. "The workshops are limited to fifty students," he said. "Someone or something worthwhile invariably turns up in those. At the start, I have to get over the three impossible questions, of course: '*How* do you write?' and '*Why* do you write?' and 'Where do your ideas come from?' "

"And your answers?" we asked.

"To the first, I say 'It's something you know if you're a writer,' " Albee replied politely. "To the second, 'You write because you're a writer.' To the third, I usually say 'Schenectady.' I've been going out to the universities for fifteen years. I find it fascinating to see the changes in the students from the activist days to these, the ostrich days. They all want to get a good job and vanish. They don't believe that political participation makes any sense. They feel they can't do anything to make democracy work. I like talking to them because—in theory, at least—people of that age have not completely made up their minds, so maybe I can get at them. I don't like living in a vacuum. I believe there's a strong relationship between people's being aesthetically informed and their being able to govern themselves."

"Any other reasons for going?" we asked.

"Yes—I always learn something," Albee said. "Somebody asks me a question, and I hear myself giving an answer, and I suddenly find out something I'd never realized before. For example, one student said to me, 'Your characters never have last names. Why?' I said, 'I'd have given them last names if I knew what they were.' It was something I hadn't realized before. Also, I love travelling. And the lectures pay nicely, given the vicissitudes of the theatre. I'm told W. H. Auden used to go out and do thirty readings in thirty days. That could be a rat race. I never do that."

"What do you do in your workshops?" we asked.

"Discussions. Scenes. How at the age of twenty they figure out how to get into the mind of a fifty-five-year-old person. How to learn to differentiate between characters. Things like that. It's very easy when you're very young to fancy you're a writer. I read their plays. You end up reading a hundred plays, and if you're lucky you'll find someone to encourage."

"What generosity!" we said.

"It's responsibility," Albee said. "You've got to encourage talent. It's an *obligation.* This last tour was wonderful. But I didn't know when I left that it would coincide with the closing of the play. The critics." He gave a small smile. "The critical response to the creative act." He shook his head. "People think the critics are giving facts, not opinions," he said. "We had ten favorable reviews and ten unfavorable reviews, but the economics of the theatre are such that you can't keep plays open with mixed reviews. And it's becoming harder and harder for a serious play to get produced. In 1962, it took seventy-five thousand dollars to produce 'Who's Afraid of Virginia Woolf?' This year, 'The Lady from Dubuque' required three hundred thousand dollars to produce. I know my plays. I know my chances. Every single play of mine has had mixed reviews. Right down the middle. Walter Kerr said about 'Virginia Woolf' that it had a 'hole in its head.' The *News* said it was 'dirty.' Back in the old days, what the critics said would hurt. Now I know that you can't permit yourself to let it destroy you. Or even hurt you. After having eighteen plays produced, I've learned a few things. One, never expect anything but disaster. Two, there's not necessarily any relation between what you've done and what the critics say. Three, the ultimate judgment of your work probably won't be made for seventy-five years, and unless you're exceptionally lucky you're not going to find out how it comes out. The producers of 'The Lady from Dubuque'—there were seven of them, including Richard Barr, a decent and honorable man who has been involved in the production of all but one of my plays in New York—refused to make a fight for the play. It would probably have cost forty thousand dollars to mount an advertising campaign, and they refused to do it. I was disgusted that they didn't fight, but that was their business decision. They were shortsighted, though. If they had kept the play going for one more week, they would have been eligible to have a forty-per-cent share in the subsidiary rights—and I've already agreed to productions of it in Zurich, Vienna, and Stockholm. The German critics were at the opening and wrote wonderful reviews, and Stefani Hunzinger, the German agent who initially arranged for the production in West Berlin of my first play, 'The Zoo Story,' in 1959, is arranging to have 'The Lady from Dubuque' produced in West Germany. I've taken beatings from the critics before. My play 'Malcolm' closed after *seven* performances." Albee laughed, and polished off the last of his lunch. "I'm not against having critics," he said. "But I'd be happiest if the drama critics were poets or novelists. People who know something about the arts are the best critics. We need critics, because there's always the danger that you're missing something. Unfortunately, now what they do is tell me what I should expect commercially. But those thirty-second wonders on television are the real critical disgrace. So many in the commercial audience come to see plays because of what television says to them. If I have any nightmare, it is that I wake up and discover that the critics have been right. I couldn't do a cheerful, carefree little play about death even if I wanted to. There's nothing more embarrassing than to watch a serious writer try to do a potboiler—unless it's watching the funny, situation-comedy writer try to get serious."

"Why not go back to Off Broadway?" we asked.

"I disapprove of the idea that a serious play has to be economically punished," Albee said. "It's so much easier to do plays in a favorable, protected environment, but people around the country think the nature of the theatre is determined by what is done on Broadway. It's safer to do a play in a three-or-four-hundred-seat theatre. The economic pressures are less crushing. But it's unhealthy to give in to them. I keep fighting against it."

"What's next?" we asked.

" 'Lolita'—an adaptation of Nabokov's novel which I wrote in part because I was so deeply offended by the movie version—will be produced soon, with Donald Sutherland. Also, I'm on the Artistic Directorate of the Vivian Beaumont Theatre, at Lincoln Center, and I've started collecting plays for a production this fall of one-act plays from the United States, Canada, and Latin America, in the Mitzi Newhouse Theatre, a lovely little theatre. About three hundred seats.

Safe." Albee grinned. "In a few days, I'm going off for the State Department on one of those cultural-exchange trips I do a lot of. To Venezuela and Colombia this time. I've been involving myself with Latin-American writers and their problems—their repressive governments, the establishment theatre's lack of enthusiasm for anything new, the way the avant-garde theatre is automatically labelled leftist, the lack of communication between the countries. I'll be discussing their woes, making new friends, and then, on my own time, going to see those wonderful waterfalls and Indian settlements."

"Staying put for a while after that?" we asked.

"I like to be a moving target," Albee said, with a far from weary grin.

✦ *Mr. Bell*

A BIG feed and assorted festivities were put on last week by the American Telephone & Telegraph Company at Lüchow's, where *the* message—emblazoned on clumps of helium-filled white balloons, on buttons, on posters, on the aprons of dozens of waiters and bartenders, on souvenir gifts of T-shirts, ceramic cups, and highly polished brass plated cases holding an Indian-head penny dated 1882—was "The Bell System Celebrates a Hundred Years of the Phone at Home."

Hosts: many jovial-mannered, three-piece-suited corporate types, handing out A.T. & T. business cards that identified them as having titles like Advertising Director-Marketing and Media Relations Manager and Vice-President-Residence Marketing. Guests: the press, big and little, general and trade; television announcers, commercial and cable; decorators and designers; a lot of very thirsty and very hungry anonymous people, all putting on their heads another gift, little brown derbies, and chomping away with grim concentration. Guest of honor: Don Ameche, star of the 1939 movie "The Story of Alexander Graham Bell," still thin, still tall, still with his Don Ameche mustache and his obliging good nature, and looking much younger than his age (now seventy-three), wearing a light-gray suit, a white shirt, and a light-gray necktie with dark-gray squares and red dots, and gazing around with awe and admiration at a four-foot-long chocolate-and-vanilla layer cake in the shape of an 1882-model telephone, with an earpiece of licorice; at a real antique popcorn wagon popping popcorn; at Lüchow's famous gazebo, decorated with vines of real purple grapes and with exotic flowers and feathers in the shape of birds; at a violin-cello-and-piano trio seated in the gazebo, wearing tails and playing music by Sigmund Romberg, Victor Herbert, Johann Strauss, and Irving Berlin ("All alone, by the telephone . . ."); at pretty girls wearing long Victorian velvet dresses with bustles; and at the chow tables, offering three-bean salad, baked ham with three kinds of mustard, cabbage-and-celery-seed slaw, apple-currant muffins, *darne* of Kennebec salmon, Cornish game hen with wild rice and pine-nut stuffing, roast tenderloin of beef, shrimp, oysters, clams, mussels, strawberry shortcake, and gingersnaps.

"Don, it's a very turn-of-the-century menu," one of the corporate types said to Mr. Ameche.

"Gosh, I had no idea," Mr. Ameche said. "All this!"

"I saw your movie on television," one of the Victorian-dressed girls said to Mr. Ameche. "It's like 'The Story of Benjamin Franklin.' Like that."

"Why, thank you," Mr. Ameche said. "People are always coming up to me and saying 'Mr. Bell?' And I always say 'Yes?' "

" 'Wings for the human voice,' " another A.T. & T. man said earnestly. "Don, did you see your poster?" He drew Mr. Ameche's attention to a wall poster showing various stills of Mr. Ameche as Mr. Bell, and read from it: "20th Century-Fox presents Darryl F. Zanuck's Production of 'The Story of Alexander Graham Bell,' with Don Ameche, Loretta Young, Henry Fonda, Charles Coburn, Gene Lockhart, Spring Byington. America's most thrilling story! Thrilling . . . and true! Of love so great and faith so strong that it inspired this man to endure ridicule, privation, hunger . . . to achieve the miracle of *wings for the human voice!"*

"That's right," Mr. Ameche said. "He wanted to give up working on the invention, he loved her so much. She was deaf. But she wouldn't let him give up the invention."

"Nothing compared to what *we're* gonna face from now on," said the A.T. & T. man. "With the whole field now open to competition."

"What a cast that was!" Mr. Ameche said. "Hank and Loretta and all those other good actors."

"Yeah, Don," said the A.T. & T. man. "And we can't let the public forget that *we're* the ones that gave the *real* wings to the human voice. Did you see our display of telephones, Don?"

The display: The standard 1882 phone, the first dial phone of 1919, and models all the way up to the 1982 Touch-a-Matic and Big Button.

"Design is important," said the A.T. & T. man. "These days, old is in, so we give them a new phone that bespeaks that turn-of-the-century era. Look at this model. A tiny rolltop desk. You roll it up, and inside—presto! The Stow-away!"

Mr. Ameche looked affectionately at the modern push-button model stowed away. He looked affectionately at all the hungry people surrounding him. "I like people," he told us. "I make any kind of sacrifice to make things nice. When they called me for this, of course I came. I enjoyed portraying Mr. Bell. We made the whole movie in thirty days—all on the lot. I saw Loretta three or four years ago, in California, where we both live. She looked wonderful. Loretta and Hank. It was always a joy to work with people like that. I enjoy working now, too. I did four weeks last summer in 'How to Succeed in Business Without Really Trying,' in Akron, Dayton, Columbus, and St. Louis. I did a 'Love Boat,' with Martha Scott. Of course, I didn't have as much to do in 'Love Boat' as I did as Mr. Bell. My own favorite movie, though, that I was in is 'Heaven Can Wait.' "

"How did you get the name Don?" we asked.

"From the nickname Dom, which people thought was Don," he said. "I was born Dominic Ameche. Papa's name was A-m-i-c-i, but an attorney in Minnesota, where Papa worked in the iron mines, changed the spelling for him. I never changed Dominic officially, but Don is on everything, including my passport. Would you believe that I have six children, all good children, and not one is an actor?"

"No," we said.

A Bell executive drew Mr. Ameche away to be photographed for the press, wearing a Prince Albert coat while pretending to talk on the 1882-model phone. We waited at the gazebo, ate a few of the purple grapes from the vine, and met Joe Spallino, the violinist and leader of the tail-wearing trio in the gazebo, who told us that he was making an all-out effort for the A.T. & T. party.

"We normally wear tuxedos," Mr. Spallino said. "But this is important."

Jack Hallock, the young man who had arranged the fruit and flowers for the party, urged us to eat more of the grapes from the gazebo.

"Did you see the nosegays on all the tables?" he asked us. "In 1882, these were called tussie-mussies. Very Victorian. Very Bell."

Mr. Ameche posed obligingly at the 1882 telephone for a quarter of an hour, and then he was taken in hand by an A.T. & T. vice-president (Residence Marketing), who placed him at a microphone in the gazebo, introduced him, and pointed out to the guests that the first long-distance telephone call had been made from New York City to Boston. A representative from the Mayor's office announced that Mayor Koch had proclaimed the day Home Telephone Day in New York City.

A clip from the movie "The Story of Alexander Graham Bell" was then shown on video monitors set up at various points in Lüchow's.

Don Ameche: "Ahoy! Mr. Watson, can you hear me now? This is Alexander Bell speaking to you from Five Exeter Place. Mr. Watson, come here! I want you!"

Henry Fonda (seen dozing at his post in a nearby room, then suddenly awakened by the voice over the wire, and rushing in to Don Ameche): "It talks! Mr. Bell, Mr. Bell, it talks! I *heard* you! I heard your *voice!*" Don Ameche and Henry Fonda hug each other and jump around in a dance.

In the gazebo, Don Ameche looked *very* pleased.

❖ *Alex and the Awards*

WE can count on show business every time to lure our man Stanley away from his Montauk retreat. Last week, the Thirty-sixth Annual Antoinette Perry Awards—presented by the League of New York Theatres and Producers under the authorization of the American Theatre Wing—had Stanley hanging around again with his old pal Alexander H. Cohen, the Broadway producer and impresario of last winter's "Night of 100 Stars." Cohen was executive-producing the Tony Awards show for the sixteenth consecutive year. "Tonys now real big-time television stuff, so it's lucky they have stickler for detail like Alex to handle things," Stanley said, turning over to us some notes on the occasion before heading back to the L.I.R.R.

Here is Stanley's report:

Long experience with stage people taught me *Get to theatre early,* so arrive at Imperial Theatre, on West Forty-fifth, site of Tonys—otherwise home of "Dreamgirls"—couple of hours before doors ordered locked by Alex. Theme of this year's show History of Imperial. Dress rehearsal still on. "The name of the game, folks, is Broadway," Alex telling Hildy Parks (Mrs. Cohen), writer and producer of show; Elliot Lawrence, musical director; Clark Jones, director; and scenic designer, choreographer, stage manager, big bunch of staff assistants. Alex wearing snappy maroon blazer, gray pants, horn-rimmed glasses; sitting out in auditorium at board laid over seats, with one hand on each of two multi-buttoned telephones. Hildy wearing black pants with gold-colored T-shirt. Both Alex and Hildy chewing gum frantically. "Always bear in mind what we're selling," Alex saying. "We're selling Broadway. Your show is about *theatre.*" Everybody attentive. Nervous. Opening-night jitters. Break leg, etc., etc. Live show on TV, Alex stresses. Live. Live.

Alex reviewing who getting stand-up mike, who wearing hard-wire mike (mike connected by wire), who wireless mike (mike with transmitter). Leslie Uggams, singing "Someone to Watch Over Me," getting hard-wire mike. Ben Vereen, dancing and singing "By Myself," getting wireless body mike. Elvis Presley-type character in "Joseph and the Amazing Technicolor Dreamcoat" getting wireless hand-held mike. Lot more show-biz vocab.: total track (music and vocal on tape), fish pole (mike on pole instead of broom), ambience (crowd hum), sting (one chord), bumpers (out of commercial, back to program). Much kidding around while measuring presentation and acceptance times during run-through, with fake presentation of awards, fake award classifications, fake acceptance speeches. Examples: "The nominees are: Amanda Plummer, Christopher Plummer, and Josephine the Plumber." Also, "Thank you for this award. I can't pass up this opportunity to insult my agent in public." Also, "And the winner is: Nancy Reagan for 'Table Settings.'" And "Best Performance by Usherette," "Best Program Peddler," "Best Dresser Stage Right." All delivered by highly self-appreciative young alumni of Alexander H. Cohen enterprises. Much levity. Somebody in balcony taking photographs, with flashbulbs. Alex on job. "Take a couple of cops up to the balcony and throw that photographer out of there!" Alex says.

"Prior to telecast, the band has to be in the pit and *playing* at eight," Alex instructs. "The doors will be literally closed and locked at five minutes *to* eight." Alex worrying about Nedda Harrigan Logan, president of Actors' Fund, scheduled to accept special Tony, presented by Jason Robards, in honor of Hundredth Anniversary of A.F. "Nedda comes from the audience, has to go up those very, very steep steps to stage," Alex says. "It's so terribly dark. I'd better go fetch her from the audience. I'll cue that into my script."

Hildy asks, "How about Lillian Gish? How about Ginger Rogers?"

"They're spryer than I am," Alex says. "Remember, folks. Everybody must be in black tie, ladies in formal gowns. That means *everybody* in the house. Ushers wear their regular black uniforms. Everybody else is to be in black tie. Cameramen. Sound men. Stagehands. Engineers. Everybody. This is Broadway going out live via satellite to a hundred million people in the United States and Canada, in Europe, Japan, Hong Kong."

Alex turns to Gerson Werner, Imperial manager, white-haired gent with gold-rimmed specs, already wearing his tux. "It's too hot in here," Alex says. "It's got to go low."

"It's seventy," Werner says.

"Seventy will be *seventy-eight* with the audience here," Alex says. "Too warm. The temperature in this theatre has got to go down! Our audience will be here an hour longer than the ones for 'Dreamgirls.' "

Alex shifts attention to stocky, patient-looking gent— Seymour Herscher, his assistant of thirty-four years. Says, "The Tony envelopes are sealed too strongly. Last year, the presenters had a physical fight to get the envelopes open, then another physical fight to get the cards out of the envelopes. Check it out. O.K., gang. Everybody get dressed."

Alex gives me special rundown, says, "I'll dress in my office in Shubert Alley, on the floor above the Shuberts. That will save eight or ten minutes. There are thirteen hundred and seventy-eight seats in the Imperial, and I know where everybody is sitting. We know where to grab them with the cameras. Six cameras are stationed downstairs. Two hand-held cameras will be working the aisles to grab nominees. There will be two cameras in the balcony. We've got three hundred fewer seats this year, because we're in a smaller house, so we've had dozens of extra problems. There's no room backstage to take press photographs of the winners, so we're going to escort the winners over to the Barbetta Restaurant, about a block away, to see the press right after they win. Then we cart them back. While they're out, stand-ins of the same sex take their seats. We're doing seven awards —for Outstanding Regional Theatre, Outstanding Scenic Design, Outstanding Costume Design, Outstanding Lighting Design, Best Book of a Musical, Best Score of a Musical, Outstanding Reproduction of a Play or a Musical—on tape, strictly timed, before the telecast starts, so the show won't be too long. That will help keep us from running over. The pressure you're working under is good. It keeps the attention of the audience. At the Champagne Midnight Gala—the Waldorf ball after the show—there will be twelve hundred diners, and I'll be greeting every one of them. I want to know if the Fluffy Scrambled Eggs with Bacon and Sausage are fluffy, and I want to hear about it if they're cold."

Hildy comes over, says she's going home to put on formal gown. Alex says he wants to check out house, make sure it's clean. Hildy says actress nominees for musical complaining they have only eight minutes to put on dresses to accept in if they win. Hildy and Alex agree it's *their* problem. "If they can't change in eight minutes, they shouldn't be in the theatre," Hildy says.

"When we started doing this show, I was the producer and Hildy was the writer," Alex says. "Over the years, she's learned my job. She's great at it."

During show, Alex says, Hildy scheduled to be with di-

rector Clark Jones in mobile truck parked on West Forty-
sixth, both of them coördinating camera shots for telecast.
Alex shows me where he will be—in rear of theatre, beside
in-house sound console, on Plexiglas stool set up next to
headset and phone communicating with Hildy in TV truck.

"I insisted every light must be lit on every marquee on this
block," Alex says. "We're selling *Broadway*. To the *world*. The
Booth and the Plymouth are now dark. I said they must be
lit, too. We open by showing the marquees. The real marquee of the Imperial didn't appear to advantage, so we made
a special one, just for the show. It gives the show a lot of
pizzazz."

Alex nabs burly guy in bluejeans, sports shirt, sneakers,
tells guy, "You can't come in here without a black tie."

"I'm an engineer," guy says.

"You'll have to put on a black tie," Alex says. "Go to my
office in Shubert Alley. We have all the tuxedos you want.
Pick one."

To me, Alex says, "You might think it's chaos, chaos,
chaos. We had only today for dress rehearsal. This show has
on it, in a two-hour span, one solid hour of live entertainment on the air. It's especially complicated because of all the
union rules. It took us half a year to prepare the *first* telecast,
in 1967. We worked on this one in high gear for three
months. It's the most complex production schedule in television." Alex says sponsors are Lincoln-Mercury, Polaroid,
G.E., du Pont, I.B.M., American Express. Says sponsors are
interested in *class*. Alex throws chewing gum away, takes out
aspirin tin, gobbles four aspirin, says, "I can take eighteen
of these in one day. Hardly feel them. But they help when
I get a slight headache. Now I want to be sure this place is
swept up."

Follow Alex around theatre. Alex spots big trash can filled
with trash near in-house sound console, says "Remove!"
Finds mussed copy of New York *Post* on fifth-row seat, says

"Remove!" Says "When in doubt, throw it out" to few people left in theatre. Then Alex says "I think we're ready." Goes to get changed.

Back in fourteen minutes. Looking like Mr. Broadway. Neat tux, but says Hildy coming out of truck to do his studs. Finds another guy in bluejeans, asks "Who you with?" Guy says "Backstage." Alex says "Then *get* backstage!"

Audience arrives. Elegant. Dressy. Amanda Plummer, up for Outstanding Performance by a Featured Actress in a Play, skinny, cute, in lacy white dress, white stockings, white shoes. Katie Kelly, TV critic, skinny, cute, in black silk knickers. Tommy Tune, up for Outstanding Direction of a Musical, six feet six, skinny, cute, in tux with *white* bow tie, doing little dance on way to seat.

"I want you to do a good job tonight," Imperial manager tells Alex. "That's a joke," manager explains to me. "We have a running gag." Manager cracking up.

Alex onstage. Explains show to audience. Jerry Wexler, Warner Brothers Records sr. v.-prez, one of eleven producers and associate producers of "Nine," tells neighbor he minds being prop for television show. Joke. Everybody coöperating. Alex says thirty seconds on show costs a hundred and twelve thousand dollars, so time big concern. "Acceptance speeches must be charming, witty, and *brief*. Ladies and gentlemen, hold your applause for the nominees each time a name is mentioned. Hold it for the winners. We will pick up three or four minutes that way." Alex asks everybody to follow yearly routine of introducing self to neighbor. Asks for moment of standing silence to remember Jack Albertson, Susan Bloch, Melvyn Douglas, Lee Strasberg, Lotte Lenya, others who have died since last Tony Awards. Welcomes Governor Hugh Carey, former Mayor John Lindsay, ASCAP president Hal David, and others. Gets awards for Regional Theatre, Scenic Design, Costume Design, etc., etc., taped fast. To be used on air during breaks. Explains how winners to go off stage right, have trophy taken away for engraving, be escorted to Barbetta, then carted back. All winners to go center stage after finale. Warns winners to be careful about going up curved, steep staircase to stage. Says take it easy. Says no high jinks. "This is not the Grammy Awards," Alex says. "Please do not wave at the cameras."

Alex takes place on Plexiglas stool in rear. Tells Hildy over telephone, "The only time you cut is when I tell you to cut. Only when you hear from me. Otherwise, don't make a single move." Alex very unhappy about inadequate air-conditioning. As show starts, tells theatre manager too hot. Even unhappier when first minute of telecast is lost to house, thus blowing wonderful opening showing marquees. During break for commercial, Alex onstage again, explaining to audience they missed beautiful opening but television audience saw it intact. Rest of show plays just about as planned. Alex escorts Nedda Harrigan Logan up steep steps. Nobody trips. Winners very happy to win. Amanda Plummer says she doesn't believe it. Tommy Tune dances down aisle, dances dance of thanks onstage. Alex smiling benevolently. Alex locates Marvin Hamlisch, Lucie Arnaz about to do presentation routine together, gets them to speed up routine. Gets extra one-minute commercial in before cut-off. Show runs only twelve minutes over. After finale, all winners together on center stage. Everybody telling Alex he did it again.

◆ Remembering Picasso

LAST week, in a glassed-in office of the West Fifty-seventh Street Gallery of Sidney Janis, eighty-five-year-old art ex-hibitor *extraordinaire,* who was one of Pablo Picasso's first American friends, and who helped bring Picasso's "Guer-nica" to this country from France in 1939, Carroll Janis, the younger of Sidney's two sons, fortyish-looking, wearing bluejeans, tan running shoes, and a tan velour sweater over a pink tennis shirt, was sitting on a corner of a desk talking on the telephone about arrangements for the gallery's open-ing, on October 25th—the hundredth anniversary of Picasso's birth—of an exhibition of two hundred and fifty photographs, all by David Douglas Duncan, of Pablo Picasso. In the gallery's four exhibition rooms, the white-painted walls were blank. On the floors, carpeted in beige, were rows and rows of photographs, mostly in black and white, measuring ten or twelve inches by fifteen, and mounted on ragboard. Standing upright in a corner was a big photograph, in color, about forty inches by sixty; a mounted dye transfer on a thick panel, it showed Picasso in 1962, from the rear, seated in a chair in the large salon of his château at Vauvenargues, the room bare of usual furniture but with a couple of unframed Picassos on easels and one in the fireplace.

Duncan, wearing a blue-and-red checked sports shirt

open at the collar, brown corduroy pants, brown socks, and no shoes, was tiptoeing among his photographs, rearranging them, studying them, straightening them, getting them ready for the walls. He picked up one showing Picasso and his second wife, Jacqueline, eating at their kitchen table and laid it beside a photograph of Picasso kidding around as he embraced his wife. Duncan, a Mid-westerner who has lived for many years in the South of France, near where Picasso lived, looked the same as he has for decades: deeply tanned, thin, boyish, talkative, exuberant, and eager, as always, to share some of his endless enthusiasm for Picasso as both man and artist, which had led him to bring out four books of photographs of Picasso—"The Private World of Pablo Picasso" (1958), "Picasso's Picassos" (1961), "Goodbye Picasso" (1974), and "Viva Picasso" (1980).

An elevator door opened. Into the gallery stepped Paloma Picasso Lopez Sanchez, the thirty-one-year-old daughter of the artist, who is a jewelry designer now working in New York City. Trim, attractive, energetic, with straight black hair hanging almost to her earlobes, Mrs. Lopez Sanchez is about an inch taller than her five-foot-two father. Except for a red wool French beret with metal grommets, she was all in Saint-Laurent—navy-blue leather jacket, straight skirt of navy with white pinstripes, red-white-and-blue silk print blouse with a bow at the collar, red leather belt, black stockings, navy leather pumps trimmed with red around the instep. She also wore dark-tinted Italian glasses and a single piece of jewelry, of her own design—a gold ring set with rubelite and amethyst. She glanced at the photographs spread out on the floor and then, with a pleased smile, embraced Duncan, who grinned at her with unrestrained approval.

"This is what I wanted you to see," Duncan said. "This is our birthday present to your pop." He led her closer to the photographs on the floor. "This is not really an exhibition of photographs," he said. "The work of art here is your father."

She gave a little laugh. "Dave, it is very impressive," she said. "Very impressive." She looked up at him with large, Picasso-duplicate brown eyes.

Duncan looked as though he had just been presented with a dozen Picassos.

"And Sidney Janis is not charging one dime to get in here," he said. "This is going to be a *celebration.*"

Mrs. Lopez Sanchez carefully walked along a row and looked down at a photograph of a spectacularly beautiful little black-haired girl sitting with Picasso in a café and eating an ice-cream cone. "He was always buying me ice cream," she said.

"Paloma, you know your English is astonishing," Duncan said. "Extraordinary. Perfect."

"I can do the British accent if I want to, but it's pretentious," she said seriously.

"Do you remember where that photograph was taken?" Duncan asked.

"Café des Belges, Juan-les-Pins," she said. "It was 1957."

"What a memory!" Duncan said. "You have the same memory as your pop."

"I remember it because my brother Claude and I spent so much time looking up at the Sputnik," she said.

Carroll Janis ambled over and was introduced. "It's all starting to shape up," he said.

"There are so many here I've never seen before," Mrs. Lopez Sanchez said.

"I had such an opportunity," Duncan said. "Nobody was ever self-conscious in front of the camera."

"This picture," Mrs. Lopez Sanchez said, going over to one of the few photographs in color. "This one wearing the Indian war bonnet."

"Gary Cooper brought him that," Duncan said, with delight. He pointed to the photograph of Picasso-mugging-as-Indian-chief. "Remember when he grabbed that bull's tail that someone had given him and put it on as the Indian's hair?" he asked, with further delight. "He was the greatest mime of them all."

"I would be sitting with him, and suddenly he would put on a funny hat or a plastic nose," Mrs. Lopez Sanchez said. "They were always sending him things."

"Every day was Christmas," Duncan said.

They walked slowly and carefully between the rows of photographs.

"Here I am making faces out of leaves," she said. "He was always working on the dinner table. When I came, he would say, 'It's O.K. Stay. But don't open your mouth.' I always had a second breakfast with my father. His breakfast was always the same: dry toast and Caro, a coffee without caffeine. He was homeopathic. He was careful with foods."

"He never drank anything alcoholic," Duncan said.

"I liked the big vicuña quilt he had on his bed, summer and winter," she said. "And his moccasins, with the fur inside. I'd walk in his shoes."

They looked at photographs taken at the beach. "A driver would take us all to the beach," she said. "My father never learned to drive a car. He would say that when he was poor he couldn't afford a car and then when he was rich he could afford a driver, so he never drove himself. We'd stay at the beach till five. We'd take pedal boats out."

"And here he's permitting himself to be sketched by one of those beach artists," Duncan said. "They never left him alone."

"He used to go to that beach, La Garoupe, for years before it became popular," she said. "One day, I read a book that said that my father and the Gerald Murphys and Hemingway and Chanel started going to that beach in the summer.

Before that, nobody ever went there in the summer. It was too hot. They went to Deauville. Now La Garoupe is too crowded."

They looked at photographs of Picasso and his children with a goat.

"Esmeralda," Duncan said.

"I don't know how it arrived," she said. "One day, a *bull* arrived—a big fighting bull. He said, 'I don't want it here.' We sent it back." Pointing to a picture of a large Boxer lying on marble steps at the front door of Picasso's house, she said, "Ian! I was sort of raised by this dog. I called him my milk brother."

"He put that dog in many paintings," Duncan said. "Do you have this one?" He indicated—in a photograph—a painting of a girl jumping rope.

"Yes," she said. "When we divided the paintings, I chose this rope-jumping painting of me, and the rope-jumping sculpture of me cast in bronze. I love it. We divided the paintings among us. I think we're six: Jacqueline, then Maya, Claude, and me—we're the children—and Marina and Bernard, the grandchildren. And the French government. It took twenty-five per cent of everything." She pointed to a photograph showing a Picasso bronze sculpture of a baboon. "That is the one he made of Claude's cars," she said, laughing. "Claude's two plastic cars. My father made it so fast. He stuck the cars together to make the head. He put on a broken spring of a toy to make the tail. He made ears of the broken handles of two coffee mugs. Then he sent it all off to be cast in bronze. My brother was furious, because his toys were taken away from him."

"You can see the cars," Duncan said, outlining them with a forefinger, as Carroll Janis bent closer to see the sculpture. "The top of the baboon's head, and the bottom."

"I never knew about that," Janis said. "Toy cars," he said. "Sculptured in bronze."

"My brother has it now," Mrs. Lopez Sanchez said. "He loves it."

"The man had a perfect boxer's stance," Duncan said as she turned her attention to a photograph of Picasso pretending to box. "He was in constant motion. And here's how pure his vision was." Duncan was now pointing to a photograph of a painting of Jacqueline. "He made at least thirteen great portraits of Jacqueline, all dedicated to her. She has all of them. And there's another one. On a thin sheet of steel. He painted her profile on it and then cut it out as a sculpture. In this photograph, it's very late at night. Picasso and Jacqueline are sitting here, with the profile in metal of Jacqueline illuminated in the background."

"Did she come to the exhibition last year at the Museum of Modern Art?" Carroll Janis asked.

"Without anyone's knowing about it," Duncan said. "The week before the show closed, she came here, and we went every day."

"There's *your* dog!" Mrs. Lopez Sanchez said to Duncan.

"Do you remember Lump?" he asked as they looked at a photograph that showed Picasso, a small dachshund nearby, making one of his plates with a representation of the dog on it.

"I liked that dog," she said.

"That's the day he asked me, 'Does Lump have his own plate?'" Duncan said. "I said yes. So he asked me, 'Does he have a plate with his *name* on it?' I said, 'He can't read.' So your father said, 'How do you know?' And he made that plate for him."

"Here I am, when I was seven, at the dinner table again with my father," Mrs. Lopez Sanchez said, picking up one photograph. "He was making a linogravure with a gouging knife. And I was drawing at the same time. With crayons."

❧ *Electronic Rock*

FIVE o'clock. A recital, with drinks and hors d'oeuvres, given by The United States of America, a new (eight months old) rock group of five musicians and a vocalist from Los Angeles, who describe themselves as an electronic rock band. This was their first appearance in New York, and it took place at Judson Hall, where a Columbia Artists Management man greeted us with the words "We are the first classical agency to take on a rock group." He had an expression of hope on his face as he went on, "The big word these days is 'diversify'—like I.T.&T. going into the fishing-tackle business or what-have-you. It's a brave new world." There are six long mirrors in Judson Hall, and they reflected and re-reflected the scene: a stage set with six upended coffin-shaped metal boxes, sprouting numerous control knobs, and with electric keyboards, an electric violin, an electric bass, an electric guitar, and electric drums. At the sides of the stage were setups for a seven-piece marching band and for a string quartet, which were going to augment the sound of the Electronic Rock Band. The audience that was gathering for the augmented sound seemed to be evenly divided between adherents of the miniskirt, corduroy-pants, and undisciplined-hair cookie pattern and tired mufti-clad friends and associates of Columbia Artists Management. Everybody was busy gobbling up the food—egg rolls and little meatballs. As they were chewing, one of the band musicians stepped to the mike onstage and said, "The United States of America will now do their duty on this stage here in this great country of ours." One of the mufti-wearers said to another, with a laugh, that he expected the music to break the mirrors. Malcolm Terence, a young man with a blast of red curly hair and a matching mustache, introduced himself to us as the manager of The United States of America and told us he was looking forward to presenting his group here in the East at C. W. Post College, on Long Island, and then at Columbia. "It's very easy to sell this band," he said, or shouted, in our ear as the music started. The band played numbers called "The American Metaphysical Circus," "Love Song for the Dead Che," "Machine No. 2," and "The American Way of Love." In addition to the music, which had electronic vocals sung by Dorothy Moskowitz, there were films projected over the heads of the players by a man whom Terence identified for us as Bill Kerby. "Kerby is the real hero!" Terence shouted. "All these films were compiled by him at the U.C.L.A. film school! All the students at the film school this year are asking our permission to use our records for their sound tracks! We're very flattered!" The films consisted of three simultaneous projections—brief clips of odd machinery in motion, African witch doctors, piles of garbage, an Indian chief on a horse, a dead body, a camel, a girl crying, a tiger walking in a jungle, Max Baer battering Primo Carnera, the nose cone of a jet liner, Adolf Hitler making a speech, Storm Troopers, traffic jams on a parkway, and many other quick glimpses of this and that, which seemed to us to be in fine accord with the music. It was all rather soothing, in a nervous way.

"All our musicians are incredibly talented!" Terence shouted to us. "They all went through classical and avant-garde music, and now they want to do their own thing!"

"What's that?" we shouted back.

"Rock and roll," he answered. "Augmented by exotic foreign rhythms and electronic music and all the classical stuff."

Somebody from Columbia Records, which has just issued The United States of America's first recording, called "The United States of America," told us that they are the first rock group to use tapes (their own) onstage and the first to use an electric drum. "Their sound equipment is the ultimate," he said. "And Faye Dunaway just came in."

✦ Truffaut—I

WE'RE fresh from a delightful visit with François Truffaut, the twenty-eight-year-old director, producer, and co-author of "The 400 Blows," which many people consider the best of the group of independently produced and inexpensive French movies that have come to be known as "the new wave," and which *some* people consider the best movie about children ever made. M. Truffaut was in town to accept the New York Film Critics' Award to "The 400 Blows" as the best foreign-language film of the year, and his stay here was both brief and crowded, but when we called on him, at his suite in a midtown hotel, we found him outwardly calm and ready to talk endlessly, in French, about films, films, films. Earnest, good-humored, slightly built, and boyish-looking, M. Truffaut told us that he is known in Paris as *"le petit Truffaut."* This is his first visit to America. His wife, who stayed home to take care of their year-old baby, has often visited this country and could have given him plenty of advice on what to see and do but took pains not to, knowing, said *le petit,* that with him everything sooner or later boils down to films.

We noticed that M. Truffaut, otherwise smartly turned out, was wearing brown felt bedroom slippers, and he explained that his feet hurt. "Not from sightseeing but because my shoes don't fit," he said. "They never fit. I hate to go shopping, and so become impatient and buy the first pair of shoes I try on. When I was a boy, my feet always hurt; I was a weakling in the eyes of my parents, who liked hiking and sent me to live with my grandmother until I was eight. I was always in revolt against adults, and I was always hungry. Today, as it happens, I'm not hungry; I had an excellent lunch at Le Pavillon. It was quite a change for me, because in Paris I usually eat at Manny's Bar, an American snack bar on the Rue Washington, where there are hamburgers and a pianist who plays jazz and songs by Jean Constantin, who composed the music for 'The 400 Blows.' A song from the film—'Comment Voulez-Vous?'—is going to be recorded in this country by Frank Sinatra, which gives Constantin much pleasure."

"The 400 Blows" is Truffaut's first full-length movie. Like most of the other new-wave movies, it was shot with a crew of under a dozen people. The production cost about a hundred thousand dollars, a third of which was contributed by Truffaut's father-in-law, a retired film distributor; another third of it had come to Truffaut in the form of a bonus from the French government for some short subjects, and the remaining third he collected from friends. "Our new wave would never have come into being if it hadn't been for the young American Morris Engel, who showed us the way to independent production with his fine movie 'Little Fugitive,' " the little Truffaut said. "Not to be tied to tremendous sums of money serves the aesthetics of film very well. A working-class apartment or a street in Montmartre is incomparably more real and intimate than anything one might create in a studio. Furthermore, a small crew is a great help to an actor, especially an inexperienced one. The fewer people he finds around him, the more natural he is. In shooting most of my scenes, I send away everyone but the cameraman."

It's no wonder that "The 400 Blows" is about children, for

its maker has long been preoccupied with them. "Even as a child, I loved children," he said. "I have very strong ideas about the world they inhabit. Morally, the child is like a wolf—outside society. In the early life of a child, there is no notion of accident—merely of *délits*—while in the world of the adult everything is allowed. From the age of eleven until now, I've seen three thousand films. Of the lot, there have been only four I have liked that were about children: 'Zéro de Conduite,' which was directed by Jean Vigo, a Frenchman who died at the ridiculous age of twenty-nine, and who has had the greatest influence on my work; the 1931 Russian film 'The Road to Life'; Rossellini's 'Germany Year Zero'; and Engel's 'Little Fugitive.' In all the others, the children are betrayed. What is important about a film that deals with a child is the child himself. Why should children be shown on the same level as anybody else or anything else, whether it is a white mane or a red balloon? It is not necessary to add ideas or sugary sentiment to what the child is. Moreover, in a film about children it is not necessary to condemn the adults. On the contrary, since the public is always on the children's side, it becomes necessary to find the maximum excuse for the adults' conduct. Another thought. Most films about children make the child frivolous and the adult serious. Quite the other way around! In a film, when parents give a present to a child, the parents are shown acting solemn and the child overjoyed, but in real life the child is nearly always disappointed with the present and looks angry, and the parents take it away and cheerfully start playing with it. You have to be extremely tough in making a film about children, yet I admit that for me it's easier to make a film about a child than about an adult, as it would be easier to make a film about a wild animal than about a tame one. It's my belief, by the way, that an actor is never so great as when he reminds you of an animal—falling like a cat, lying like a dog, moving like a fox."

Truffaut is putting the finishing touches on his second movie, called "Shoot the Pianist." "I wasn't sure how to end the film, so I took my actors to Grenoble and stood them about outdoors, in the snow. It's a theory of mine that when you don't know what to do next in a film, you should go outdoors; something comes to you there. The film is about a timid man and his relation to society, to women, and to his brothers. The family is Armenian and is named Saroyan. I used that name because I've read and admired the works of William Saroyan. My third film will be called 'Le Bleu d'Outre-Tombe'—in English, 'The Blue Beyond the Grave' —and will deal with the conflict between the old teachers in a lay school, for whom teaching is a *métier*, and a new teacher, for whom teaching is a religion." Truffaut sighed happily, looking forward, we gathered, to the difficulties implicit in that theme. "I can be reproached in many ways for my faults," he said, as if to take himself down a peg or two. "I'm lazy, and when the day for shooting a film arrives, I don't have a finished script. Then, too, I've a tendency to go in for polemics; I make pictures in reaction to pictures I don't like. The result is that I may find myself changing my notions about what I want to do right in the middle of making a film. And on days when I'm feeling merry I shoot merry scenes, and on my gloomy days I shoot gloomy ones." He smiled and pushed himself back up a peg. "So far, these strange methods satisfy me, and I see no reason to work in any other way."

◆ Truffaut—II

EARLY in 1960, when we first had a talk with François Truffaut, whose latest movie, "The Wild Child," has been a great critical success, he was twenty-eight and was making his first visit to America—to accept an award for the first movie he directed, "The 400 Blows." At that time, we found him earnest, good-humored, slight of build, and boyish-looking, and he told us that he had seen three thousand movies. We saw him again when he was thirty-two and had come here for the opening of his fourth feature film, "The Soft Skin." He looked exactly the same. He had by then directed "Shoot the Piano Player," "Jules and Jim," and his part of the trilogy "Love at Twenty," and he had seen seven hundred more movies. The other day, we saw him for the third time, in his midtown hotel suite. (He still speaks very little English, and, as before, his American friend and colleague Mrs. Helen Scott, who has done the English subtitles for some of his movies, and who is co-author with him of a book about Alfred Hitchcock, modestly provided a marvellous interpretation.) At thirty-eight, he still looked just about the same, except for a bit more fullness in his face. He had seen eight hundred and fifty movies since our second talk, and he had made six—"Fahrenheit 451," "The Bride Wore Black," "Stolen Kisses," "Mississippi Mermaid," and "Bed and Board," in addition to "The Wild Child."

"How about the past ten years?" we asked him. "Have

they gone the way you wanted them to?"

He took a good half minute to reflect before he answered. "I think they have," he said, finally. "Except, sadly, for the death of several people. Actors. Françoise Dorléac, the star of 'The Soft Skin,' and Nicole Berger, who played the pianist's wife in 'Shoot the Piano Player,' and Albert Rémy, who played the father in 'The 400 Blows.' Also, Guy Decomble, who played the teacher in 'The 400 Blows,' and Catherine Lutz, who played the lady detective in 'Stolen Kisses.' And there were writers. William Irish, who wrote 'The Bride Wore Black,' and David Goodis, the author of 'Shoot the Piano Player.' Several of them died in bad car accidents. And there were filmmakers whom I didn't know but loved a great deal. Jacques Becker. Jean Cocteau. This is what strikes me most about these years."

"Aren't movie directors supposed to become hardened to human suffering?" we asked. "Aren't they supposed to become toughened by their business?"

"It is a hard, cruel métier, but it's really not a question of becoming hardened to human suffering," Truffaut said. "It's just that people of my age seem to have less connection with death, less connection with older people. So we seem to react strongly. For example, I started to correspond with Henri Pierre Roché, the author of the book 'Jules and Jim,' on which I based my film, when he was seventy-three. Then I became a filmmaker, but I kept delaying making the film. Roché kept sending me letters telling me it was a very urgent matter to make this film. I sent him a picture of Jeanne Moreau and wrote to him that I thought she should be the girl in the film. He answered, 'Bring her to me quickly.' But he died before he could meet her. And I am angry with myself that I didn't make the film during his lifetime. One often feels guilty toward the dead, if only because they perhaps sent a letter to which you didn't reply."

Truffaut looked a little sad. Then he smiled. "There's a scene I would like to have in a film. About an elderly and prominent man. A young man comes to see him, to get something from him, to learn how to achieve prominence and success. The old man has facing him this young man— virile, healthy, ambitious. All the old man tells him is 'Play golf. Sleep eight hours a night. Do not smoke. Do not eat too much. Be sure not to put on weight.' " Truffaut laughed out loud. "I have always wanted to do this scene in a picture," he said. "I will *have* to do a picture that will let me have this scene."

"Are you taking care of yourself these days?" we asked as he reached for a package of Celtique cigarettes, took one, lit it, and inhaled deeply.

He shrugged. "I never eat much," he said. "I like to eat while I am doing something else, like watching television. I like eating in America. Eating is less solemn here."

"Do you notice anything different about things here since your last visit?" we asked.

"The traffic seems to be worse," he said. "You hear more police sirens. I may not have enough contact with life here, but I have an impression of quiet here, compared to Paris. On the surface, social relationships here seem to be less tense. The events of May, 1968, in France made relationships between people in France much tougher. De Gaulle had truly depoliticized France. When he was in power, you met people and you didn't bother to find out what their views were. In May, 1968, therefore, we found ourselves in a situation we were not ready for. Now people who are having trouble with money or with themselves have become very aggressive. The élite are ashamed of being favored, so they go to a great deal of trouble to justify themselves. Each Frenchman reacts in a defensive way, as if he himself had been accused. If you go into a store in France, the salesgirl gives you the impression that her life is a failure. Here, in the building occupied by United Artists, I see the elevator man calling to a boss to hurry. That would be unthinkable in France. England has those class differences but without the hostility. In France today, the small tradesmen, who used to be the kings, are bitter and angry. When I was a child in France—between the ages of eight and twelve, during the Occupation—I would be sent, like other children, with food tickets, to the grocer. The grocer was the king. With the grocer, I was always humble and sneaky. To this day, when I go to a grocer, I am always surprised if I am greeted by a smiling face. Now supermarkets are opening all over France, and the small tradesmen are angry. The same is true of the farmers. They remember how, during the war, Parisians came on their bicycles with bags on their backs and left with fifteen kilos of potatoes. We used to say of the farmers that they got so rich during the Occupation they needed *lessiveuses*—laundry tubs—to store their money in. The farmers, the small tradesmen, the salesgirls—they are full of hatred in France today."

"You really think things are better over here?" we asked.

Truffaut took a good minute to think before answering. "I suspect that the deaths of the two Kennedys and the malaise caused by the Vietnam war may have had an effect on people that is similar to the effect on France of May, 1968," he said. "One has the feeling that Americans are always ready to start their lives anew. Perhaps I have the view of a European. But I always feel the American health. Americans seem to be bigger and taller. Their blood *must* be better. They still are believers in sport and fair play. I prefer America, but people tell me that I wouldn't be able to stand it if I tried to live here. I never stay long enough to be weary of it."

"Any plans for movies you're going to make?" we asked.

"Vaguely, I'd like to make a film about life in France during the Occupation," he replied. "It would not be concerned with the Germans, or with the Resistance—it would be about the many Frenchmen who simply waited until it was over. During the war, France was compelled to be completely French."

"What about the romantic notion of all those French underground fighters?" we asked. "All those wonderful people in the Resistance?"

Truffaut gave a big laugh. "One out of thousands was like that," he said. "Many of the others were sitting on their bicycles going after the potatoes. In my neighborhood, for instance—Pigalle—if German soldiers asked how to get to the Folies-Bergère, people *might* direct them the wrong way. It was that kind of Resistance." He gave another laugh.

"Any other ideas for new movies?" we asked.

"Yes," Truffaut said. "I would like to make a film about the making of a film. One film that is important for all filmmakers is Fellini's '8½.' There is great truth in it. But it deals with what happens *before* the shooting. What I have in mind is a film about the shooting. It would show a scene badly played, the rushes, the cutting—things like that."

"Ten years ago, you said that of all the movies you had ever seen there were only four you liked that were about children," we said. "Have you liked any movies about children since then?"

"One," Truffaut said. " 'The Two of Us.' Made by Claude Berri."

"How about your shoes?" we asked. "You used to say they always hurt."

"Not anymore. When I saw myself on the screen, walking, in 'The Wild Child,' in which I play the part of the doctor, I noticed that my legs did not move right. So I went to a doctor. Now I have my shoes custom-made, and they feel fine."

"And your children?" we asked. "How is their taste in movies?"

"Developing," said Truffaut. "They don't live with me, because I am divorced, but I see them constantly. And I constantly take them to see movies. Laura is eleven, and I took her with me to see 'Gone with the Wind.' She said, 'It's the most beautiful movie I have ever seen.' Eva is eight. She compelled me to see 'Mary Poppins' twice. Because I saw it through her eyes, I loved it. Most of the time, I wind up liking the same movies they do."

♦ *Truffaut—III*

WE'RE speeding up the intervals between talks with François Truffaut. We saw him first in 1960, when he was
twenty-eight and was being awarded all kinds of honors for
his first feature film, "The 400 Blows." He had seen three
thousand films by then. We saw him again when he was
thirty-two, and had made three more feature films and seen
seven hundred more. Then we had a talk with him when he
was thirty-eight, with six more films made and eight hundred and fifty more seen. Last week, we had a talk with
Truffaut at forty-one. He had seen four hundred more movies. He had made three more, the most recent of which, "Day
for Night," is about people making a movie. In 1970, he had
told us, "I would like to make a film about the making of a
film. One film that is important for all filmmakers is Fellini's
'8½.' There is great truth in it. But it deals with what happens *before* the shooting. What I have in mind is a film about
the shooting. It would show a scene badly played, the
rushes, the cutting—things like that." Well, Truffaut did
exactly what he said he wanted to do. "Day for Night" was
shown at the opening of the current New York Film Festival,
and it got a great reception from critics, audience, and fel-
low-filmmakers. The actor-character in it played by Jean-
Pierre Léaud, who played the young hero of "The 400
Blows" and many other Truffaut films, seems to be forever
going to see movies.

First, an up-to-date report on Truffaut himself: He is getting more and more lovable with age (by the time he's eighty he'll probably be a cross between Mr. Chips and Jean Gabin), and he is more and more in love with movies and moviemakers. He's gradually getting heavier around the midriff, but he still manages to look boyish. He says his hair gets grayer after each film he makes. He still smokes Celtique Caporals, though some of his friends have tried to convince him that smoking shortens one's life. His two daughters—Eva, now twelve, and Laura, fourteen—have turned into stunning young beauties, and he travels with color photographs of them that he took himself. He does not plan to make another film for about two years. Instead, he is going to work on some books: a collection of his early articles for *Arts, Les Cahiers du Cinéma,* and other publications; a day-to-day journal of the making of "Fahrenheit 451"; and perhaps the same for "Day for Night." He keeps getting invitations from colleges and universities to visit them—to talk or not to talk—but so far he has managed to stay away, except from Harvard. Their interest in movies is fine, he thinks, but intellectuality about movies without enthusiasm may not be such a good thing. (This opinion was given very deferentially and kindly.)

The big step forward in his life recently, Truffaut told us, was a concentrated attempt to learn to speak and to read English. He told us about it, with wry amusement, when we saw him at his suite at the Plaza, on the eve of the opening of the Film Festival. He spoke partly in English, and the rest of the time we made out with the help of a pretty young lady named Hilary James, who is the head of the magazine department of Warner Brothers, the company releasing "Day for Night" in this country. We will give you some of Truffaut's English phonetically, as we got it—along with some French—because it sounded very pleasant.

"Ze first English book I have read eez 'Memo from David

O. Sel*zneeck,*' " Truffaut told us. "Eet eez ay great book. *Extraordinaire!* I liked heez mem*o* about Ingrid Bergman wiz ze explana*tion* for why she had to change her name. He wrote in anozer mem*o* ze ver*ee* best name eez Ver-on-i-ca Lake, ze way eet sounds. Ze sylla*bles*. Ver-on-i-ca Lake. *Extraordinaire!*' That's the general idea.

Truffaut told us that he had spent six weeks in West Los Angeles last summer for the sole purpose of taking an intensive course in English at the Michel Thomas School of Languages. He lived in a small bungalow at the Hotel Bel-Air, he kept a red convertible parked out in front, and most of the time he led a monklike life: getting up early, driving to his lessons, spending five or six hours a day just with his teacher, Michel Thomas, having dinner alone in his bungalow while watching television or trying to read the Los Angeles *Times.* He had a little kitchen, with a refrigerator, in which he kept only mineral water. He would order his meals over the telephone. "Always ze same," Truffaut said. " 'Weel-you-have-my-break*fast*-brought-up-in-my-bungalow? I-would-like-black-coffee-and-some-toast-and-some-orange-juice-zat's-all.' And for ze deenair 'I-would-like-sirloin-steak-medium-rare-wiz-sa*lad*-romaine-wiz-vinaigrette-dressing-wiz-creamed-spin*ach*-wiz-black-coffee-and-one-yogurt-zat's-all.' "

We'll try to give you the rest of what he told us in straight translation. "I arrived in Los Angeles two days before the Watergate hearings started," Truffaut said. "And so I started learning English with the help of the hearings on television and with the reports in the newspapers. When I got up, because of the time difference, the hearings were already on television. The very first thing I did was turn on the television. While shaving, I would fix the mirror to reflect the television screen. Before I left the bungalow for my lesson, I would hear most of the morning session of the hearings. Then, with my teacher, I would read the newspaper reports about them. Just Michel Thomas and I alone, in his small office, with three goldfish in a bowl on his desk, and, on the walls, signed photographs of the movie stars he had taught French to—Grace Kelly, Gene Kelly, Barbra Streisand. Then we would go to a restaurant for lunch and, immediately, back to his office. For contraction of verbs—'would, would-*ent*,' 'could, could*ent*.' " Truffaut gave a shrug. Then he said, in a kind of singsong, " 'I was*ent* going to tell you zat I was going to buy it for you, because I did*ent* want you to know.' " He paused and smiled, and then added, "I learned that sentence very well, but so far I have not been able to find an occasion to use it."

Truffaut told us that the Watergate hearings were much more fascinating to him than any film, and so much the stronger because there were no commercial interruptions during the showings. As soon as he got back to his Bel-Air bungalow, he would turn on his set again and watch the hearings over his dinner. "It seemed that John Dean was a much stronger character even than Humphrey Bogart," Truffaut said. "John Dean was Jean-Louis Trintignant. And John Dean's wife is Kim Novak—with a face that is rather animal and passive at the same time. The detective—the one who carried a coin changer on his belt, Ulasewicz—is Victor McLaglen. And Senator Ervin is Charles Laughton. What a big lesson for civilization, this democracy in action! I watched them all. Every morning and every night. It was amazing. I was impressed by the way their families clustered behind them. That is unimaginable in Europe. And the way John Dean's wife changed her dress every day. In Europe, it would never happen, to make public that they have money enough for that. Amazing! John Mitchell was so arrogant the first day. By the fourth day, he was putting his hand over his face, and my pity was going out to him. *Très arrogant*. But he was ready to crack. I can say very well now, 'To-ze-best-of-my-recollec*tion*-at-zis-point-in-time.' But I have no occasion to use that sentence, either."

"Did you do anything else in Hollywood?" we asked.

"Only, every few days I would drive out to see Jean Renoir, where he lives in Benedict Canyon," Truffaut said. "He is now busy dictating his memoirs. We would talk and talk about movies. About what this friend or that friend is making. How they are doing. I got to know him better in six weeks in Los Angeles than I had ever known him in France. He is so interested in what filmmakers are doing. I thought he was very content with the great films he had done, but he told me they were only a fourth or a fifth of what he would like to have done. He wanted to know all about Jeanne Moreau, because he would like to have shot a film with her. Also, we laughed a lot. About Hollywood parties, where you have to sit and eat with a plate on your knee. Renoir never eats from a plate on his knee. With Renoir, food is very important. With me, an hour later, I can't even remember what I ate."

"How did you like life in general in Hollywood?" we asked.

"I became attached to the style of it," Truffaut said. "It's the first time in my life I felt I'd like to live anywhere but in Paris. It's much more slowed down—you never see one car overtaking another—and the vegetation is so lush. Yet you get all the same efficiency you get in New York, the same services. Hollywood has a sort of colonial charm."

♦ *Truffaut—IV*

FRANÇOIS TRUFFAUT's visit to the Fourteenth New York Film Festival, which opened with the showing of his nineteenth movie, "Small Change," was also the occasion of our fifth talk with him since 1960, when, at the age of twenty-eight, he made his initial visit to the city, in connection with his first feature-length movie, the now famous "400 Blows." By this time, Truffaut, at forty-four, feels like a kind of relative, so we started by picking him up at Kennedy Airport on his arrival, via T.W.A., from Paris, and bringing up to date our chart of Truffaut statistics.

General appearance: Practically the same as it was sixteen years ago. Hair a mite more iron gray. Horn-rimmed glasses worn almost constantly. Complexion showing hardly any exposure to fresh air or sunshine. Midriff with perhaps a *hint* of a paunch.

Use of the English language: Terrific. Proved the effectiveness of the intensive course in English that he took in the U.S.A. just before our last talk, in 1973, when he practiced his grammar by watching the Watergate hearings on television and memorizing key phrases like "To ze best of my recollec*tion* at zis point in time." He reads books in English. ("I read 'Ze Final Days,'" he told us. *"Extraordinaire!* I also read 'I Remember Eet Well,' by Vin*cente* Minnel*li*. But I cannot read ze novels in English. Ze *vocabulaire!* Ver-ree difficult.")

Use of an interpreter: During public appearances and during long interviews, as a time-saver. Accompanying him this time was his longtime interpreter and colleague Mrs. Helen Scott, who did the English subtitles for "Small Change."

His daughters: Laura, now seventeen, is very serious, wants to be a professor of literature, and has just finished reading Simone de Beauvoir's "Memoirs of a Dutiful Daughter." Eva, now fifteen, wants to be a fashion designer. Both girls have parts in "Small Change."

Interest in clothes: His main concern is still wearing shoes that don't hurt his feet. He has them made to order. He was wearing a Francesco Smalto suit of oatmeal-colored linen, made in Italy. (Explanation, given to us with an almost wicked grin: "My Cardin period ees *over*. When Cardin bought a theatre and renamed eet Espace Pierre Cardin, I objected. Ver-ree pre-ten-tious. Ver-ree stupid. I would not wear Cardin to ze best of my recollec*tion* from zat point in time." And from zis point in time we will drop the accent.)

Interest in, and judgment about, food: Nil. ("T.W.A. food very good. Very good chicken.")

Watching television in France: "Our television is cultural, our films are frivolous. The opposite of television here. I do not like the color television. I have on my television set a gadget for turning off the color."

Self-appraisal compared to the way he felt ten years ago: "I feel the pressure of not having much time ahead of me when I am not pleased with my work. I have so many films in my mind to make. It becomes urgent to make progress."

Compared to self in 1960: "I was more timid. I was more worried."

Practical differences in his working life between then and now: "Lately, it has been much easier to obtain the money for the films. All they ask is 'How much does the kid want this time?' "

Freedom to make whatever he wants to make the way he wants to make it: The same as it has been all along—complete. "But I have the advantage of giving them the scripts in French, and they do not read French."

How he thinks about each new film he makes: "It is one more stone in the wall."

How much his films cost to make: "Small Change" cost about seven hundred thousand dollars, which is seven times as much as "The 400 Blows" cost. About one-twelfth of the cost of "Jaws." About one-twentieth of the cost of "The Godfather, Part II."

How many movies he has seen since 1973, when he told us he had seen, since he was eleven, four thousand nine hundred and fifty: Five hundred more.

How many movies he has directed since then: Two more —"Small Change" and "The Story of Adèle H."

How he happened to get into Steven Spielberg's movie so far entitled "Close Encounters of the Third Kind" as an actor, playing the part of a French scientist, a specialist in U.F.O.s, for which he will have to go to Benares, India, in January, and for which he has already had to go to Mobile, Alabama, and Gillette, Wyoming, where some of the movie has been shot: Spielberg telephoned him in Paris and told him he liked the way Truffaut wore an old-fashioned wristwatch and always wore a necktie. "I told Spielberg, 'I am not an actor. I can only play myself.' He said, 'Good.' The picture started filming on May fourteen, and, oh, my goodness, it still is not finished. I wanted it clear they could fire me if I am not good. I never asked any questions. I made it a point not to bother Spielberg. Jeanne Moreau once told me, 'On every picture, you must love everybody except the one who becomes the scapegoat.' I followed Jeanne Moreau's advice. I made Julia Phillips, the producer, my scapegoat. Every time I find something not to my liking, I say I am sure it is the fault of Julia Phillips."

Where he goes for a vacation: Only to the Beverly Hills Hotel. He sits by the Beverly Hills Hotel pool and reads. He finds the place calm and appealingly quiet. He never goes *into* the pool. He does not swim. He does not play tennis. He does not go to the beach. He does not go to parties. He does go to visit Jean Renoir, who lives in Beverly Hills, and who recently finished writing an autobiographical novel, entitled "Friends, I Have Just Become 100 Years Old," and they talk endlessly about movies and people involved with movies. And he does visit the Larry Edmunds Cinema & Theatre Bookshop, on Hollywood Boulevard. ("It is the best shop for film. *Fantastique!*")

Interest in going back to Mobile, Alabama, or to Gillette, Wyoming: Nil. "I might as well go to Cherbourg as to Mobile. The countryside near Gillette is beautiful, but compared to French countryside you think you are on the moon."

Interests outside of movies: Nil.

Interest in movies: Still all-consuming.

Patience and seriousness with which he meets questions from interviewers: Incredible. Question from Joseph Gelmis, of *Newsday:* "How do you renew the man so that the artist can function?" Answer: "One works with what happens to one in the first twelve years of life, and this base is inexhaustible."

What he did this time in New York: He watched "Small Change" at the Film Festival, attended an opening-night party, and had a press conference and half a dozen interviews.

After we had met him and driven with him to his hotel, he did not come out for forty-eight hours. When he did come out, we took a taxi with him and Mrs. Scott to Cinemabilia, a bookshop and gallery at 10 West Thirteenth Street, where Truffaut wanted to look for new books about movies.

"You should see the pileup of film books at his home and in his office!" Mrs. Scott said in the taxi. "But he knows where everything is."

"It is a good collection, yes?" Truffaut said mildly.

"He's a compulsive file-keeper," Mrs. Scott said. "He has everything arranged on shelves and in drawers, *alphabetically*. When he comes over to my flat in Paris, he goes around fixing up *my* books alphabetically."

Truffaut shot into Cinemabilia like a retriever. He didn't waste any time on small talk. He concentrated completely on the business at hand. Quickly, he picked up the new issue of Andy Warhol's magazine *Interview,* because it contained an article on Jeanne Moreau. He also took *Film Fan Monthly,* issue of June, 1968, because it had a list of Alfred Hitchcock's films for TV; "A Standard Glossary for Film Criticism," by James Monaco; the new issues of *American Film* and *Women & Film;* "The Name Above the Title," by Frank Capra; "Harlow," by Irving Shulman; "Don't Say 'Yes' Until I Finish Talking," by Darryl Zanuck; and greeting cards that had still photographs from old movies on the front. "Nice," Truffaut said, taking five "Design for Living" with Fredric March, Gary Cooper, and Miriam Hopkins, An Ernst Lubitsch Production, cards, and three "River of No Return" starring Robert Mitchum and Marilyn Monroe cards. He flipped through a bin of vintage-movie stills, mostly of "The Little Rascals," but passed them up. He glanced without interest at a book entitled "Focus on 'Shoot the Piano Player'" and passed it up, along with a dozen other books about him or his movies. He autographed a paperback edition of the script of his movie "The Wild Child" for the bookshop owner, and then, looking disappointed, he retraced his steps and glanced over the stock again. "Nothing new," he said.

"Film students were in here a few days ago and bought practically everything," the proprietor of the bookshop said.

Truffaut had accumulated what looked to us like an enormous load of stuff, but he still looked somewhat disappointed. On the ride back to his hotel, however, he immediately started paging through the books and magazines, and seemed to feel better. We dropped him at the entrance. Before going through the revolving door, he turned around, held his load of books aloft in a kind of farewell wave, and lifted his head to them in triumph.

❧ First and Only

THE New York City Fire Department has three hundred and fifty-seven companies, all with red fire engines except Engine Company 65, our next-door neighbor, at 33 West Forty-third Street, whose fire engine—or, in firefighting parlance, "apparatus"—is a pale lime green. Why?

"It's an experiment in better visibility," John Mulligan, assistant commissioner in charge of public relations, told us over the telephone from his office, at 110 Church Street. "The lime-green apparatus is the first in a thirty-seven-million-dollar replacement program. She was made by American LaFrance at a cost of ninety-six thousand dollars. She's a cause. A point of contention. Recognition versus visibility. Yellow or green is supposed to be easier to see. She is lime yellow, or, officially, federal safety yellow, sometimes called national yellow. She is called chartreuse and slime green by those loyal to red. They are detractors, so to speak."

"O.K. to go over to see how she's doing?" we asked.

"Take some facts with you," Mulligan said. "She's the first and only, so it's too early to have figures. By next year, we plan to have ten more—made by Mack, now low bidders at a hundred and thirteen thousand each—and then we'll have something other than conjecture. She's only been in service since July. We've had a lot of pro and con. Keep in mind we're the busiest fire department in the world." Mulligan, who was the speediest talker in our reportorial experience, went on, "Not the biggest. Tokyo is the biggest. They have eighteen thousand firefighters, and they do fewer than eight thousand fires a year. Tokyo still has red. We have eleven thousand five hundred and ninety-nine, and we do three hundred fires a *day*. Last year, we did a total of one hundred twenty-seven thousand eight hundred and seventy-six fires, but it wasn't our peak year, which was 1976, when we did one hundred fifty-one thousand and seventy-nine fires. We're up on emergencies this year, but we're cutting down on false alarms, thank God. A fireboat can pump twenty thousand gallons a minute, and that gives you an idea when you realize that this one and only pumper pumps *one* thousand gallons a minute, which is typical of our pumpers, red or green. So we can't relate any of that to color. A lot of our firefighters think this new apparatus is a horrible color, but that's because they want traditional. I've driven in three cars—one black, one blue, and one red. Red gets them every time. But the public, I'm told, likes the green. Especially the women."

"We'll have a look," we said.

"Hold it," Mulligan said. "It's not true that we've *always* had red. Red dates from about 1916, with the arrival of motorized apparatus. Before that, only pumpers were red—the hose wagons, the ladder trucks, and the water towers were cream-white with maroon trim and fenders. It's not unusual to have different colors around the country—yellow, red-white-and-blue, you name it. Salt Lake City has green, but they are switching to red. Our fire-alarm boxes and the lights over them are still red. In 1731, the original fire apparatus, a hand-operated pumper that came from England and pumped seventy gallons a minute, had a *green* body with *brown* wheels. It was wood. You can see it at the American Museum of Fire Fighting, in Hudson, New York.

We're heavy with history in this department. This green apparatus was the one stored in the second City Hall in history, at Wall and Nassau, where John Peter Zenger was imprisoned for nine months in 1734 and 1735, and he probably heard the firefighters drilling with this green apparatus. It's also where George Washington took the oath of office in 1789, and where our Bill of Rights was passed. In the presence of *green*, not red."

Fact-fortified, we visited the controversial apparatus next door, and thought it looked splendid. A shade lighter, in our opinion, than lime green. With a lot of gold leaf. "CENTURY NEW YORKER" in large gold letters on the sides. "KEEP BACK 200 FEET" in silvery letters on a red background on the rear. Illustrations of red apples on the exhaust-stack cover. The apparatus looked very shiny, very new, very modern, and raring to go as it faced the door of its landmark habitat (dedicated in 1898), which has white tile walls, a brass sliding pole, and, alongside, neatly stacked black leather helmets, black rubber boots, and black Nomex coats, all banded with yellow safety stripes.

Company Captain Robert Kearns, meticulously garbed in officer-on-duty navy pants, light-blue shirt, navy necktie, and black military-type shoes, gave us the lowdown on the apparatus. "She gets more yeas than nays," he said. "Especially from women. They go for the bright color. They're impressed. Personally, my men would prefer her to be red, but they also like having one of a kind. You stand out. Besides, this apparatus replaced a 1971 pumper that was old and tired, that was rusting away. The fire pump leaked. The engine oil leaked. The transmission oil leaked. Everything was loose. This is a beautiful pumper. Solid. She rides well, with power steering, which is great in midtown traffic, and flow meters that tell the pump operator the number of gallons of water being discharged. Look at this deluge nozzle." Captain Kearns jumped on the apparatus and pointed to a big object in the middle. "This nozzle weighs fifty pounds. The old one weighed a *hundred* and fifty, and it required two men to lift it. This takes one. And this electric siren! It's variable. It allows for three different sounds. First, there's the regular fire-engine whine. Then, there's a repeated 'wow-wow-wow.' Finally, if I press a button I can get a high-low siren—the quavering type of siren you hear in Europe. When I come to an intersection, I usually change the tone from the regular fire-engine whine to the 'wow-wow-wow.' And look at these crew-riding positions." He opened the door of the cab and sat down in one of the seats. "The firefighter just leans back, puts his arms through the straps, and—presto!—into the smoke mask. He's ready!" He demonstrated how a firefighter gets into the mask contraption. "It's not just the color that gets me. It's the apparatus as a whole. Firefighters are into tradition. We've been wearing the same kind of helmets for a hundred years. We are all *attached* to red. Nick Mancuso, head of the Uniformed Firefighters Association, will dispute the contention that yellow is a safety factor. In the rearview mirror, he'll tell you, surrounded by hundreds of yellow taxicabs, you'll see a blanket of yellow, and lime green is not that much of a distinguishing factor."

Captain Kearns led us up to the front of the station and stopped at the house-watch desk, where a large, framed color photograph of the lime-green engine was hanging. "We're really *proud* of her," he told us. "There's a lot of competition between the companies. The horseplay never stops. We're constantly criticizing each other. Everybody in Sixty-five thinks Sixty-five is the greatest, and it *is.* So if we take a ribbing over the green, that makes us unique, and we're not going to admit to preferring red. We have green T-shirts with a drawing of the apparatus and the words 'The Mean Green—First Again.' And we go along with the safety idea that green is much easier to see—especially in fog or in twilight, at five o'clock in the afternoon on a rainy day, or with smoke or snow affecting light conditions. We like it when a poem is written about our apparatus—as it was by Mal Levy, the dispatcher in the Manhattan Central Office. I'll read it."

THE NEW LOOK

Tradition died and by the book,
One-hundred-sixteen years it took;
I speak of apparatus "red"—
Which color, science says, is dead.

Defenders deem it for the best,
As proved by laboratory test;
But those that care, know otherwise—
A lime-green shade offends their eyes!

When arsonists their candles lit,
'Neath sardine cans whose oil would spit,
Much help arrived all shiny red—
Extinguished and went back to bed!

No self-respecting torch today,
Would even light one up for pay;
Mere waiting for would him demean—
Arrival of a Green Machine!

Ask "Sixty-five," all those who doubt,
"Lime-Green" may put the fire out;
The problem that the men must lick,
Arriving at the job . . . sea-sick!

◈ Eleven Thousand Lawyers

OUR man Stanley took a brief vacation earlier this month in San Francisco, where the American Bar Association was holding its hundred-and-fourth annual meeting—the largest one in its history. We asked Stanley to look in on this phenomenon, and he obliged, with the following report:

What to do about eleven thousand lawyers, plus their families, running all over San Francisco, filling thirty hotels, hogging all places on cable cars, polishing off supply of Boudin's pizza bread, practically demolishing baby-shrimp and crabmeat cocktails on Fisherman's Wharf, monopolizing sightseeing boat trips to Alcatraz? Only thing lawyers not exhausting is great San Francisco unpolluted air. Consider covering A.B.A.'s Young Lawyers Division program Coping with the Law Office Blues. Or Tax Aspects of Planning for the Second Marriage After Divorce. Or Crisis in Criminal Defense Funding. Decide against. Pass up lawyers' dramatic productions, including "The Trial of Sacco and Vanzetti— Re-Creation of the Famous Trial and Retrying of the Case Using Current Federal Rules of Evidence." Pass up "Anatomy of a Marital Settlement—Live Mock Negotiation of a Complex, but Not Atypical, Marital Case, Staged in Three 'Acts' (Custody, Finances, Taxes)." Pass up serious stuff like Two Resolutions Relative to Religious Discrimination in Law School Admissions. Also Two Resolutions Requesting the A.B.A. House of Delegates to Rescind Its Policy Adopted Last January Opposing Discriminatory Membership Policies in Private Clubs. Dig through a hundred and seventeen tons of material describing other highlights. Also Major Speakers List—one thousand one hundred and sixty-one Major Names, from Aberbanel, Arthur, New York, N.Y. (Topic: "Death on and Over the Water"), to Zunker, Jerry, Bar Counsel, State Bar of Texas, Austin, Texas (Topic: "Avoiding Litigation Against Bar Associations").

Decide to go to A.B.A. Opening Assembly at San Francisco Opera House, for appearance of major Major Name, former Secretary of State Alexander M. Haig, Jr. No explanation given by A.B.A. for choice of Haig as bigwig of official opening of nine-day convention. Seems to be biggest deal to hit Bay Area since Clark Gable emerged in one piece from earthquake. Word out Haig getting big fee for appearance: twenty thousand dollars, plus expenses. Haig apparently ordered special six-star security arrangements. Most of press ordered to be inside Opera House by 8:30 A.M. Further orders: No press conference. No interviews before speech or after speech. No copy of speech before speech. No photo opportunity for closeups. Entire audience, including media, to remain seated after speech until departure of Haig from building.

Opera House filling up dutifully with lawyers. Stationed in upper box is seven-piece orchestra, with members wearing tuxedos, playing "The Sound of Music." Walt Tolleson's orchestra. Nice beat. In five other boxes, photographers, television reporters, TV cameramen squashed together, all very cranky, making cracks about twenty-thousand-dollar fee, about being pushed around, about not being allowed to talk to local politicians or to A.B.A. officials waiting for Haig backstage. Reporters skeptical. Objective. Independent. Good "Front Page" stuff. *Wall Street Journal* man says, "I'm getting a plane ticket to Washington to hear the *real* Secretary of State."

Three Supreme Court Justices waiting backstage in clump. Mr. Justice Byron R. White. Mr. Justice Lewis F. Powell, Jr. Mr. Justice John Paul Stevens. Polite, tough, icy Justices. Ask Mr. Justice White for opinion of Haig as choice of opening speaker. Get high-class judicial answer: "I have no comment on that." Ask Dick Collins, A.B.A. information man, why Haig. Get sensible answer: "Last year, at the New Orleans Hilton, Haig filled the ballroom." Collins gives straight facts: "Caspar Weinberger is coming, but he is *not* being compensated. Only Haig and Marvin Kalb."

Talk to Richard O. Gantz, Anchorage, Alaska, lawyer, also backstage. Get another splendid legal reply to the question about Haig: "I can't really give you a definitive answer, because I'm too busy figuring out where I'm going to sit. There are scores of us up here on the stage with Haig. I'm on the board of governors. We're at the head table, so to speak."

Ask Gantz why no pictures of Haig. Get another terrific answer: "After all, this is a function for our members."

Dick Collins wants to add facts about magnitude of meeting: "We have sixteen hundred subcomponents. We have sixteen foreign Bar Association presidents, on the *stage.* We have hundreds of different Bar Association presidents. Can't fit them on the stage. We have fifty-eight tons of Wangs, file cabinets, and so on, shipped from A.B.A. headquarters, in Chicago. We have five hundred and seventy-four judges, some on the stage, some off. We've got to introduce a hundred and ten people before Haig can open his mouth."

Collins says over two thousand lawyers and their families will be out front. Look. Opera House only half filled. Go back to TV, photographer, press buddies in media box. Eric Risberg, A.P. Gordon H. Stone, San Francisco *Examiner.* Etc. Good guys. Share crouching space. Share inside info.

"Strom Thurmond couldn't make it," somebody says.

Somebody else says, "The rumor is Haig is going to speak

off the cuff. For twenty thousand smackers, not worth *preparing* a speech for lawyers." Adds that Haig appearance just showoff stuff. Key issue at convention is Lawyer-Client Confidentiality. "That's the biggie," he says. Knowledgeable fellow.

Proceedings start. Houselights down. Walt Tolleson's orchestra playing "I Left My Heart in San Francisco." Lady in long gown—Marianne Kent, famous in California—singing words. Screen onstage. Cable cars pictured onscreen. "San Francisco" playing while Golden Gate Bridge appears onscreen. Fine spirit.

Introductions next, with time for bows, applause. Geoffrey Lane, Lord Chief Justice of England. Leon Jaworski, Second Century Fund Chairman. Lawyers from Spain. Judges from Australia. Lawyers, judges from Hong Kong, Mexico, France, Venezuela. Past A.B.A. treasurers. Diverse mob. Press buddies dozing.

Houselights go up as m.c., distinguished fellow named Ernest T. Guy, from Chicago—big thatch of gleaming brown hair, tuxedo with blue ruffled shirt—announces Navy Precision Drill Team "will perform a very spectacular drill." Wow. Twelve-man team—one woman, one black—in white helmets, white uniforms, white gloves, with gleaming rifles, take next seven minutes demonstrating discipline, discipline, discipline. Impressive tricks with rifles. Lots of footstamping. Sharp commands. Haig not in sight. Too bad. Just his stuff. Why Navy Precision Drill Team for lawyers? Nobody knows. Then announcement by m.c.: Governor Edmund Brown, Jr., unfortunately in Oklahoma at Governors' Conference, so Brown's legal-affairs secretary, Byron Georgiou, to give official welcome. Georgiou says that California has eighty-four thousand lawyers, more judges in Los Angeles County than in all of England, one lawyer in San Francisco for every seventy-two individuals. Big hand. Then city welcome from S.F. Mayor Dianne Feinstein. Looks efficient. Takes opportunity to tell lawyers she hopes they vote yes on handgun control, S.F. first large American city to vote for handgun control, twenty-two thousand people killed by handguns in U.S. in 1980, but now S.F. setting good example for other cities to save lives. Mild applause. Leon Jaworski follows with report on Second Century Fund: almost thirty thousand lawyers, plus more than three hundred law firms, gave ten and a half million bucks to Fund, for public-service projects. Jaworski looking chubbier than in Watergate days. Praises "selflessness of the American legal profession." Loud, long applause.

Press buddies restive. Been sitting cramped in box for hour waiting for Haig. Now David R. Brink, outgoing A.B.A. president, starting speech. Begins with quote from Ambrose Bierce defining "a bore as 'a person who talks when you wish him to listen.' " Good laugh. Finishes twenty minutes later—impressive courtroom-delivery manner—advising lawyers to choose road of "rule of law among nations." Applause.

Finally, Haig introduction. Quick bio by m.c.: Grad of U.S. Military Academy, 1947. Served in Japan, Korea, Europe, Pentagon, Vietnam. Military assistant to Kissinger, January, 1969. Fourteen trips to S.E. Asia, in the course of which he helped to set up Nixon visit to China, 1972. Appointed Chief of Staff by Nixon, 1973. Retired from Army, June, 1979. Appointed Secretary of State, January, 1981. Resigned, June, 1982.

Haig natty, as usual—gray suit, white shirt, red-white-blue tie. Looks on top of world. Smiling. Tells joke-writer-type joke—à la Bob Hope, Henny Youngman, Ron Reagan. Says, "Only a few weeks ago, I could travel all over the world in my own planes any time I liked. Now I can't leave home without my American Express card." Gets laugh. Tells more pal-to-pal jokes—about telephoning "Ed Muskie," "Cy Vance," "Henry," about shared letdown feelings. Gets chuckles. Throws out another one-liner: "A few weeks ago, I was fourth in line of succession; today I have to struggle for a precedence in a checkout-counter line at the supermarket." Losing audience. Quickly tells lawyers glad to be there. "In a room with thirty-six hundred attorneys, I'm sure I'll learn how to deduct the three-Martini breakfast I just had." Audience coming back a little. But still no Johnny Carson Show smash guest comic.

Cameras going click, click, click. Photographers looking grim. Haig saying decade of nineteen-eighties "particularly difficult as we seek to strengthen the rule of law." Jokes over. Lawyers settle back in chairs. Haig says, "Marxism-Leninism perverted the rule of law." Trying for academic level. Making voice go up and down, as if following elocution teacher's instructions. Jumps to another thought: "American foreign policy must be bipartisan." Bounces quickly from idea to idea, slipping in intellectual references; self-consciously gleeful. Peculiar. Seems to be discussing appeasement, confrontation, negotiation among nations. Refers to "a fine balance of the Hegelian dialectic, if you will." Gives little giggle at this brainy but unapropos reference. Seems to be against U.S. confrontation with our allies. More references to "Marxism-Leninism." Then gets on familiar ground for moment, says he agrees with Cap Weinberger that we must reverse the decline of our defense capabilities. Delivered in manner of politician telling political convention he's against high cost of living. Then returns to brainy-type references, castigates people who would "contemplate each other's navel." Castigates "proclivity of developing leaders to latch on to Marxism-Leninism." Says, "Marxist jargon is a locomotive for social change but never an engine for economic development and social progress." Says only the West brings economic development. Knocks "sloganisms and sophistries of Marxism-Leninism." Says emphatically, "I go to bed each night thanking God that I don't preside in the Kremlin!" Brezhnev undoubtedly glad to hear this.

Lawyers in audience give Haig nice hand.

"Nobody can get out till Haig leaves!" m.c. calls out after Haig exit. "The doors are locked!"

Take advantage of captive audience to sample lawyers' reactions. Identification easy, because lawyers wearing badges. Start with Ogden W. Fields, Godeffroy, New York. Unusual lawyer. No mincing words. Gives blunt answer: "I got the feeling he's running for President." Bert Early, Chicago: "Well, I'm a low-profile person." Larry Dagenhart, Sr., Charlotte, North Carolina: "We've got to have something like that for this audience. Do you know how to get to Candlestick Park?" Larry Dagenhart, Jr. (thirteen years old): "It kind of put me to sleep." C.D. Peterson, State Justice, St. Paul, Minnesota: "Sobering and predictable." James R. Greenfield, New Haven: "A very two-handed speech." Sidney S. Baron, Pontiac, Michigan: "Full of sound and fury. Not worth twenty thousand." Priscilla Schechter, Smithtown, New York: "Very impressive. He tailors his suits like a Marine, with more white shirt showing than all these legal types here." Norman Redlich, Dean, N.Y.U. Law School: "Expensive." Leon Jaworski: "I comment only about jurisprudence." Right idea.

◆ *Between Sets*

IN the current fuss being made over the fiftieth anniversary of the Waldorf-Astoria and its list of marvels, we start our own list of Waldorf marvels with Jimmy Lyon, who plays the piano in Peacock Alley every Tuesday through Saturday from 6 to 10 P.M. Jimmy Lyon not only plays hundreds and hundreds of songs—practically any song you can come up with—but reharmonizes and arranges them on the spot, making many of them better musically than they were to begin with. In fact, he raises playing the piano in a cocktail lounge to an art. Mr. Lyon is a dapper, distinguished-looking, Cole Porterishly elegant man in his fifties. He has silver hair parted impeccably on the left, boundless good nature, and an attitude of quiet, alert camaraderie toward all who sit and drink in the Alley, or even enter it, immediately making them feel that they're in for a very special treat. His piano is a Steinway grand in a fruit-wood casing. (The piano was owned by Cole Porter, who lived at the Waldorf for the twenty-five years before his death, in 1964.) Behind him is a contemporary chinoiserie screen with representations of pheasants, herons, and white peacocks. Off to his left, on a shelf, is a stuffed peacock in a wooden cage. Around him is a lot more chinoiserie—including mirrors on the walls—along with the softest, coolest leather love seats in town. Also fresh geraniums in vases on the tables and surprisingly nutritious cocktail tidbits, including plantain chips. While Mr. Lyon plays, observing everybody who comes and goes, people tramp past the fruit-wood piano on their way to meals in the adjoining dining room; some stop to ask Mr. Lyon if the piano is really *it;* cocktail drinkers talk, laugh, and call out request numbers to Mr. Lyon; glasses clink; fans sitting near the piano eagerly present Mr. Lyon with lists of song titles they have brought along, and he receives the lists just as eagerly and proceeds to play the songs. With all this going on, usually at once, Mr. Lyon blithely, calmly cuts loose with his music. When we got to hear him, we invariably come out feeling better than we did when we went in.

"When did all this start?" we asked Mr. Lyon the other evening, during one of his take-fives.

"When I was born, in Morgan Village, near Camden, New Jersey," Mr. Lyon replied courteously, and, at our urging, he gave us this biographical rundown:

"There was always a piano in our house. My father, a machinist in a shipyard, came from Glasgow, and my mother from Belfast. My father played the piano in the key of F-sharp and never put his thumbs on the keyboard. He was exuberant. Nobody laughed better than he did. He would sit at the piano and play and sing 'There's Somebody Waiting for Me' and other Harry Lauder tunes. My mother liked him to sing 'As the Wig Wig Waggle of His Kilt.' I was an only child, and the piano was all mine whenever I wanted it. I started playing it by ear at four. I had my first lesson at eight, stayed with the lessons for a year, then started playing on my own. We moved to Collingswood, New Jersey, when I was about thirteen, and I went to Collingswood High School. At thirteen, I started taking piano lessons again, this time with J. Blaine Saltzer, who wore spats, but I think I might have taught him more than he taught me. He'd say, 'Play "Embraceable You" the way *you* play it.' And he'd sit there listening carefully. From the time I was thirteen until

I was eighteen, I'd practice six hours a day, after school and at night. At Collingswood High, I had a ten-piece jazz band and played during lunch hour and at dances. When I was seventeen, I played piano with a commercial band at the Birdwood Club, near Collingswood, on Tuesday and Saturday nights. We'd play special arrangements for dancing. Gershwin, Rodgers, Porter, Kern—all the giants.

"One day, I came home from school, put the radio on, and heard some jazz being played on the piano that stopped me cold. Harmonically, it sounded unbelievable. It sounded like *two* pianos. It was Art Tatum. That same day, I got into my car, a '32 Plymouth, and drove ten miles to Philadelphia, where I grabbed every Art Tatum record I could find. I took six records home and stayed up all night long listening to them. Art Tatum's harmonic structures were way ahead of everybody else's. I still listen to those records today, and I always learn something new." Mr. Lyon paused, smiled, shook his head as though he were still in a state of disbelief, and said, "Art Tatum became the greatest influence in my life."

"After that?" we asked.

"The Second World War, and I was drafted," he said. "I wanted to be a pilot, but my vision was only twenty-thirty. However, I qualified as an aerial gunner, and I was sent to Atlantic City for basic training. We'd go to Convention Hall to watch training movies. One day, we marched in and saw this guy onstage playing the piano. I thought, 'This guy must know Eisenhower.' Then a staff sergeant got up and said he was looking for show-business talent. I volunteered to play the piano. 'Do you know how to fake?' he asked me. 'Do you know "My Heart Stood Still"?' Well, *I* wound up playing the piano onstage there for a year and a half. Then I was sent to Greensboro, North Carolina, where I got a call one day from the local fire chief, who said the piano player for their Y.W.C.A. dance was sick, and asked me to fill in.

For twenty-five dollars. When I got to the hall, I sat down at the piano to practice, and a guy walked in looking like Abraham Lincoln and dragging a guitar. He said, 'Sounds mighty fine. Can I play along?' He had huge hands. 'Gimme an E,' he said. 'What do you want to play?' I asked. 'Whatever you say,' he said. I started playing, reluctantly, but this guy turned out to be *fantastic.* He was a sign painter, and his name was *Tal Farlow.* I made him come up North. He's one of the greatest. At the moment, he's with Red Norvo." Mr. Lyon looked at his wristwatch and said he had to get back to his piano in a few minutes.

"How did it go from then on?" we asked.

Mr. Lyon gave us a quick summary: "Joined the Gene Williams Band. Went on the road with June Christy, who had left the Stan Kenton Band to go out on her own. Did a tour with Stan Kenton's forty-piece orchestra. Did a four-month tour with Benny Goodman's sextet. Got married. My wife, Chris, was a singer with the Gene Williams Band. We have two kids —Jim, Jr., who's getting his doctorate in psychology in Berkeley, and Pamela, who's helping to manage a discothèque in Fort Lauderdale. While my kids were growing up, I was at the Blue Angel for nine years, playing seven nights a week, with my trio. Jimmy Raney on guitar and Beverly Peer on bass. We played for almost everybody who had a show there—Carol Burnett, Dorothy Loudon, Johnny Mathis, the Smothers Brothers, Harry Belafonte, Phyllis Diller. When the show was over, the trio would go into the bar and play jazz. After the Blue Angel folded, in 1964, I signed with MCA and took the trio all over the country playing jazz. Mabel Mercer used to sing at the RSVP, across the street from the Blue Angel, and come over to see the shows. In 1958, she had asked me to do an album with her, and with my trio and a drummer, for Atlantic Records. It was called 'Merely Marvellous,' and it was a great hit. Then, in 1968, I got a call from Mabel. 'Jimmy, will you do me a favor? I've got a concert in six days with Bobby Short at Town Hall, and my accompanist can't get back from Paris in time. Will you do it?' Then she said, 'If you won't do the concert, *I* won't do it.' I said, 'We'll have to rehearse around the clock.' Then I found out the concert was going to be recorded by Atlantic Records. I had to learn twenty new songs. I must have lost a pound for each song. At Town Hall, we were still rehearsing upstairs while Bobby Short was on downstairs. The place was packed. People were sitting on the stage. When Mabel walked out onstage, the whole audience got to its feet. I didn't fill out my clothes for weeks. In 1970, Mabel asked me to be her accompanist on a steady basis. I stayed with Mabel for eight years, until she went on a sabbatical, which she is spending in her house in the country. I was never conscious of a lyric till I met Mabel. She's the greatest storyteller. Nobody sings a lyric the way she does. Nobody."

Mr. Lyon got up to go back to his piano. "I have great respect for the melody the composer wrote," he said. "If you don't know the melody of a song, you don't know the song. Harmonically, the songwriters left a lot to be desired, but that is not their fault—they weren't exposed to the harmonies we know today, thanks to the genius of Art Tatum and players such as Cy Walter and George Shearing. It also helps to have some knowledge of the lyrics in the back of your head, to interpret a song correctly. The composer supplied the feeling in the music, the vitality, the spirit, which so often was a spirit of simple cheerfulness."

Mr. Lyon went back to the piano and played a set. We listened. Show tunes by Rodgers, Porter, Duke, Youmans, Coward, Arlen, Coleman, Weill, Schwartz, Sondheim, Gershwin, Kern. Music by Duke Ellington (in a class by himself). Standards like "It Had to Be You." Out-of-the-mainstream songs, by composers like Alec Wilder, of the kind that Mabel Mercer sings. When he was asked to play a terrible song, he'd turn it into something else by working up a whole new harmonic structure, by embellishment, by his particular phrasing. He wound up his set with Paul Desmond's "Take Five," played, as it was composed, in five-four time.

"It's not what you play but how you play it," Mr. Lyon told us in *his* next take-five. "I don't have hard and fast arrangements. I never play the same song twice the same way. People sometimes ask me how I arrive at my 'changes.' I just *hear* them. I learned by making mistakes, and if the mistakes sounded good I kept them in. If I don't know a song, I hear it a few times and I can play it. My job is to play what people want. Because I'm playing Cole Porter's piano, I get more requests for 'Night and Day' than for any other song. Talking doesn't bother me in here. People come in here to talk, and I don't demand the attention a singer gets. If I can reach one person, it's a good night. Every now and then, if I feel that nobody at all is listening, and if I start to get bored, I find myself doing things for fun. One night, I played songs with girls' names in the titles for almost an hour. I played 'Laura,' 'Margie,' 'Peg o' My Heart,' 'Emily,' 'Ida,' 'Dinah,' 'Stella by Starlight,' 'Samantha,' 'Rose of Washington Square,' 'Rosalie,' 'Dolores,' 'Fanny,' 'Diane,' 'Lilli Marlene,' 'Mame,' 'Mary,' 'Maria,' 'My Gal Sal.' I just kept playing and playing. Every time I finished a song, I'd think of another one. 'Nancy with the Laughing Face,' 'Louise,' 'Georgy Girl,' 'Sweet Lorraine,' 'Waltzing Matilda,' 'Jennie Rebecca,' 'Bess, You Is My Woman Now.' After about an hour, I heard somebody laughing, long and loud. It was a very affluent-looking Japanese businessman, and he was sitting with about half a dozen other affluent-looking Japanese businessmen. When he caught my eye, he called out ' "Hello, Dolly!" ' and my night was made."

❧ Davis on Dogs

OUR dog-groomer, dog-partisan friend Mel Davis gave a few unsettling cries of anguish about his profession the other day while he worked—in his establishment, a cozy, warm, tidy place on East Forty-ninth Street near the East River—on a ten-year-old small miniature apricot poodle named Goldie, who stood on a grooming table as though transfixed by the shop's windows, which were opaque with steam against the icy blasts outside. "I'm so upset about what's happening with dogs," said Mr. Davis, who is, as half the poodle owners in town know, a small, faithful, puppy-like man, with a small, faithful, puppylike face, who believes that every dog has the right to look naturally beautiful, and who measures all people by the way they recognize that right. Wearing pastel-green slacks and a gaudy flower-patterned sports shirt open at the collar, Mr. Davis sat on a bar stool, his heels hooked over the top rung, and clipped away at Goldie's fluff, shaping a kind of halo on top of her head. "Every time I go out on the street and see the way dogs look, I feel so depressed," Mr. Davis said. "All around me, I see long, low dogs with haircuts shaped to make them look like walking coffee tables. Short-backed dogs look as though their heads were pushed up against their behinds. Has mass production reached the point now where all dogs are made to look alike, no matter what the breed, and with no artistry and no styling? I know it's been happening with books and with clothes and with television programs and with movies and with medical doctors and with politicians and with the faces of people. But *dogs!*"

Goldie gave Mr. Davis a look of sympathetic gloom.

"Don't the owners see the travesties that are made of their dogs?" Mr. Davis asked. "Don't they see how badly their dogs are patterned? I feel so *sorry* for the dogs—and for the owners, too. I see so many shaved bodies, with full legs but with a small, scissored head, making the dog look so unbalanced, as though he came out of a barber school on the Bowery. Can you imagine schnauzers and other terriers not being made to look like the precisely tailored creatures they should be? The other day, I met a woman whose schnauzer looked like a poodle. She didn't know how her dog should look. But the *dog* knew. He came to us so unhappy. Well, we did a complete restyling. The dog looked so serene, and the woman was hysterical with joy."

Goldie wagged her tail.

"Who knows or cares these days about how to enhance the personality or conformation of the dog?" Mr. Davis asked. "The trouble is, first of all, with the grooming schools. They appeal to the students to learn and to go out fast and earn a living in grooming. The students are dog lovers, and are sincere in their efforts. But how much can they learn in a crash course in a few months? Can an artist be taught to be an artist in the first place? We interview and audition quite a few of these graduates, but we rarely find anybody with real talent. We try to encourage the youngsters to start at the bottom, doing rough clipping, washing, drying, and brushing, and leave the styling to our talented groomers—at least, until the youngsters *learn* something. But no, these youngsters want to start immediately at the *top.* Their attitude is, once they are graduates they are immediately qualified to do it *all.*"

"Sounds familiar," we said.

"To commercialize an artistic profession is to me an outrage," Mr. Davis went on. "Our clients are very fussy. When we have a new client, at first we observe the animal and suggest the correct cut. Some of these cuts are very intricate and require more than just a basic style. A Dutch clip, or a modified Dutch clip, must give the effect of a poodle wearing a jacket or pants. If you mess up on *that,* the poor dog looks as though the pants were falling down. If only these would-be groomers would attend *one* all-breed American Kennel Club–sanctioned dog show and observe the charges of the professional handlers, they would learn more in one day than in an entire course taking months."

Mr. Davis picked up clippers to trim Goldie's nails, and she trustingly held up one paw. "Poodles are treated the worst," he said. "The textures of their coats are so varied that the formula of the shampoo has to be chosen with care. We happen to have developed our own, with high-protein content. It makes thin-coated poodles look virtually heavy-coated, while our woolly woollies become manageable, so that we can scissor and style them easily. Each poodle has an individual look. Nobody should ever forget that."

Mr. Davis looked Goldie in the eye, and she gave him a fervent wag of the tail.

"Heads have to be designed and cut to capture the true personality of each poodle," Mr. Davis said. "Every day, I go out and see dozens of horrible pinheaded dogs. When these dogs flex their ears, a horrible point appears on the top of the head. Horrible. This is what you get when you let a book-learning groomer do it. I'm so miserable when I see that Happy Hooligan look."

Goldie looked alarmed.

"It's O.K., Goldie, not you," Mr. Davis continued. "I have seen legs clipped starting from incredible angles, so that they look as though they were just hanging there, defying the laws of gravity. Tails are made to look like witches' brooms. And the mustaches! Some of them only people of Diamond Jim Brady's time would wear."

Goldie cringed.

"When I do Goldie, I start from the base of the neck and work toward the shoulder line and blend it in down to the full leg," Mr. Davis said. "You're done, Goldie. I'll give you your yellow bows."

As Mr. Davis tied the bows on Goldie's head, behind her ears, he almost smiled. "I took a walk yesterday," he said. "The unhappiest walk of my life." He looked solemn again. "I started from the Forties, where every dog looked either matted or the object of a different kind of indifference on the part of the owners. I saw one Afghan hound who actually had a tied-up topknot, à la Yorkie. I saw a freshly groomed schnauzer sporting a closely trimmed poodle face and a hula skirt with legs to match. Then I saw a beautiful Yorkshire terrier with so many ribbons and bows its whole head was hidden. One head bow is sufficient for a Yorkie. Only an idiot doesn't know that. In the Fifties, I found a glut of Lhasa apsos and Shih Tzus that had been 'economically clipped,' so the regal look of these beautifully coated breeds was ruined. When I reached the Sixties, I saw a cocker spaniel with a completely shaved skull, instead of a topknot blended into the dome. And again the hula skirt, like the one on the poor little schnauzer in the Forties, *plus* sloppy, un-rounded paws. Then I saw some poodles with full puppy clips without shapings. They resembled little cigars. In the Seventies, I saw more guess-what-we-are poodles and pulis."

"All right," we said. "Specifically, what are the main faults you found with the poodles?"

"The legs were clipped so high the dogs looked as if they were walking on stilts," Mr. Davis replied. "The heads were too small and tightly cut, so the dogs looked as if they were wearing caps. The bodies were shorn too close—usually with injury to the animal, revealed by discolored hair over the skin wound. Tails sometimes looked like bananas instead of nice little pom-poms. The ears weren't blended to the side of the head, so I knew there had been deep scissoring, cutting away precious hair that had taken years to grow."

Goldie was ready to leave, looking satisfied with herself.

"*She* knows," Mr. Davis said.

◆ W. A.

WILLIAM ALFRED, the playwright and Abbott Lawrence Lowell Professor of the Humanities at Harvard, is in town preparing for the opening of his new play, "The Curse of an Aching Heart," starring Faye Dunaway, who appeared in Mr. Alfred's first play, "Hogan's Goat," sixteen years ago. At that time, we spent an exhilarating afternoon with Mr. Alfred, walking around with him in the South Brooklyn area in which he had spent most of his pre-Harvard life, and which he loved. He had made the area the locale for "Hogan's Goat," which tells about an Irish Catholic couple in 1890—they had married outside the Church and felt guilty about it—and he has made the same area the locale for "The Curse of an Aching Heart," which is about a Brooklyn woman of thirty-five (the daughter of Josie Finn, the character who caused trouble for the Miss Dunaway character in "Hogan's Goat") looking back over her life between the nineteen-twenties and the nineteen-forties, the decade in which the play is set. This woman, as Mr. Alfred puts it, "comes to decide that her life has to it a daily glory."

Now we have had the pleasure of spending another afternoon with Mr. Alfred, this time in Manhattan, in the Lenox Hill area, where he lived between the ages of four and a half and nine. For the first year and a half, he boarded, and later he was a day student, at St. Ann's Academy, which used to be on East Seventy-sixth Street near Lexington. He attended Mass at the Church of St. Jean Baptiste, which is still at Lexington and East Seventy-sixth Street, and he moseyed around the Third Avenue shops with his father, a bricklayer, and his mother, a telephone operator, when they weren't working and had the time. Mr. Alfred keeps a second home —a tiny apartment—in this area, in addition to a house in Cambridge. The apartment is a very short walk away from the Church of St. Jean Baptiste, where Mr. Alfred now attends Mass every morning on his way to the theatre for rehearsals of his play.

This is what Mr. Alfred gave the press agent for "The Curse of an Aching Heart" to say about his new play: "Santayana once wrote that everything in nature is lyrical in its ideal essence, tragic in its fate, and comic in its existence. Being, then, is the dazzle each of us makes as we thread the dance of those three rhythms of our lives. My hope is that 'The Curse of an Aching Heart' occasionally captures the dazzle as water captures light."

I. The Apartment

A third-floor walkup, over Orwasher's Bakery ("Fresh Bread Daily") on the ground floor. Inside the building entrance, fading brown stencillike representations of flowers on mustard-colored walls. Rickety tile stairs. Rickety brown-painted door to the apartment. Mr. Alfred opening the door to us, looking only a hint affected by the passage of sixteen years: the same dark, ascetic face, the same large brown eyes, the same strong impression of innocence, deep humor, compassion, and good will. He was wearing a gray flannel suit, a dark-blue shirt with a button-down collar, a gray-and-blue striped poplin necktie. We stepped directly into a comforting little kitchen with a window.

"I'm making you a cup of tenement-house coffee, freshly perked," he said. "I love the smell. Especially with its being so cold outside."

The kitchen was shining clean. A rectangular wooden table with oilcloth on the top. Under a board cover, a bathtub, old-fashioned, with legs like a puppy's. Refrigerator and stove doll-house size, but a full-sized percolator on the stove. To the left of the kitchen, a diminutive bedroom. To the right, a living room only slightly larger, with sofa, floor-to-ceiling bookshelves, an armchair, an old black-and-white television set, a sewing table used as a desk. The room's two windows, with a fire escape outside, looked out on other windows, other fire escapes.

"It's compact, like a ship, in here," Alfred said. "It's only a hole in the wall, but I love it. I love the neighborhood. I got the place right after my father died, eight years ago, for a hundred and seventy-five dollars, and today it's only up to two hundred and ninety-five dollars and eighty cents. The landlord, Mr. Braun, is a very nice man. When I had my heart attack, in Cambridge, two years ago, my lease was up, and I told Mr. Braun I didn't know whether I'd be coming back, but he held the place for me without a lease, and he didn't raise the rent."

We had the coffee, out of delicate blue-and-white china cups, in the living room, at the sewing table. On the walls: a crucifix; a Picasso print, in a brown wooden frame, of peasants in a field, resting; a "Hogan's Goat" poster featuring the name of Ed Begley; a small eighteenth-century wash drawing of country musicians by Jean Baptiste Le Prince.

"I think he did some of the murals for the Hermitage," Mr. Alfred told us. "I found the painting in a thrift shop. I got it for twenty bucks. I got a genuine 1790 Coalport-china teapot in another thrift shop for only eighteen bucks. My mother loved china; she collected it. In a way, I'm still buying presents for somebody who isn't here anymore. I love the thrift shops. My mother loved them. They used to be all up and down Third Avenue. The best one was the one called Stuyvesant Square—it's now moved over to Second. They can't pay the Third Avenue rents. We dressed out of the thrift shops. Beautiful things. We always had the most beautiful clothes. I bought this tie I'm wearing in a thrift shop yesterday. Fifty cents." Mr. Alfred laughed an openly joyful laugh. We picked up from the sewing table a small nineteenth-century clock in a gilded brass case, its works visible through glass, its face, with Roman numerals, enamelled in pale green.

"Faye gave it to me for Christmas," Mr. Alfred said. "It winds up with a key. It's a travelling clock. Faye knows I used to collect clocks."

Mr. Alfred started packing some items into a dark-green Harvard book bag. "I've been helping get the props for the play," he said, identifying each item before he packed it away. "The *Staats-Zeitung und Herold,* because there's a man on the streetcar in the play who carries one. The paper still looks the same as it did fifty years ago. A bottle of toilet water—Florida Water. I got them this brass shovel with a black handle—brought it from Cambridge. My mother used this Louis Sherry candy box as a sewing box. I like to have things that are mine on the set."

Time to go. Mr. Alfred put on a black topcoat with a velvet collar and a worn-looking dark-gray fedora, and opened the door of his apartment. A heavy aroma strongly suggesting well-seasoned pot roast.

"It's from the apartment across the hall—my neighbor, a Hungarian lady," Mr. Alfred said. "She's always cooking. The smells drive you crazy. And in the kitchen you can see from my windows there's a French couple. In the worst heat of summer, she cooks him eight-passenger meals. It's a wonderful mixture of old and young in this building. Young people just making their way. Everybody friendly with everybody else. My laundry is *William's* Chinese Laundry, on East Seventy-eighth, and I get my hair cut at *Alfred's* Barber Shop, around the corner. Maybe I'm getting loopy, but it helps make me feel I was meant to be here." He laughed.

Mr. Alfred left most of his lights on in the tiny apartment as he closed the door. "My mother would say, 'You're making Edison rich,' " he said. "But I like the lights on when I come home. It's less lonesome."

II. The Church

As we emerged from Mr. Alfred's building, the cold hit us like a sharp wallop. Mr. Alfred hunched his shoulders and led us a block west and a couple of blocks south, directing our attention to various points of dazzle on the way: the thrift shop where he got the Coalport teapot; the top floor of the little four-story building where his parents had an apartment in the early nineteen-thirties, and where a young German called Willy did odd jobs for them and slept on a Cogswell chair and an ottoman in their living room, because it was during the Depression and "you took people into your home off the streets in those days"; the bookshop with a fancy red drapery in the window which framed a fake ice-cream soda and a real begonia plant, and with books that included a "Special, $11: 'Chandor's Portraits' by Malcolm Vaughan, Foreword by Deems Taylor"; the Save on Income Tax Preparation shop; the newspaper-delivery shop; Ellen O'Neill's Supply Store, with a window completely occupied by a mannequin wearing a long, Victorian white lace dress.

"I haven't stopped teaching at Harvard during this rehearsal time," Mr. Alfred told us. "Luckily, this is Reading Period—the time for the kids to consolidate what they have studied and to write their term papers. I've read twenty-five papers and have another twenty-five to go, by the kids in my course in Old English Literature from the Beginnings to the Norman Conquest. I also teach a playwriting course and have five honors' tutorial students, along with four more I couldn't say no to, in independent studies. I get presents for all my girl students in this Supply Store, and for the boys, too. They have wonderful old things. Buttons. Picture postcards. You can get the weirdest things in there. I found a postcard that reminded me of 'Krazy Kat' humor. It showed a boy and a dog. The boy is saying, 'If you laugh and smile all the while, How will the streetcar fare,' and the dog is saying, 'Bite him, Fido. He's got no suspenders.' I like it especially because a streetcar figures in the new play. Wait till you see our set. Our set designer made us a real streetcar that goes on a real track all around the stage. Be careful!" Mr. Alfred held us back, out of the path of an aggressive, speeding taxi. "My mother used to say, 'They'll kill you; it's on their way,' " he said, giving his all-out laugh.

At Third and Seventy-sixth, Mr. Alfred said, "And here's where the Third Avenue 'L' station was. Where this pizza parlor is, there used to be a cigar store, where my parents got cigar coupons for me. I never knew how to save money, so I collected cigar coupons instead. I got a dime allowance. I tried to save it, because they told me you were supposed to save. Not much success. I've never been good with money." Mr. Alfred stopped suddenly and looked north on Third Avenue. "I was going to say, 'Let's go to Rappaport's Toy Bazaar,' but I just remembered it folded last year, after being in business for ninety years. I always think of their celluloid saxophone. It smelled of celluloid and nail polish. You turned the crank, and it played 'Pop Goes the Weasel.' "

Inside the Church of St. Jean Baptiste. "There's been a white dove trapped in this church for several days," Mr. Alfred said, looking around as we sat down in a pew at the rear. No dove to be seen. On the dome in the center of the transept: "CHRISTUM REGEM ADOREMUS DOMINANTEM GENTIBUS." On the clerestory of the Baroque church, stained-glass windows illustrating the Old Testament: the sacrifice of Isaac; Abraham offering tithes to Melchizedek; Cain and Abel; God talking to Adam and Eve after the Fall. Within the dome: the Twelve Apostles. More stained-glass windows below: scenes of the Eucharist, including the feeding of the multitude (the miracle of the loaves and fishes). Around the church: the fourteen Stations of the Cross. Several confessionals. Up front: the altar. To both sides of it: the devotional candles.

"My father used to light candles to the Infant Jesus of Prague when he wanted to win the lottery," Mr. Alfred whispered to us. "He never won." He laughed.

There were half a dozen other people in the church. Two of them were men, sound asleep. A third man had a loud, body-shattering cough The others were elderly women.

"Every Friday, all of us from St. Ann's Academy would have Benediction," Mr. Alfred said. "A priest would give the sermon. The following Friday, he'd come back and you'd be asked how much you remembered of the sermon. If you remembered enough, you'd win a holy picture. I'd win maybe once every three weeks. I was a great woolgatherer. Instead of listening to the sermon, I'd be thinking of what we were going to have for supper. Look! There's the white dove! Isn't that amazing?"

Nobody else in the church seemed to notice the dove, which was sitting on the altar.

"When I reached seven—the age of reason—I made my First Communion here," Mr. Alfred said. "You wore an Eton collar, a white Byron tie, and a bow of white silk on your sleeve. You wore short black pants, high black shoes, and black lisle stockings held up with a rubber band, which would always break, and then your stockings would get sucked down into your shoes in a lump. Two days after the First Communion, I was confirmed—that was done here at that age. Cardinal Hayes came. I'd never seen anything that magnificent. His embroidered white-and-gold gloves! His white-and-gold cope, and his gold mitre! An enormous ermine cloak covered the pillars. It was so opulent, like something out of old history books. And Cardinal Hayes gave you a light slap on the face—to show that you must suffer for your faith."

On our way out, we looked at an empty glass case.

"It used to hold a relic of St. Ann," Mr. Alfred said. "It was supposed to be her thumb bone. It was wrapped in linen, with Latin writing all over it. It was kept downstairs in my day. You kissed the glass—you wiped it before and after you kissed it. Before, in case the person ahead of you had a cold and forgot to wipe it."

In the vestibule, we stopped to read a brass plaque: "IN GRATEFUL REMEMBRANCE OF THOMAS FORTUNE RYAN, DONOR OF THIS CHURCH. TO HIS PRINCELY GENEROSITY, PROMPTED BY A LIVING FAITH, THE CLERGY AND PEOPLE ARE DEEPLY INDEBTED. OF YOUR CHARITY PRAY THAT HIS SOUL MAY ENJOY FOR EVER, REFRESHMENT, LIGHT AND PEACE. DIED NOVEMBER 23, 1928. R.I.P."

"I was probably around here on the day of the funeral," Mr. Alfred said.

A small elderly woman wearing about three coats against the cold came over to us in the vestibule and asked Mr. Alfred for the time. He said it was a quarter to three. She told him that she had to wait for a friend who was coming from her job at the Lenox Hill Hospital, and she started away.

"Oh, you dropped your Kleenex," Mr. Alfred said, picking it up and going after her.

"Bless you. You're very kind," the woman said.

"It's warmer if you go inside the church," Mr. Alfred said.

III. The Theatre

Outside, on the steps of the church, Mr. Alfred pulled his hat down closer to his ears and stood for a moment, blinking at D'Agostino's, on the other side of Lexington Avenue. We walked over with him to 170 East Seventy-seventh Street.

"This is where the school's soccer yard was," he told us. "I was pretty good at soccer, because I had big feet. I was always fouling people with my feet. And here, next to it, was the dormitory where I slept. It was just like the one in the movie 'Zéro de Conduite.' Rows of beds up and down. I was in such a state of blues. I had one friend—Maurice, who was three months older than I was. He was very sweet to me. He had a pen—you looked through it and you saw the Tour Eiffel. And Brother John was a lovely man. He knew instinctively about children. He knew when you were blue. But he didn't condescend to you. A very grave, very sweet man. A year in that place, though, seemed like a century. I hated it. About thirty years ago, when the school was still here, I came to see it. All the Brothers I knew were gone. I had been having nightmares that I was still at St. Ann's. I felt I might lay the dreams to rest. I don't know when they tore the place down. Well, I'd better be bringing the props to the theatre," he said, pulling his hat down farther, against a sharp wind. "I don't like to miss the rehearsals. Those actors! They are so *good!* Oh, my, they break your heart. They make me cry. Every time. They're afraid for me on opening night. They want to put a paper bag over my head."

We got into a taxi and headed down to West Forty-fourth Street. "Wait till you see our theatre," he said. "It's the Little Theatre. Built in 1912 by Winthrop Ames, one of Guthrie McClintic's first employers. It held two hundred and ninety-nine people in those days. Now it's got a balcony and holds four hundred and ninety-nine. It has a beautiful Georgian front. And it's right next door to Sardi's. Four stories high. Winthrop Ames used to have his offices over the theatre. A very dignified-looking man. McClintic used to say that Ames looked like a Velázquez cardinal. Ames went to Harvard. Class of 1895. I looked him up, because his initials, W.A., interested me, if you don't mind my getting loopy again."

Inside the Little Theatre, it was cozy and warm. A spectacular-looking multilevel set—a revolving sculpture of a latticework of pipes suggesting a fire-escape landscape—had a realistic streetcar on a track. The set designer was conferring with the director. The lighting man was testing his set of color cards against the stage. The actors were walking around the stage, across the stage, onto the stage, off the stage. Mr. Alfred told us that the production cost three hundred and seventy-five thousand dollars, and that five main producers and fifty independent investors had put up the money. "Nothing from me," Mr. Alfred said. "Not since my ten-cents-a-week allowance have I held on to money. Watch, now. What you're looking at up there is Bond Street and Third in South Brooklyn, in back of a disused brewery. The audience is the Gowanus Canal. Watch."

The streetcar onstage began to move on its track. Mr. Alfred looked as though he needed to have a paper bag put over his head.

Following are the dates of *The New Yorker* issues in which the stories in this book appeared:

Takes   June 14, 1969

Revels   August 5, 1972

Bartók in the Morning   March 30, 1981

Halloween Party   November 17, 1980

Nixon's Walk   December 7, 1968

Secretary Shultz   May 24, 1969

Two People in a Room   February 25, 1967

An Educated Person   December 4, 1978

Hits   September 14, 1968

Composer in Tartan Cap   December 21, 1968

The Return of Mr. S.   January 4, 1982

Ralph Bunche   January 1, 1972

Popov   December 30, 1972

Aboard   June 26, 1971

Sermon   August 3, 1981

Narrator   May 4, 1981

The Shave   March 10, 1980

Rehearsal   October 30, 1978

Adlai Stevenson   July 24, 1965

Arrival   October 7, 1974

On the Great Lawn   October 3, 1981

Quick   September 25, 1978

Albee   March 3, 1980

Mr. Bell   February 22, 1982

Alex and the Awards   June 21, 1982

Remembering Picasso   October 19, 1981

Electronic Rock   March 30, 1968

Truffaut—I   February 20, 1960

Truffaut—II   October 17, 1970

Truffaut—III   October 15, 1973

Truffaut—IV   October 18, 1976

First and Only   December 7, 1981

Eleven Thousand Lawyers   August 30, 1982

Between Sets   October 12, 1981

Davis on Dogs   January 26, 1981

W. A.   January 25, 1982